Marriage Wars in
Late Renaissance Venice

STUDIES IN THE HISTORY OF SEXUALITY
Guido Ruggiero, *General Editor*

Further volumes are in preparation.

MARRIAGE WARS IN
LATE RENAISSANCE VENICE

Joanne M. Ferraro

OXFORD
UNIVERSITY PRESS

2001

OXFORD
UNIVERSITY PRESS

Oxford   New York

Athens   Auckland   Bangkok   Bogotá   Buenos Aires   Cape Town
Chennai   Dar es Salaam   Delhi   Florence   Hong Kong   Istanbul   Karachi
Kolkata   Kuala Lumpur   Madrid   Melbourne   Mexico City   Mumbai   Nairobi
Paris   São Paulo   Shanghai   Singapore   Taipei   Tokyo   Toronto   Warsaw

and associated companies in
Berlin   Ibadan

Copyright © 2001 by Joanne M. Ferraro

Published by Oxford University Press, Inc.
198 Madison Avenue, New York, New York 10016

Oxford is a registered trademark of Oxford University Press

Library of Congress Cataloging-in-Publication Data
Ferraro, Joanne Marie, 1951–
    Marriage wars in late Renaissance Venice / Joanne M. Ferraro.
      p. cm.
    Includes bibliographical references and index.
    ISBN 0-19-514495-3; 0-19-514496-1 (pbk.)
      1. Marriage—Italy—Venice—History.   2. Renaissance—Italy—Venice.   I. Title.
HQ630.15.V465 F47 2001
306.81'0945'31—dc21   2001016336

Frontispiece: Titian (c. 1488–1576). *Miracle of the Jealous Husband,* fresco (1510–1511).
Padua, Scuola di Sant'Antonio, Sala Capitolare. Photo: Scala/Art Resource, New York.
A doubting husband fatally punishes his innocent wife for suspected adultery,
an injustice that calls for the intervention of St. Anthony of Padua.

Venice parish map courtesy of Instructional Technology Services, Graphics,
San Diego State University. Adapted from R. Diana (1961) in G. Bortolan,
Il patriarcato di Venezia (Venice, 1974), 609.

9 8 7 6 5 4 3 2 1

Printed in the United States of America
on acid-free paper

For

ELSA

and in memory of

AARON

ACKNOWLEDGMENTS

IT IS ALWAYS a pleasure to acknowledge the riches that family, friends, colleagues, and benefactors bring to the scholarly experience. The research for *Marriage Wars* was generously financed by the Gladys Krieble Delmas Foundation, the American Council of Learned Societies, and the College of Arts and Letters and the Office of Faculty Affairs at San Diego State University. A sabbatical as well as a semester leave under the California State University Research, Scholarship, and Creative Activity Program provided time away from the university to write the manuscript. Translations from the archives are mine.

In Venice I benefited greatly from the help of Michela Dal Borgo and Sandra Sambo, senior archivists at the Archivio di Stato, who not only showed me the way through the 160 kilometers of dusty documents over the years but also offered the warmest of friendships. Moreover, the Patriarchal Archives were a delightful discovery, both for the rich collections and for the able staff. I thank the director, Don Bruno Bertoli, and Francesca Cavazzana Romanelli, whose scientific direction of the archival staff has made this treasure trove of documents readily accessible to the scholarly community. Archivists Manuela Barause and Yousrit Boulous provided helpful assistance.

Over the course of a decade, I received invitations to test and refine earlier versions of the material in this book in several venues. I wish to thank all the scholars who generously gave their input at these seminars, held at the Center for Culture and Literary Criticism at Harvard University; the Harvard Center for Renaissance Studies at the Villa I Tatti; the National Institute for Renaissance Studies in Florence; the Science and Research Center of the Republic of Slovenia, Koper; the Istituto Storico Italo-Germanico at the University of Trent, Italy; the Research Seminar on Gender and the Department of History at Pennsylvania State University; the European Colloquium at the University of California at Los Angeles; and the Feminist Research Colloquium at San Diego State University. Among these, the Istituto Storico Italo-Germanico at the University of Trent stands out as host to a unique and stimulating interdisciplinary seminar on marital litigation in early modern Europe. I thank Professors Silvana Seidel Menchi, Diego Quaglioni, and Francesca Cavazzana Romanelli for bringing together a talented group of legal and social historians to grapple with approaches to the history of marital conflict. I am particularly grateful to have worked with Paolo Prodi, Lucia Ferrante, Daniela Lombardi, Giovanni Minucci, Elena Brambilla, and Anne Jacobson Schutte at these meetings.

Venice is a unique and special place to conduct research, and writing a book is a long and arduous journey. For more than two decades I have enjoyed the friendship and collegiality of many accomplished scholars across the disciplines as well as the pleasure of continually meeting new ones who promise to take Venetian studies in new directions. It's been a pleasure to exchange ideas over dinner, coffee, on a walk through the *calli* and *campi*, or over a drink at the wonderful Venetian *osterie* with Edward Muir, Rona Goffen, Stanley Chojnacki, John Martin, Sally Scully, Laura McGough, and Monica Chojnacka. At home in the United States, many more friends have generously given me helpful guidance. Mathew Kuefler merits a special acknowledgment for reading the entire manuscript, offering thoughtful criticisms, and being a valuable sounding board for my ideas and queries. William and Aimee Lee Cheek, Joe Elliott, Oliva Espin, Brian Giguere, Myron Greene, Reva and Gerson Greenburg, Neil Heyman, Kathy Jones, Harry McDean, Barbara Rosen, Norman and Emily Rosenberg, Rosalie Schwartz, Francis Stites, and Paul Vanderwood all helped me develop my approach to this project over the years, and I heartily thank them. Joanne Donahoe has been an excellent M.A. student and a fine research assistant. Elyse Katz Flier has provided her expertise in the history of Renaissance art as well as offering many years of friendship and collegial support. With her, it is time to thank my other *amici di cuore*, Marilyn Boxer, Michela Dal Borgo, Sandro Bosato, Laura Giannetti Ruggiero, and Guido Ruggiero, for the special place they hold in my life. Guido deserves special thanks, for leading the way to new adventures in Venetian studies and for being an exemplary mentor to me and many others in the historical profession. He has given much to many. Finally, closest to home, I want to include my sisters, Sadie Hemphill and Ann Maimone. Hamlet, my Renaissance cat, provided warm companionship during the preparation of this manuscript, and a few critical pawprints as well.

My parents, Corrado and Jennie Ferraro, fostered my close connection with the history and culture of Italy early in my life, and with this work I honor their memory. I was happy to accept additional tutoring (and parenting) Venetian style from Elsa Dalla Venezia, her sister Edda, and her brother in-law Ezio Crosara. A kind and wise Venetian woman, Elsa has generously introduced a long line of scholars new to Venice to the city's customs and manners while providing them with a family experience in her home. To her above all I owe my familiarity with Venetian dialect, my developed tastes for Venetian cuisine and *alta moda*, my experience with family and neighborhood life in Venice, and much more. I dedicate this book to Elsa and to the memory of my great nephew Aaron Mortrell. Gifted with insight and creativity that exceeded his mere twelve years, the eye and pen of an artist, and a vivid imagination, Aaron gave me energy and brought me the greatest joy.

San Diego, California   J. M. F.
February 2001

CONTENTS

VENETIAN MONEY

DUCAT   A money of account, not represented in coinage. It was based on silver currency and was equivalent to 6 *lire di piccoli, 4 soldi*; or, alternatively, to 24 *grossi* (Venetian groats). In 1561 and 1608 the state minted silver and gold coins of the same value as the ducat of account.

LIRA DI PICCOLI (pl. *lire di piccoli*)   Money represented in coinage. It was divided into 20 *soldi*.

SOLDI   Money represented in coinage. A twentieth of a *lira*. Each was equivalent to 10 *denari*. Between 1551 and 1565 the average daily wage of a master builder was 29.5 *soldi*; between 1628 and 1630, it was 67.7 *soldi* a day. A journeyman in the building trade received approximately two-thirds as much.

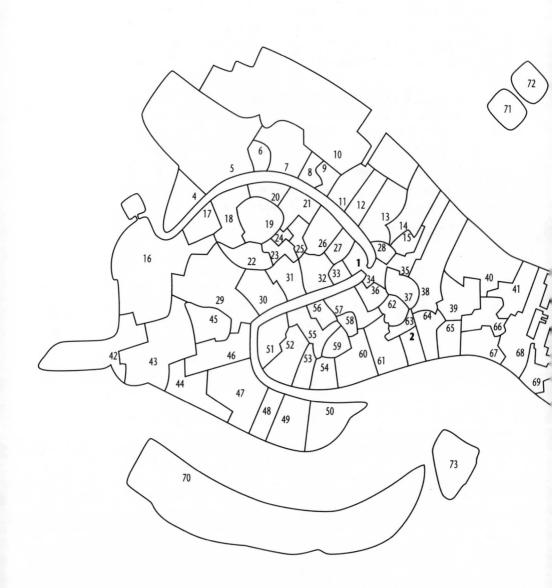

MAP OF VENICE PARISHES

1. S. Giacomo di Rialto
2. S. Marco
3. S. Pietro di Castello
4. S. Lucia
5. S. Geremia
6. S. Lunardo
7. S. Marcuola
8. La Maddalena
9. S. Fosca
10. S. Marciliano
11. S. Felice
12. S. Sofia
13. Ss. Apostoli
14. S. Canciano
15. S. Maria Nova
16. S. Croce
17. Ss. Simeon e Guida
18. S. Simeon Grande
19. S. Giacomo dall'Orio
20. S. Zandegolà
21. S. Stae
22. S. Stin
23. S. Agostino
24. S. Boldo
25. S. Maria Mater Domini
26. S. Cassiano
27. S. Mattio
28. S. Giovanni Crisostomo
29. S. Pantalon
30. S. Tomà
31. S. Polo
32. S. Aponal
33. S. Silvestro
34. S. Bortolomio
35. S. Marina
36. S. Salvador
37. S. Lio
38. S. Maria Formosa
39. S. Severo
40. S. Giustina
41. S. Ternita
42. S. Nicolò dei Mendicoli
43. S. Angelo Raffaele
44. S. Basegio
45. S. Margherita
46. S. Barnaba
47. S. Trovaso
48. S. Agnese
49. S. Vio
50. S. Gregorio
51. S. Samuele
52. S. Vidal
53. S. Maurizio
54. S. Maria Zobenigo
55. S. Angelo
56. S. Beneto
57. S. Luca
58. S. Paternian
59. S. Fantin
60. S. Moisè
61. S. Geminiano
62. S. Zulian
63. S. Basso
64. S. Giovanni Novo
65. S. Provolo
66. S. Antonino
67. S. Giovanni in Bragora
68. S. Martino
69. S. Biagio
70. S. Eufemia
71. S. Cristoforo (S. Pietro di C.)
72. S. Michele (Murano)
73. S. Giorgio (S. Eufemia)
74. S. Elena (S. Pietro di C.)

Marriage Wars in
Late Renaissance Venice

INTRODUCTION: READING TEXTS AND
BUILDING CONTEXT

*Do you think all the good qualities of men and all the good qualities of women
that historians claim are true? You should know that it is men that have written these things, and that they never tell the truth if not in error; and because
of their envy and ill will towards women, they rarely say good things about
us. Rather they praise their own sex in general and themselves in particular.*
                                            —Cornelia, in Moderata Fonte,
                              Il merito delle donne (Venice, ca. 1592)[1]

THIS WORK EXPLORES stories of failed intimacies that circulated in
the neighborhoods and courts of late Renaissance Venice, a city whose
historical record of marital litigation is extremely rich. It captures six-
teenth- and seventeenth-century individuals and authorities working
to keep the last few threads of troubled marriages from unraveling, or
untying the knots that held them together. The stories ring with contemporary relevance. Failing relationships badly marred by domestic
violence, betrayals, sexual problems, and economic woes still occupy
the attention of the mass media and generate debates about moral and
social issues among legal and health care professionals, community or-
ganizations, and audiences around the world. Married Venetians faced
similar problems, rooted in generational differences, avarice, philandering, betrayed loyalties, and marriage strategies that prioritized family
honor, class, and wealth over affection and compatibility. Their bu-
reaucratic structures and modes of communication were somewhat
more limited than those of the modern world, but they were still prepared to confront the challenges of domestic conflict. Their response
to family strife offers us significant insights into the history of attitudes
toward intimacy, domestic partnership, and marital breakup.

The time frame of this study, 1563–1650, represents an important
historical watershed. It was the century following the Council of Trent
(1545–1563), an event that marked the resurgence of the Catholic
Church as a force affecting many aspects of domestic life, particularly

the regulation of marital relationships. Theologians at Trent sharply defined the rites that made a marriage contract binding, an important turning point in the history of Catholic marriage. Prior to Trent, the Church had permitted the free expression of mutual consent between partners to be the only requisite for a valid marriage. France had regularized the marriage celebration, but in the rest of Europe a freedom of form had prevailed. A family model of marriage developed that prioritized social status, wealth accumulation, and inheritance. It hinged in part on arranged marriage, formalized in notarized contracts. As the post-Tridentine Church attempted to reassert its power over European society, the considerations that went into the family model of marriage were potentially made vulnerable by the new reforms, which did not insist on parents' consent to betrothal and marriage nor give parents any veto power. The Church prioritized the sacrament over the contract. At the same time it made new presumptions to be the ultimate authority over the validity of the contract, an intrusion upon customary practice. Ultimately the free will of the partners took precedence over parental wishes. Theologians at Trent also emphasized the absolute indissolubility of marriage, which was defined by canon law as a permanent union before God. The Church based the sacrament on Matthew 19:6—"What God has joined together, no man may put asunder." However, canon law did allow a separation of bed and board, such as when, by mutual agreement, husband and wife expressed a preference for religious vocations; when either spouse committed adultery; or in instances of extreme cruelty, where life and limb were in severe danger.[2] Theologians at Trent also reminded Catholics that all marital disputes had to be brought before the ecclesiastical courts.

Judicial records in the Patriarchal Archives of Venice provide the opportunity to assess the impact of Tridentine marriage reform as well as the Church's role in regulating marriage and marital breakup. In the century following the Council of Trent, both parents and children proved reluctant to follow the new rules on marriage and annulment, which frequently clashed with their individual desires. Financial concerns guided parents to arrange marriages for their children without allowing them veto power, while the children, favoring passion over parity in wealth and status, often tried to circumvent or thwart their parents' plans. In Venice, arranged marriage best served the patriciate, a closed, constitutional elite that had practiced endogamy for centuries, but the city's marital litigation reveals that parental control of marriage was not limited to the upper class. Nor was it limited to fathers and brothers. Children from ordinary households were expected to honor the wishes of parents and guardians as well, and mothers were strong figures of authority. Still, arranged marriage, predicated on a gendered view of relationships between women and men that did not accommodate the needs of everyone alike, was resisted. Ironically, the Tridentine reforms that defined how a marriage contract became binding gave some unhappy couples hopes of annulling their vows.

The post–Tridentine Venetian state was not a passive partner in the regulation of marriage, an institution that was vital to its stability. The Patriarch of Venice, who presided over marriage suits, was a member of the city's constitutional elite. Moreover, a good number of secular tribunals actively dealt with problems related to domestic conflict, ranging from assault and homicide to the expropriation of property. They strove to ensure proper maintenance of wives by husbands as well as to protect dotal wealth. The late sixteenth and seventeenth centuries was a period of growing secularization, with European states like Venice making greater claims to authority over institutions, including marriage. The flood of marriage suits did not ebb over the course of the seventeenth and eighteenth centuries, with the result that Venetian patricians sought to play an ever greater role in their regulation, in order to guarantee the stability of the aristocratic state.

Beyond shedding light on the impact of ecclesiastical and state authority over marriage, judicial records in Venice underline the importance of the broader community in regulating this vital institution. The city's inhabitants worked alongside ecclesiastical authorities to maintain the cohesion and continuity of the family and its wider networks of alliances, and they joined civic authorities and lawyers in mediating property disputes and accusations of the expropriation of goods. Friends and neighbors doubled as accountants, investment brokers, and arbitrators for litigating couples. Priests, along with kin, servants, and neighbors, claimed the insight that comes with experience, and served as sixteenth- and seventeenth-century family and marriage therapists. Midwives counseled and assisted women in sexual education, gynecological and obstetric care, and family planning. Female servants helped reluctant brides on their wedding nights and tried to assist battered wives. Neighbors continually censured and disciplined misbehaving husbands, wives, and children. Thus, the role played by communities in domestic disputes is critical to the exploration of the Venetian marriage wars. Supplicants, neighbors, and kin divided or collaborated on the issues of abandonment, domestic violence, forced unions, non-consensual sex, sexual dysfunction, and marital separation. The court investigations draw attention to the expectations and family responsibilities of men as well as of women. They reveal gender differences, including the ways in which men's responses to domestic problems differed from those of women. Finally, they illustrate differences between ordinary people and those within elite circles.

The court depositions archived by the Patriarchal Chancellery provide insight into scholarly debates in European cultural studies over how best to access and interpret the actions and sentiments of ordinary people.[3] My approach to this discussion will be to evaluate the internal properties of the court narratives, to go beyond the problem of broken unions present in the depositions to capture moments of personal intimacy, and to shed light on modes of communication and ordinary patterns of daily life. Depositions for the Patriarchal Court were inherently biased records. Supplicants and witnesses approached their examiners with the purpose of persuading the judges to take sides. With the help of parish priests and with ecclesiastical lawyers as advisers, they marshaled evidence and fabricated stories to win an express cause. Their stories contain a repertoire of tropes, rooted in canon law, conveyed by priests, lawyers, notaries, and perhaps other officials, and then tailored to the disputing parties' or their witnesses' individual situations. Even if the testimonies were deliberately slanted, they reveal individuals' hopes of remaking their lives and identities. Moreover, the stories had to ring true to the judges who weighed the significance of the depositions.

Success in achieving a chance for self-renewal depended in part on the litigants' skills in self-presentation. While lawyers built arguments based on canon law, the evidence from the disputing parties and their respective supporters had to sustain the legal structure of the case. Moreover, the strength of any testimony depended in large part on the credibility and moral characters of the witnesses. Within these important parameters, then, the depositions of supplicants and their witnesses allow us access to their modes of agency. That is, they reveal individual capacities to exert powers of decision, to act, and to fabricate narratives that might result in favorable judgments. The court narratives demonstrate skill both in using community gossip and in telling plausible stories before the courts.

The transmission of gossip was the community broadcasting system for domestic drama in sixteenth- and seventeenth-century Venice. Its power to organize codes of conduct and to regulate behavior knew few limits. Gossip was also a means of selectively assembling fragments of "what happened" to fashion a convincing narrative. It was filtered through shopkeepers, itinerant vendors, and a cast of other neighborhood characters, who in turn supplied their versions of situations and events to the courts. Plausible stories had a reciprocal relationship with cultural values; performance was both a product and a creator of standards, codes, and conventions. Learning what was a viable story in sixteenth- and seventeenth-century Venice and what was too far-fetched to be believed or accepted gives us templates for virtuous wives, reliable husbands, and obedient children. My assumption, borrowed from narrative psychologist Mary Gergen, is that individuals understood their lives through familiar cultural forms, gathered over their lifetimes from friends, neighbors, family, and authorities, and from a cultural repertoire of moral and social codes and conventions.[4] Rather than read the self-descriptions of deposing husbands and wives as reflections of their actual experiences, we may view them as appropriations from a cultural repository of stories that became synthesized as personal narratives.

Using language as evidence, however, presents its own complexities and ambiguities. The court depositions offer no certainty of social experience, but at the same time they cannot be reduced to language alone. There are several ways to understand the representations of supplicants and witnesses: they may reflect their own experiences, even if they are not necessarily aware of them, or they may have been directed by the lawyers. Still further, they may be voluntaristic, or, in the process of telling their stories, supplicants may have re-created themselves: the honest courtesan establishing herself as a virtuous wife; the adulterous wife describing herself as the unfortunate victim of an impotent husband who could not satisfy her desire for children; an obedient daughter who became a mature woman with needs and choices of her own; a husband who pandered his wife shedding tears of affliction, claiming to have borne the brunt of adultery.

Although there is no definite evidence for how annulment or separation narratives were transmitted among ordinary people in late Renaissance Venice, it is plausible to suggest that the authorities attached to the ecclesiastical court who routinely dealt with marital litigation furnished the structural framework for the stories. Lawyers presented the pleas of disputing spouses in conformity with canon law. The Patriarch and his vicar determined agendas of questions, and notaries from the Patriarchal Chancellery routinely took down the depositions.

The men and women who went through the court process, either as litigants or as deposing witnesses, then undoubtedly conveyed their experiences to others through the gossip networks. Together, then, authorities who shaped court experience, and ordinary people who went through the process, created a culture of marital litigation that took into account local custom and behavior.

The ecclesiastical investigations indicate that married women, more often than married men, called upon established institutions to protect their welfare and interests. Canon law and the Patriarchal Court were legitimate paths to changing marital status, and special patrician-run secular courts, established after 1553, furnished the mechanisms for protecting and recuperating dowries. The reasons more women than men turned to these courts are many. Women were more likely to be subjected to forced marriage, under constraint from parents and kin. Although men, too, were pressured to take spouses chosen by their parents, they may have been more reluctant to accept the negative consequences of disobedience, particularly if it meant disinheritance or disrupting the continuity of the patriline. Moreover, as husbands, they could simply abandon their wives or form new relationships without seeking the help of the courts. Generally they turned to them only when they feared losing dowry resources or hoped to gain sole control of them.

Wives, on the other hand, did not necessarily have the financial resources to sustain themselves if estranged from their husbands. Moreover, it was not honorable for women to live independently or outside of wedlock. Female honor rested with marriage, taking vows as a nun, or, following a failed marriage, living in an asylum for women. Unsurprisingly, the stories brought to the Patriarchal Court illumine the precarious state of unmarried women who did not enter asylums or convents: they generally ended up as domestic servants if they were fortunate, or as prostitutes if they were not. More surprising, however, are the admissions of *married* women working as prostitutes and in this way supporting their husbands. Without the help of kin or Catholic reform institutions, they tried to protect themselves against the dangers of illness, dishonor, destitution, or worse, some with more success than others. For some unhappy wives either contemplating separation or suffering the consequences of abandonment, the dowry was the only income to which they might lay claim. It is understandable, then, that they would turn to the courts to protect or recover the nest eggs that had been deposited with unreliable or incompatible husbands.

But dowries alone do not answer the question of why the ecclesiastical court was largely a women's court. It is also highly significant that the Church recognized free choice in the making of marriage.[5] The narratives of the women who deposed before the Venetian Patriarchal Court demonstrate some cognizance of this policy and of how it could help them improve the quality of their lives. Suffering abandonment with no possibility of remarriage, or the indignities of forced marriage, sexual dissatisfaction, or abuse from a misbehaving husband, led these women to work actively toward bringing about change. They not only refused to stay in unhappy relationships; they also expressed the desire to join with partners of their choosing. In bringing these lawsuits, Venetian women found support from kinsmen, servants, and neighbors, across generational, class, and gender lines. Moreover, authorities exhibited some understanding of women's desires for self-improvement.[6]

In the chapters that follow, I employ narrative techniques, allowing the dramas of the court investigations to unfold as stories, while at the same time contextualizing and interpreting these texts to unravel the intertwined and often unsystematic workings of Church, state, and community in regulating marriage and sexual behavior. The analysis highlights the laws and institutions in place to deal with failed marriages and domestic conflict, and assesses the ways in which the competencies of Church and state overlapped.

The depositions in the ecclesiastical investigations are a treasure trove for the study of self-presentation, showing how husbands and wives cast themselves before the courts and how lawyers participated in writing and directing their dramatic scripts. I suggest that the scripts not only expressed norms and interpretations of the family but also elicited new ones based on the stories of ordinary people living in Venice. Chapter One, "A Snapshot of Venice at the Twilight of the Renaissance," establishes the broader context for the stories, including the urban landscape; Venetian modes of transportation and communication; the city's social, political, and ecclesiastical structures; and the judicial activity of the Patriarchal Court in a comparative context with both Catholic and Protestant regions north of the Alps. Chapters Two through Five represent the major themes heard in the Patriarchal Court after 1563: petitions for annulment, based on coercion or on failed efforts to consummate unions, and petitions for a separation of bed and board, based on cruelty and neglect. The requests for dissolution of marital bonds submitted to the ecclesiastical tribunal were grounded in a formal language of complaint deriving from canon law. At the same time, however, there is a performative dimension to the testimonies, recorded in dialect, that casts light on the idiosyncrasies of Venetian values and attitudes as they separated out in terms of class and gender.

In Chapter Two, disputes between parents or guardians and children over forced unions and nonconsensual sex provide the raw material for an analysis of the scripts that supplicants presented to obtain annulments. This chapter highlights the life circumstances and strategies of women in their late twenties who claimed to have experienced arranged and forced unions a decade or so earlier, in their teens. They use Tridentine definitions of marriage to prove their own unions were invalid. Chapter Three, "Bedtime Stories," focuses on themes of sexual impotence. According to canon law, a marriage that could never be consummated was not valid. Claims of illness and gynecological problems reveal much about attitudes toward sex and intimacy as well as contemporary medical knowledge, the legal power held by midwives, and the rivalry between physicians and midwives. Chapter Four, "Concubines and Courtesans in the Courts," explores the illicit or clandestine relationships of concubines and courtesans whose quarrels with their aristocratic partners or their partners' kin brought them to both ecclesiastical and secular courts. The chapter offers important insights into the intimate living arrangements of married patrician males in adulterous relationships and unmarried patricians in intimate unions. Female partners express a sense of entitlement before the courts, refusing to be cast off as convenient but temporary commodities. In Chapter Five, "Tales of Violence, Hunger, and Betrayal," wives petition the ecclesiastical court for permission to separate. The chapter focuses on descriptions of bad husbands within failed marriages. Women claiming to be victims of attempted poisoning, battery, neglect, abandonment, sodomy, pandering, and adultery used the masculine operational code of honor to challenge their husbands' reputations before the community. Chapter Six moves from the Patriarchal Court to the Venetian secular tribunals for an analysis of the legal strategies women and men employed to preserve property when their marriages were on the edge. It also examines the state structures in place to protect the property of husbands and the dotal goods of wives, and looks at the role of arbitrators, selected from among the couple's friends and family, in settling property disputes. Finally, it compares women's attitudes about dowries with those of men.

My approach has been influenced in important ways by specific historical debates and the published work of several historians. One category is the ongoing methodological debate about the relation of the "historical" to the "fictional," a debate in which deconstructionists challenge positivists over the existence of absolute knowledge outside situational context.[7] Deconstructionists literally disassemble the historical narrative, drawing attention first to the historian's selection of data and individual interpretation, as well as to the inherent biases in the historical record. The main line of argument is that facts are "made," not discovered. It is my view that the stories of the ecclesiastical court lend themselves to this type of analysis, and that what is described must be approached with the utmost scrutiny. The work of Natalie Zemon Davis, particularly *Fiction in the Archives*, a book about how people narrated, and in the process also constructed, the realities of their lives, is a good model of analysis.[8] It was Davis who first characterized court testimonies as a mixed genre: first, as a judicial supplication to persuade the courts; second, as a putatively historical account of past actions or observations.

My own work considers the legal constraints and cultural assumptions that shaped the stories of supplicants and their collaborators in Venice. Even if the depositions were mediated by the notaries of the ecclesiastical court, the record of the vernacular enables us to approach the actual words and sentiments of the individuals. The strictures of canon law, contemporary social and cultural norms, and individual imagination also shaped the constructions in important ways. Familiar patterns in the narratives pose limitations for the historian whose aim is to get at "what happened." What emerges is that the investigations of the Venetian Patriarchal Court are replete with unspoken secrets and contrived lies, with "fictions" in the sense that the narratives are constructed by lawyers, supplicants, and witnesses. Experience may be presented in the form of a well-crafted narrative, but one should not presume such linear and neat explanations. There is no sharp dividing line between history and fiction, as Hayden White has aptly pointed out.[9] The depositions for the Patriarchal Court draw attention to the problems of crafting historical narrative from evidence that has been constructed for a purpose, in this case by supplicants and their lawyers for the adjudicators grounded in canon law. Real or imaginary, the Venetian tales of broken marriages document human will and agency, and furnish a repertoire of court stories in a situational context. I am suggesting that the successful plots for annulment or separation were passed on in neighborhood gossip as well as by specialized lawyers. Deposing witnesses availed themselves of both of these resources.

My analyses will also follow the model suggested by Joan Scott in

Gender and the Politics of History by questioning categories of analysis in gendered terms.[10] For example, what did adultery signify to supplicants and witnesses as men and women? To state prosecutors, lawyers, or priests as men? To family and community? Did men use accusations of adultery differently than woman? Viewing gender as an important determinant of human experience broadens the conceptual framework of the sixteenth- and seventeenth-century family by illuminating women's actions, by drawing attention to men's participation in family life, and by breaking down purported divisions of private and public.

Elsewhere, Scott draws attention to the limitations in giving historical subjects fixed, essentialized identities.[11] In this view, there is no one universal, permanent subject status for women, workers, peasants, or other created categories. Instead, identities are ascribed, resisted, embraced, and changed through discursive processes. The archival sources I have consulted afford the opportunity to remove women from venues that prioritized public politics or the transmission of family estates through male lines. They illumine snapshots of Venetian women as subjects exercising individual choice. Women responded differently to their life circumstances, according to their diverse situations and statuses. Some acted rather than simply being acted upon. Some used language creatively in court depositions to resist or to liberate themselves from oppressive conditions and prescribed roles. Above all, some used the courts to effect change.

These conceptual tools allow for an exploration of the extent to which Venetians were able to choose marriage partners or to break their marriage ties successfully, and to protect themselves and their property during the separation process. It is instructive to measure this degree of success in a comparative context. European states increasingly claimed more authority over domestic life in the sixteenth and seventeenth centuries.[12] Particularly in early modern France, Sarah Hanley has found that the efforts of the *noblesse de robe* to secularize family law, and thus obtain absolute jurisdiction over their children's betrothals, worked in lockstep with the growth of the absolutist state. Some scholars also emphasize that the new Protestant teachings and the resurgence of the Catholic Church reinforced patriarchy,[13] constricting young adults' opportunities to choose marriage partners over their parents' wishes. These conclusions find validation in prescriptive writings as well as in studies of elite family behavior, where concerns about wealth conservation and status limited options. In fact, this is the case with aristocratic women in Venice, as recent scholarship has amply illuminated.[14] People from the popular orders in Venice, in contrast, lived by a more flexible set of rules, and could ignore or reject prescribed social and moral codes. Among them were orphans, children with abusive parents or guardians, concubines, courtesans, and couples who concluded mésalliances that crossed class boundaries.

Resourceful individuals outside of Venice also exercised flexibility within the patriarchal framework. Two studies of women's agency in the Renaissance that have generated discussion are those of Lusanna, the fifteenth-century daughter of a Florentine artisan, who took Giovanni, her patrician lover, to court when he reneged on his promise to marry her[15] and of Bertrande de Rols, the sixteenth-century French peasant, popularized in *The Return of Martin Guerre*, who accepted the imposter Arnaud de Tille as her husband, despite the grave consequences she would face if her secret was discovered.[16] The experiences of Lusanna, a woman who turned to the courts for redress when her clandestine relationship collapsed, and of Bertrande, an abandoned wife who defied social convention to acquire a new husband, raise a series of questions that can be applied to late Renaissance Venetians: Were men and women able to work with or around formal legal structures to satisfy personal goals?[17] Were ordinary people able to have more influence outside political life, in the context of a neighborhood community? Did women outside elite circles break marital bonds more easily than daughters and wives within them? Systematic examination of sources like the Church depositions, which record the voices of men and women and trace their behavior, will enable us both to draw a clearer picture of the options available to them and to evaluate their powers to make choices in their own interests.

None of the storytellers discussed here necessarily achieved his or her goals. The outcomes of their attempts to receive favorable judgments, of course, were tied to many variables, among them the attitudes of the individual judges who heard their cases. Yet in late Renaissance Venice it is significant that the odds were good that women in troubled marriages would be allowed to dissolve their nuptial ties, a reality that provided them hope of changing their domestic circumstances. This work sustains the view that the institutions of public life—Church, state, community, and family—gave women in failing marriages some latitude to make choices. From these institutions women of many classes also received hope, direction, protection, and support. Much like today, in sixteenth- and seventeenth-century Venice, troubled marriages generated popular discussion and sparked community involvement.

"I have no intention of returning to him. I cannot believe Justice would require this."

A SNAPSHOT OF VENICE AT THE
TWILIGHT OF THE RENAISSANCE

VENICE WAS REPUTED to be among the most serene republics in Europe, offering safety and tranquillity to the diverse communities of people living within its waters. The sun, however, had almost set on the Renaissance Maritime Republic by the late sixteenth century. The city witnessed riots precipitated by adverse conditions. Foul weather in 1569–1570 and 1590 had brought the hardships of famine, and the collapse of the coinage system in 1602 prompted bakers to refuse debased coins as payment for bread.[1] The potential for siege also caused apprehension. The naval conflict with the Turks (1571–1573) had reached the very gates of Venetian frontiers in Istria and Dalmatia, fueling fears of Turkish conquest. Moreover, the city's economic life sagged from the strains and disruptions of war.[2] Then came another form of siege. Fleas infected with *Pasteurella pestis* inflicted the horrors of plague on the population in 1575–1577 and 1630. Trade and industry fell into a downward spiral after 1580, and by 1620 the city was no longer a European center of economic gravity. Nobles and other prosperous citizens scrambled to convert investment capital into passive income, such as rents and loans, and inherited fortunes took on greater importance, creating fissures among heirs. Textile workers and other artisans also felt the hardships of economic contraction, making it necessary for them to find other income-generating activities in order to subsist. Despite all these setbacks and reversals, however, the Constitution endured, and from the viewpoint of outsiders, Venice bathed in the myth that its inhabitants enjoyed exceptional peace and political continuity.

Even the urban geography was a metaphor for stability: *La Serenissima*, the Most Serene Republic, as Venice was called, was built on venerable piles of Istrian pine, driven more than twenty feet into a compressed bed of sand and clay and hardened over ten centuries. In 1493 the diarist Marin Sanudo marveled at the absence of fortified walls or

Facing page: Aerial view of Venice. Photo by Joanne M. Ferraro.

gates to lock in Venice at night.[3] In contrast to the sentries who guarded other European cities, the sea was Venice's night watchman.

Although geography fed the perception that the inhabitants on the lagoon were cushioned from surprise intrusion, it did not offer the same illusory feelings of security to Venetian neighborhoods. The threat was not physical but social and psychological, connected to notions of reputation and honor. Venetians, like other people, were subject to domestic conflicts that emanated from the hearth but inevitably spilled over into the neighborhoods, and sometimes flowed into the courts. Their disputes were by no means closed affairs: the geography of the city did not lend itself to privacy, nor did the culture. In the late sixteenth century the urban landscape measured only seven miles in circumference. Venice's geography fostered tightly knit neighborhood communities in close communication with one another. The neighborhoods were actually clusters of islands connected by bridges of wood or Istrian stone and filled with innumerable waterways (*rii*) that led out from the Grand Canal. Houses were densely packed along a labyrinth of streets (*calli*) radiating out from squares (*campi*). Some had sun roofs; others had balconies; still others, only windows. It was easy for Venetians to see into their neighbors' houses, to hear their voices through the walls, and to study their laundry hanging out the windows, ideal occasions to fuel their imaginations.

Modes of transportation in Venice also lent a special intimacy and interconnectedness to its inhabitants. There were two ways of getting about: on foot and by boat. Sanudo tells us the Grand Canal and the hundred-plus waterways were continually in movement, with too many watercraft to be counted. A galley service connected the Lido, a long strip of colonized land two miles away, to the Grand Canal. Patricians went about in beautifully ornamented, pitch black gondolas rowed by servants; more ordinary folk used rowboats, took one of the ferries that crossed the Grand Canal for a *bagattino* (a small coin), or walked the long way around the city. Alternative modes of transportation offered different perspectives on both routine and unexpected events. Little escaped the notice of astute observers of city life along Venice's maze of streets and canals. Moreover, Venetians knew, or at least recognized, their neighbors; strangers and newcomers were easily sighted and noted. People pondered over daily events, and they talked about them.

The Grand Canal served as the city's main artery, splitting Venice into two unequal parts, each with three districts divided into parishes. The larger, northeasterly part included the districts of Castello, San Marco, and Canareggio, and the other part encompassed the districts of Santa Croce, San Polo, and Dorsoduro. Castello, an important site for our stories, was the home of the Venetian Patriarch, the patrician who held the highest ecclesiastical office and who resided with his canons on San Pietro, an island linked to Venice by a long wooden bridge. The Arsenal was near by, and its workers, both women and men engaged in the armsmaking industries, often figured in the Patriarch's investigation into broken marriages. The Patriarch collaborated with a vicar trained in both Roman and canon law. Sometimes the vicar examined supplicants at his residence near San Geremia, in the district of Cannaregio. Other times the Patriarch and the vicar together held ecclesiastical court at Castello. They considered the arguments of lawyers who specialized in canon law and marital breakup, together with evidence from deposing witnesses.

St. Mark's, the largest square in the city, was the official site of Church and state. It was graced with a unique Byzantine-Gothic cathedral of remarkable beauty, the Doge's Palace, and the meeting halls of the government councils and courts. The picturesque Bridge of Sighs connected the Doge's Palace to the prisons in 1600. Adjacent to the piazza on the Grand Canal, a special mooring was the venue for judicial sentencing, hanging, burning, and other punishments.[4]

Patricians meted out secular justice and deliberated on matters of state in St. Mark's Square. Several courts and policing institutions that the characters in our stories frequented were attached either physically or bureaucratically to this site, including the Avogaria di Comun, the Signori di Notte, the Giudici del Procurator, and the Giudici del Proprio. The patricians who presided over them were not professionally trained lawyers, but had gained their positions through right of birth into a closed, constitutional oligarchy of a few hundred families. The three *avogadori* were state prosecutors who held office for a year. They had wide-ranging powers to arraign and arrest criminals; to have malefactors brought before the Doge, the criminal Court of the Forty, or the Senate; to propose proceedings; and to attend the meetings of these deliberating bodies, whose decisions they could overturn. The *avogadori* heard all complaints of assaults on persons and accusations of adultery. The Signori di Notte were Venice's night watchmen, one for each of the six districts of the city, whose *calli* and *campi* they patrolled in search of weapons and robbers. In these capacities they were sometimes called on to police domestic disruptions among violators of civil order. Other magistracies lodged at St. Mark's Square held competencies in marriage disputes as well. The Procurator and Proprio, respectively, protected wives' dowries against insolvent husbands and saw to it that widows received their dotal patrimony upon their husbands' death.

Leaving St. Mark's on the northeast side, the city's principal economic artery, the Merceria, linked the square with an important commercial hub, the Rialto Bridge. In 1588–1592 the architect Antonio da Ponte replaced the bridge's old wooden structure with a single marble arch, ninety feet in length, reaching from one side of the Grand Canal to the other. Both sides of the Rialto Bridge were flanked with shops and markets where secret meetings of lovers and opportunities for gossip took place. Vendors and gondoliers became valuable character witnesses in the ecclesiastical investigations because their activities provided occasions to observe the interaction of their customers. The exchange house of the German merchants, another gathering point, lay nearby. Men and women who did not attend the Wednesday market at Campo San Polo or the Saturday market at St. Mark's could find a large meat market, a fish market, and many other stalls at the Rialto. Men purchased sexual services at the Rialto, as well as at a number of brothels at St. Mark's, San Luca, and San Cassiano in Carampane.

Venetians sorted themselves into several classes: nobles, citizens, artisans, and various unskilled or lower classes. Dress codes, housing, and behavior served as visible signs of status. Both noblemen and male citizens wore long black robes, caps, and hoods, which made them the most difficult to distinguish on sight. Noblewomen flaunted a variety of jewels and finery: costly necklaces, rings of precious stones, and enormous pearls. We read about these items of clothing in the marriage disputes, for they were often points of contention between husband and wife. How individuals dressed was also an important descriptive element in the disputes, a visible sign of real or desired standing in society. Women's dress codes symbolized not only class but also marital status and reputation. Noble maidens wore veils and long tresses, and sometimes black capes. Women might, it was said, make purchases at favorable prices if clothed as maidens, connoted by a white kerchief, than dressed in the married fashion. For the most part, noblewomen donned silk, and were it not for the Senate's sumptuary laws limiting conspicuous consumption, so men complained, they would be even more extravagant. Cesare Vecellio's costume book offers us detailed descriptions of how Venetians dressed in public and in their homes. Vecellio classified maidens, wives, widows, servants, courtesans, and prostitutes separately and according to contemporary codes of honor.[5] Sobriety, expressed through subdued tones, signified a reputable woman. Colorful garb was relegated to the reaches of the home, away from the public eye or visiting guests; if worn in public, in Vecellio's account, it suggested waywardness. Servants' dress was quite plain: "frocks of tawny fabric, that Venetians call reddish brown, or some other dark color, such as peacock blue."[6]

Besides class differences, Venetians might sort themselves according to place of origin, for the city was home to people of many ethnicities. Although population data for the sixteenth and seventeenth centuries are incomplete and often contradictory, patterns suggest that, like other early modern cities, Venice's population fluctuated dramatically.[7] In the two plagues that ravished the city in 1575–1577 and 1630–1631, Venice lost a quarter of its population during the first and another 30 percent during the second.[8] Episodes of catastrophic mortality truncated households and brought profound disruption to family life. Heavy immigration from the countryside, some fifty thousand residents from the mainland, replenished the city. The Patriarchal Court records identify their places of origin as well as their occupations and ages. Skilled laborers as well as migrant peasants came from the territories of the Venetian regional state, which stretched as far west as Bergamo and north to the Friuli. Thriving clusters of German merchants, Orthodox Greeks, Turks, and Ashkenazi and Levantine Jews added to the mix. Language, or dialect in the case of migrants from the Italian Peninsula, distinguished individuals and groups from one another. Large-scale immigration to Venice no doubt created a perceived need to regulate marriages with newcomers, whereas commerce and warfare, in contrast, took husbands away and left the courts to deal with deserted wives who sometimes found new partners. Episodes of catastrophic mortality, moreover, threw the secular tribunals regulating dowries and inheritance into a whirl of activity.

Nuptial rates in Venice are impressionistic, making it hard to calculate the percentage of marriages that ended in annulment or separation.[9] Analisa Bruni's demographic study of the parish of San Salvador includes marriage rates for the period between 1575 and 1631. A total of 921 marriages occurred during that time, with annual figures as low as eight and as high as thirty, based on parish populations ranging from 1,969 in 1581 to 1,351 in 1632. Thus, for many years, the number of marriages relative to the total population of the parish added up to less than a percentage point. Moreover, 22 percent of the 921 were widows who remarried.[10] Michela Dal Borgo's study of the parish of San Zaccaria offers figures of between five and sixteen marriages per year at the churches of San Giovanni Novo (1608–1612) and San Severo (1591–1610).[11]

Marriage was for those whose financial capacities permitted it. Noble families practiced restricted marriage to conserve wealth, whereas common folk depended on scraping together a living to start a household. This by no means meant that people did not pair off. As our stories reveal, many had common-law marriages, rather than the legitimate unions that would be entered in the parish registers. In noble families, in which only one son married, the single brothers especially forged relationships with women whose labels ranged from prostitute, courtesan, or concubine to foster child or ward. Sometimes these relationships were permanent but clandestine, threatening to disrupt family inheritance practices. The marriage disputes are particularly revealing of women's claims to legitimate unions, much to the consternation of the noblemen's natal kin. Other disputes were quarrels between people who legitimately married but later came to regret it, taking to the courts their hopes of refashioning their lives and their identities. These are the principal subjects of our stories.

Going to Court in Post-Tridentine Venice

Word of the Church's regulations on marriage and separation reached the Venetian community in a variety of ways. First, the Venetian patriarchs accepted the responsibility of transmitting the decisions of the Council of Trent to parishioners. Even Giovanni Trevisan (1559–1590), who had voted against the *Tametsi* decree at Trent, reiterated the rules expeditiously. Beginning in 1564, he instructed parish priests to repeat them regularly at Mass. The first year priests received instructions to announce the rules every Sunday to parishioners, and every Christmas and Easter thereafter.[12] Trevisan's successor, Lorenzo Priuli (1590–1600), formalized the Tridentine regulations in Venice by making them into juridical norms. The new rules, however, were not necessarily respected or enforced. Thus, Priuli had to emphasize throughout his term that legitimate marriage rites required the presence of a parish priest who knew the couple.[13] Knowledge of the reforms also spread, in all probability, through the Venetian community through the activities of the Patriarchal Court. The presence in Venice of this important ecclesiastical tribunal and of experts in canon law who specialized in marital litigation made legal norms and practices local news. Word of the legal results presumably spread, publicizing the Tridentine rules.

The Venetian state also worked to regulate and stabilize the institution of marriage, passing laws that were complementary to the Tridentine reforms. The Republic recognized the Church council and accepted its deliberations. During these same years Venice and the Papacy joined to combat heresy; Venice hosted the Inquisition, and some of its own patricians sat on the tribunal.[14] Still, there were limits to the cooperation between the Republic and the Roman Church: Venice consistently refuted papal claims to jurisdiction over temporal affairs within its domain.[15] The Republic itself wanted to supervise the moral life of the polity, first, by keeping one of its own patricians in the office of Patriarch, and, second, by passing secular legislation and providing judicial enforcement.

Although for the most part the Patriarchal Court in Venice adjudicated petitions for annulment or separation,[16] breach of promise suits shifted to the secular arena during the late sixteenth century. Broken betrothals had long been a source of anxiety for civic authorities in the medieval cities of northern Italy.[17] The stability of marriage as an institution was vital to their social and political equilibrium. Moreover, women whose honor had been compromised were excluded from the legitimate marriage market, and potentially became civic liabilities. For centuries the Venetian ruling class had upheld the institution of marriage as an organizing principle in both politics and society. Amid a general climate of growing secularization throughout Europe, the Venetian state took responsibility for guarding the honor of women.[18] In 1577 the Council of Ten, Venice's supreme judicial organ, appointed a special magistracy, the Esecutori contro la Bestemmia, to punish men who had sexual relations with women and then reneged on their promises to marry.[19] By the late sixteenth and early seventeenth centuries, then, this kind of case was more rarely brought before the ecclesiastical court. Besides the disciplinary action of the Bestemmia, the

Tametsi decree of Trent also alleviated the confusion over what constituted a binding contract of marriage. This is, for example, what happened in seventeenth-century Zurich, where the form of taking vows
was so closely enforced that breach of promise suits waned.[20]

The Venetian state, like the Church, established formal structures
that admitted the possibility of failed marriages during the mid-
sixteenth century. A Venetian tribunal, the Giudici del Procurator, handled the division of property in marriage disputes. Beginning in the
second half of the sixteenth century, a Venetian woman acquired the
legal right to place a lien on her husband's patrimony if her dowry
were in jeopardy. She also could file a complaint before this secular
court if her husband was not providing her with adequate food, housing, and clothing. A law registered in 1553 stated that both wives and
husbands had the right to present their property claims before the
Procurator.[21] Six years later, Venetian legislators established another law
authorizing this tribunal to appoint arbitrators, called *giudici arbitri* or
giudici confidenti, to help spouses decide on a fair property settlement in
the event of separation.[22] It was common for litigating couples to file
cases in both ecclesiastical and secular courts simultaneously. The
Church took up the form of the contract in annulment cases and the
quality of the marriage in petitions to separate; the state adjudicated
over broken engagements as well as property rights in failing or dissolved marriages.

Here we shall focus exclusively on stories designed to dissolve marriage, either through petitions to annul an alleged agreement or through
requests to separate bed and board. The surviving records of ecclesiastical investigations undertaken after Trent deal preponderantly with
these issues. The protocol for breaking marriage ties, either by demonstrating that the union was not valid to begin with, or by receiving permission to live apart, began with engaging a representative to plead
one's cause before the court.[23] This could be either a lawyer with a degree in canon law or a procurator (*procuratore*), someone who legally
represented the litigant. A lawyer constructed a technical defense based
on canon law. A procurator simply gathered evidence, through witnesses, to prove the assertions of a disputing party.[24] It was not obliga-
tory to have a lawyer, but there was no limit to the number of lawyers
that could be engaged to represent a party. However, the Church permitted only one procurator, who came before the ecclesiastical judges
with a special, notarized commission to represent his client. Although,

in theory, a lawyer and a procurator had separate competencies, in practice one person often functioned as both. Moreover, whether or not the legal representative was actually a lawyer, signified with *iuris utriusque doctor*, the term always used in the ecclesiastical investigations was "procurator."

The procurator drafted the main points of the case, called articles, and submitted them to the Patriarch or his vicar, together with a list of witnesses who would verify the supplicant's assertions. The vicar had authority to judge matrimonial cases, save those the Patriarch wanted to judge himself. If the Patriarch or vicar accepted the petition, the disputing parties were summoned before the court. The Patriarch or the vicar explored the articles one by one, and then formulated the dispute(s) in question in the form of propositions to be settled by judicial investigation.

The task of the procurator was to establish the facts, seeking proof from witnesses; the lawyer assumed the facts delivered to him by the procurator were true, and on them he built his legal argument. From an ecclesiastical judge's point of view, there was good reason to have both a procurator and a lawyer: the lawyer's duty was to focus on points of law, not on establishing facts, so he would not be tempted to suborn false witnesses. In our marriage disputes, however, the duties of the procurator and the lawyer often fell upon one person, creating the opportunity for a lawyer to coach witnesses and/or distort testimony.

Judges sometimes needed to establish the general moral character of the parties in order to evaluate their depositions. The sworn testimonies of spouses or their witnesses by themselves were sometimes insufficient. Thus, people were sometimes asked to appear before the Patriarch or his vicar at the court in Castello. Others, however, were deposed in their homes before a notary from the Patriarchal Chancellery, who recorded the questions of the court in Latin but took down the responses in Venetian dialect. The interrogations of the witnesses followed the pattern of questions the Patriarch or the vicar had prepared. The value of the depositions hinged on both the moral character and the credibility of the spouses and their witnesses.

Once the proofs of the initiating party were incorporated into the judicial acts, the opposing party, with his or her procurator, prepared remarks and criticisms. The opposing party had the opportunity to respond with contrary evidence and witnesses. Procurators for the disputing parties then stated the facts, based in canon law, and offered their pleas. In principle, but not always in practice, the judge appointed a defender of the bond (*defensor vinculi*) to sit with him during annulment disputes, and together they heard the lawyer's or lawyers' pleas. The job of the defender of the bond was to protect the nuptial union, arguing against annulment before the judge, for the presumption of the law favored the validity of the marriage. However, the defender was not always present to hear the pleas. The judges (including the Patriarch, the vicar, and sometimes one other ecclesiastical judge) reviewed the written, notarized acts gathered from the records and the witnesses, and made a decision based on points of canon law. They did not need to have *absolute* certitude, but rather *moral* certitude, a degree of conviction that excluded fear of error.

At the conclusion of the case, the Patriarch and the vicar summoned the litigants and pronounced a verdict, which hinged upon the written, notarized acts that were gathered from records and witnesses. They also indicated whether wife, husband, or both would be responsible for the expenses incurred to prepare the case and to gather and depose witnesses. Court fees were nominal, or nonexistent if the parties could not afford them. All of the procedures and verdicts were recorded. Dissatisfied parties appealed to the Apostolic Court in Rome. These documents, like the ecclesiastical investigations, form the basis of this study.

Despite what we know about ecclesiastical legal proceedings, the all-important judicial gaze of the Patriarch and his vicar eludes us. The records provide a written record of testimony but include no elaboration from the judges on how they arrived at their verdicts. What we know is that verdicts were to be based on points of law. Moreover, the sacred duties of the Patriarch and his vicar bound them to safeguard the institution of marriage in the interests of the Church. Historian Arturo Jemolo tells us that the judge was obliged to be the adversary of the party requesting an annulment, and that he was required to accede to the arguments of the defender of the bond. *Il favor matrimonii* (literally, to favor matrimony) was a dominant principle in marriage trials.[25] Canon law certainly illuminated the path to judgment, but the responsibilities of Patriarch and vicar would compel them to search the juridical souls of supplicants and witnesses in order to weigh the value of the depositions. How many witnesses did the Patriarch or his vicar actually interview, and how many did they instead come to know only from the written depositions of the notaries? It was one thing to assess

Venice, island of the Giudecca. Church of Santa Maria della Presentazione (1579), or "Le Zitelle," a refuge for endangered women founded in the sixteenth century. Photo: Osvaldo Böhm, Venice.

a personal presentation and quite another to read a deposition that had been filtered through a scribe and then interpreted and argued by legal representatives.

Did procurators coach witnesses? I would contend that the canon lawyers specializing in marital litigation indeed set the parameters for the court stories, drawing on their rhetorical skills, legal vocabulary, and knowledge of the law to supply tropes for supplicants and witnesses. Though we can never truly know what transpired between legal representatives and clients, for they left no written records, what we see is the same legal professionals consistently assisting petitioners to the Patriarchal Court, and the same terminology coming up repeatedly in the individual stories. It is more than likely, then, that the lawyers created a language of complaint over time for marital litigation, giving the annulment and separation scripts formulaic qualities. But what of the notaries who served the Patriarchal Chancellery? To what degree did their recordings provide consistency? Distort testimony? In short, what we are looking at, and what the Patriarch and the vicar were examining, were stories framed by their very own questions and recorded by the notarial personnel attached to the court. Procedures and arguments of procurators and judges were recorded in Latin, whereas the depositions were left in the dialect of ordinary folk.

Some discussion of the ecclesiastical office of the Patriarch is important to an understanding of the relationship between judge and judged in the marriage cases. Above all, it is significant that the Patriarch of Venice was not a transplant from Rome or elsewhere; he was someone grounded in the lifeblood of the Venetian Republic, someone with patrician values, with secular interests, and with an interest in preserving the stability of an aristocratically governed state that was admired throughout Europe. It is difficult to draw lines between Church and state in Venice when the highest ecclesiastical official came from the ranks of the Venetian ruling class. The patriarchate was linked both to the Venetian state and to the Papal See in Rome.[26] From its establishment in the mid-Quattrocento, this office was always occupied by a Venetian patrician elected from the Senate. The selection of a Venetian patrician for this office, together with Venice's traditional opposition of Roman authority, was highly significant: it increased the chances of greater sympathy to secular interests. Moreover, because the Patriarch belonged by lineage to the city's constitutional elite, he was well grounded in both social and Venetian affairs, and connected to networks of allies and their opponents.

Venice had long had the reputation of limiting the authority of the Church within its dominions by asserting its secular priorities. By the mid-sixteenth century, the process of choosing the Patriarch was removed from the monastic orders with links to Venice and placed in the hands of Venetian patricians, who ensured that laymen rather than clerics held this important office. The Venetian Doge Leonardo Donà justified the shift to a lay Patriarch by recalling that he had read in St. John Chrysostom "that it was often more useful to the Church to have a bishop chosen from among the advisers of a state than from monasteries or seminaries." The majority of patriarchs who presided over the marriage investigations in this study were laymen, elected between 1554 and 1619. The Benedictine Giovanni Trevisan, the son of Venetian patricians, Paolo and Anna Moro, and Patriarch from 1559 to 1590, was the only exception. It was Trevisan, as mentioned above, who integrated the reforms emanating from the Council of Trent

(1545–1563) into Venetian life, calling up his priests in 1564 for the first synod to take place in thirty-three years, and in 1561 helping to persuade Pope Pius IV to permit Venice to continue choosing its Patriarch. However, Trevisan was especially noted, and criticized in Rome, for his collaboration with the Venetian government,[27] so much so that the Papal See attempted to gain greater control over the selection of Venetian patriarchs by requiring an examination in canon law and theology before a congregation of cardinals in Rome. Venetian statesmen managed to circumvent this requirement in the elections of laymen Matteo Zane (1600–1605) and Francesco Vendramin (1605–1619), but these men almost always worked with assisting vicars who had degrees in both Roman and canon law.

The career of the lay Patriarch Lorenzo Priuli (1590–1600) exemplifies how attuned the patriarchs were to the secular interests of the Venetian patriciate. Priuli had had a full and prestigious diplomatic career before being elected to the patriarchate at the age of fifty-three, including service as ambassador at the court of Phillip II at Madrid in 1572, at the court of Henry III at Paris in 1582, and then in Rome in 1584. Very knowledgeable about the advent of Protestantism and religious division in France, he was also intimately acquainted with the Counter-Reformation politics of the Spanish Crown and the Papal See. In 1590, when he was elected Patriarch, Priuli was serving the Venetian state in another important capacity, as the governor of Brescia, one of the most important subject cities of the Venetian regional state.[28] Through his family, Priuli was also connected in important ways to the peak of the Venetian political hierarchy. Both his brother and his brother-in-law Alberto Badoer held multiple important offices during the 1580s. Several of the other patriarchs who figure in our stories had equally distinguished secular careers.[29]

Besides leading the Church in Venice, the Patriarch supervised the parish priests whose duties included performing the marriage rites. It was the Patriarch's responsibility to see to it that priests followed the Tridentine reforms. Apparently not all of them did, for Lorenzo Priuli called synods in 1592 and 1594 to insist that priests reside in their parishes. He also wanted to examine priests on points of theology.[30] Francesco Vendramin (1605–1619) set the age requirement for priests who wanted to be confessors at thirty-five or older, and required them to take an examination in canon law. Giovanni Tiepolo (1619) applied rigid Tridentism, so much so that his priests pleaded with the Doge to protect them from his encroachment on their autonomy.[31]

Priests, like the Patriarch, were deeply grounded in Venetian culture. Elected for life terms by those who owned property in the parish, the priests were greatly indebted to neighborhood inhabitants, who were in a strong position to influence their clergy. Though the marrying priest was obliged to observe the mutual consent of the marrying partners, coercion of the bride, for example, might be overlooked at the request of an influential parent or guardian. Not just accomplices to forceful parents, the priests often played important roles in the lives of their married parishioners. As the stories that follow reveal, women in troubled marriages often took advice from their confessors, asking them to help resolve their problems, to study their cases, or to refer them to experts who could help them with their troubles. The parish priest was often the first person to whom a troubled partner would turn before presenting a petition to the Patriarchal Court. Some priests even served as procurators for troubled wives.

It is appropriate to place in context the personal dramas of the couples in our stories by examining the overall activity of the Patriarchal Court in the decades after Trent. A wife, or a husband, or at times both spouses, petitioned for either an annulment or a separation. Annulment petitions were based on a variety of pleas. The most common one was from a woman who claimed she did not marry of her free consent (*a sponsalia per verba de praesenti*). Another was the claim by either partner that a sexual dysfunction had prevented consummation of the union. Still another, though rare, was a petition for annulment on the grounds that the partner had a previous marriage contract with someone else. In a maritime city like Venice, some merchant husbands disappeared on voyages. Abandoned wives remarried without petitioning the ecclesiastical court for permission, on the presumption that the spouse was dead. If the first spouse returned, the petitioner could ask for release from the first marriage, but the ecclesiastical court consistently enforced a precedent contract.

The data for annulment activity in the Patriarchal Court derive from two archival sources. One is the Acts of the Patriarch's Court, where notaries registered the requests, furnished the names and parishes of the supplicants, often identified the supplicants, and sometimes indicated the outcome. The second is the registers of verdicts. The Patriarchal Archives house far more records of requests and verdicts than collections of full-scale ecclesiastical investigations. The evidence, thus, is sporadic and does not lend itself to statistical analysis. Nonetheless, the data furnish some idea of how many people were seeking annulments or separations. Twenty-nine years were randomly chosen from the period between 1565 and 1624.[32] There were 118 requests for annulment, averaging four per year. That is probably a conservative figure, given the haphazard methods by which the activities of the court were recorded and preserved. It is significant that women initiated 75 percent of these petitions for annulment. Although in most instances the outcome is unknown, of the forty-three recorded verdicts, thirty-nine favored women. From this we can suggest that the court was a place that offered hope to some women, if not redress.[33]

The registered activities and verdicts of the court furnish a profile of the people seeking annulments. The petitioners ranged across the social spectrum, with fewer patricians than people from the common orders. This is not surprising, given the care with which marriage partners were chosen at the upper levels of society and the potential loss attached to the dissolution of an aristocratic marriage. Of those who requested annulments, more came from the middle-to-lower classes, including weavers, ironworkers, goldworkers, bricklayers, textile workers, fruit vendors, arms workers, merchants, spice merchants, and boatmen.

Petitions for separation are common in the Patriarchal Court records. The regularity with which requests for separation reached the court, sometimes as many as one per month between 1564 and 1651, suggests that men and women of all classes in this urban center thought they had a real chance to change their domestic circumstances. Sex made a difference in the plaintiffs' grounds for separation. Men's requests were based largely on accusations of adultery, and husbands made their arguments on the grounds of their wives' sexual reputation and honor. They had additional recourse besides the Patriarchal Court, because charges of adultery were often related to property disputes and thus also fell under the secular jurisdiction of the Avogaria di Comun. It was common for husbands to file for separation on grounds of adultery in the Patriarchal Court as a countermeasure against wives formally seeking to dissolve their marriage ties. A favorable judgment for the husband in this instance would enable him to keep his wife's dowry. In fact, retention of the dowry seems to have been the prime motive of men who resorted to the Patriarchal Court. But women had the same incentive to obtain a formal judgment separating bed and board, because it would secure their property and their incomes from rapacious and negligent husbands. The Patriarchal Court was a women's court because a formal judgment from the Church gave women leverage to recover their dowries, sometimes the only financial resource available to them. Women's requests, however, were often based on grounds of extreme cruelty, or on a husband's inability to provide food, clothing, and a safe living environment.

Did the activities of the Patriarchal Court actually give husbands and wives—particularly women, who filed the preponderance of suits —the realistic prospect of changing their marital status? The verdicts for the periods 1601–1607 and 1621–1626, two of the three surviving archival series which lend themselves to systematic study, show that odds were good that women would be successful in obtaining separations. During the first period, thirty wives requested separation, and eighteen of them received favorable judgments. Four husbands also made requests, and three of them were successful. During the second period, seventeen of twenty wives received positive judgments, whereas only one of three husbands obtained successful results.[34] What really stands out for both periods is the sympathy for the plight (moral, physical, and financial) of women in bad marriages. Women from all social ranks obtained hearings that offered the possibility of change.[35] Battered wives who filed suit in the Patriarchal Court in Venice found support at all levels of public life, and they could avail themselves of a variety of established institutions and public officials to aid them in their efforts to obtain favorable judgments.

It is useful here to compare Venetian figures for annulment and separation suits with court activity elsewhere in Europe. Data for marriage courts north of the Alps suggest a larger volume of annulment petitions than we have statistics for in the Venetian case. Jeffrey Watt's study of Neuchâtel, Switzerland, indicates that contract disputes far outnumbered divorce cases.[36] Moreover, plaintiffs petitioning to enforce contracts outnumbered those who wished to annul engagements. Thomas Safley's study of the diocese of Constance concludes that a third of the 11,778 cases adjudicated by the court regarded contract validity and another third consisted of consummated contract disputes. Moreover, in Constance only 15 percent of the cases that went through the court between 1551 and 1620 concerned separation;[37] 75 percent of these requests were successful. By contrast, divorce or legal separation was a possibility only for a very wealthy man or woman in sixteenth- and seventeenth-century Geneva. The most common reason for divorce both there and in Neuchâtel was adultery, and it was usually cited by males.[38] However, Protestant areas of Europe were increasingly emphasizing that husbands owed fidelity to their wives. In Zurich, 40 percent of the cases brought to court in the 1520s involved the suits of wives against adulterous husbands.[39] The Venetian marriage disputes also reveal that wives were not always patient Griseldas when their husbands were unfaithful.

Now it is time to hear the stories of the couples themselves. There are 210 records of full-scale investigations preserved in the *Causarum Matrimoniorum* for the period between 1564 and 1650. Those selected for the chapters that follow represent the full spectrum of arguments for annulment or separation that women and men brought to the Patriarchal Court. Their stories leave us with more questions than answers about their lives, but we can learn much from the omissions.

"Out of great fear of my father I said yes with my voice but not with my heart."

PERILOUS SCRIPTS, FORCED UNIONS, AND RAGGED WEDDING NIGHTS

CAMILLA BELLOTO, the forty-nine-year-old daughter of a silk weaver, petitioned the Patriarch's Court in Venice in 1617 in the hopes of obtaining a formal separation from her husband, Angelo de Bollis, a textile worker from the Friulan town of Palmanova.[1] The procurator Camilla had engaged, Pietro Abettino (a canon lawyer and a cleric), explained that her relationship with her husband had deteriorated within months of their taking their nuptial vows, twenty-five years earlier. Angelo had reneged on his commitment to support Camilla, and instead, he and his mother had offered his young bride's sexual services to a gentleman. After six months Camilla abandoned Angelo, taking refuge in her father's house in the neighboring town of Padua for a year and a half. She eventually left her father and returned to Venice, but she never again lived with Angelo. Camilla made her living from prostitution. For the most part she and her husband had been estranged since the initial separation, though mutual friends had tried to reconcile them nine years before Camilla went to court.

Camilla's deposition clearly revealed that she and Angelo had hardly experienced what could be called a marital relationship. Indeed, the prostitution and abandonment evidence made dubious the partners' intent ever to form a serious union. Camilla's petition in 1617 was in effect an attempt to dissolve all civil ties with her husband. Angelo did not object to Camilla's suit.[2] It is possible that he was interested in regularizing his marital status before God. Many couples, living in uncertain marital legitimacy, turned to the Patriarchal Court, expressing fear of divine retribution. Angelo, however, was also interested in his temporal status and in defending his honor and integrity before the Vene-

---

Facing page: Giovanni Antonio Fasolo (1530–1572). *Stolen Embrace* (c. 1568–1570). Vicenza, Villa Caldogno Nordera. Photo: Foto Archivio Storico Trevigiano/Provincia di Treviso/Assessorato alla Cultura.

tian community. While Camilla portrayed him as vile and cowardly, he insisted he was an honest Christian who earned a living by his trade and whose wife had willingly abandoned him for a life of prostitution. Camilla, he said, was "a bad woman of the worst quality," who for twenty-four years had lived "in public places" as a "public prostitute." But the witnesses from the Venetian community, crucial censors of family behavior, did not corroborate Angelo's story. None denied how Camilla earned her living, but they faulted Angelo for her sorry plight.[3] Among the worst fates that could befall a woman was to become a prostitute. It was the husband's responsibility, according to community standards, to support his wife and to safeguard her honor.

Camilla's formal statement does not offer an explanation for why she waited twenty-five years to break her formal ties with Angelo, nor does the self-defined prostitute clarify her motivation for requesting the annulment. The unspoken is tantalizing. Did Camilla have a man waiting in the wings to marry her? Could she have survived twenty-five years of prostitution? Was she already living with someone else? Did she perhaps have children whom she was eager to legitimize? Did she fear her soul was in jeopardy because of an illegitimate liaison? Was she avoiding a charge of adultery by claiming she was a prostitute? Or had she reached the end of a career in prostitution and now wished the return of her dowry? All of these are possibilities, but not reasons that would likely convince an ecclesiastical judge to grant the annulment. Camilla's first request had been for a separation of bed and board, signifying she would consent to remain formally married in the eyes of God but with independent living arrangements recognized by the Church. Annulment, in contrast, meant that there never was a valid marriage, thus offering the possibility of a remarriage. Perhaps Camilla had this in mind, for we do have evidence that she later remarried. One wonders whether her last husband aided her during the ecclesiastical inquiry, or if the incentive behind her desire was simply to sever her ties with Angelo de Bollis, but on these matters the records offer no information.

Camilla's efforts to obtain a separation from Angelo came to naught. Deliberations of the court continued from the summer of 1617 into the spring of the next year, but then the case simply dissolved. It seems Camilla and her procurator were unable to build an argument that promised successful results. However, three years after they had filed the separation request, they returned to the court with an entirely different strategy. On April 8, 1620, Abettino presented a petition for annulment—an attempt to say a valid marriage never took place. By then he and Camilla had rounded up a host of witnesses who would depose on Camilla's behalf.[4] Over the next year the case would run its course, with successful results.

The argument that Camilla and Pietro Abettino constructed for the annulment case rested on the invalidity of the marital union. Angelo, also represented by an ecclesiastical lawyer, Giovanni Rossi, did not object, and Camilla's mother and sister offered their full cooperation in making the court case. In essence, the entire family agreed that annulment was the best course to pursue, and they collaborated to reach their goal.

Camilla's story was that of a forced union, one of the most common plots in the annulment petitions brought before the ecclesiastical court. In Camilla's deposition a violent, tyrannical father, since deceased, figured as the main villain. Without a doubt, his death had liberated her as well as her mother and sister to go before the court without fearing obstruction or counterarguments. Perhaps Camilla's father was part of the reason for the long delay in her requesting an annulment. It was quite common for women to turn to the Patriarchal Court after the death of a parent or guardian. The time lapse was so long that it was possible that the priest who had presided over the union was deceased as well, so there would be no one to contest the form or celebration of the marriage rites. Camilla, sustained by her sixty-year-old mother and forty-year-old sister,[5] did not hesitate to denounce her father's shortcomings. She announced that he was a man who frequently committed adultery, who hit his wife, and who threatened to beat Camilla to death if she did not consent to the marriage.[6] It is important to note that Camilla, and her mother and sister, used her father's philandering as a weapon to defame his character, revealing that women, too, expected fidelity and were confident about expressing that sense of entitlement to the Patriarchal Court. Moreover, they stood to receive a sympathetic response from adjudicators, who were there to defend the Church's stance that sexual relations were solely for the purpose of procreation and were permitted only within marriage.

Camilla complained that her father sold her at age thirteen to Angelo for 400 ducats, which he quickly spent on prostitutes.[7] That, if true, would be an interesting reversal. Rather than providing a dowry for his daughter, she was claiming that he sold her to a knave, who would in turn try to make a living from selling her sexual services. Camilla's mother, Veronica, confirmed her daughter's claims.[8] Of her husband she complained, "He wasted the 400 ducats on women, and he led a bad life, which one does not do with loved ones. . . . My husband governed the household poorly. He kept prostitutes, fearing God very little, and he beat me and the children frequently." Veronica explained that she tried to intervene on her daughter's behalf to prevent the betrothal, pleading that Camilla would be desperately unhappy. Many times her daughter had threatened to drown herself. But the response of her late husband was so violent as to leave Veronica infirm and bedridden for forty days. Although Veronica's story is not the focus of the case, her testimony leads one to ponder her long silence: Why didn't this abused wife seek redress in the Patriarchal Court by requesting a separation? Does this point to some generational difference between Camilla and Veronica, or was Veronica simply exaggerating her description of a violent husband to assist her daughter?

Camilla's sister, Marietta, also described her father's nature as dreadful. She stated that "He was a man who lived badly, keeping prostitutes, with little fear of God. He beat my mother and us without any compassion. He came home full of anger and said dirty words that cannot be said here."[9] Was Mattheo guilty of cursing, or something more serious, such as blasphemy? Blasphemy was an offense not just against God but also against the Church, and Venetian culture in general. In the sixteenth century a special magistracy, the Esecutori contro la Bestemmia, had been established in Venice to discipline immoral behavior, including speech crime.[10] Camilla and her family were coupling the father's foul language with his sexual transgressions to put him in the worst possible light before the representatives of Christian morality.

Camilla also relied on a witness outside her nuclear family to describe Mattheo Belloto's disposition and his treatment of his family. Jacobo Justiniani, a distant relative, volunteered, "It's true that Mattheo Belloto led a bad life, and for that reason he died and he left his family in a needy state. I know his family had a hard life because of him. Camilla told me she did not want that dirty slime for a husband."[11] Camilla emphatically stated, as was common in these cases of forced marriage, that she cried for many days and nights, and that, crying, she said these words: "I do not want this husband in any way, and if my father wants me to accept him by force, I will never stay with him. I will go away." This is a variation on the standard Venetian language of complaint: "I do not want this spouse in any way." Another variation was "I never wanted him [or her]," usually followed by the explanation "I said yes with my voice but not with my heart." These phrases appear over and over in the petitions for annulment, a sign that the parties were coached by lawyers familiar with the canon laws that invalidated marriage. They were meant to demonstrate the disjunction between the petitioner's manifested consent and actual free will.

Although Camilla's marriage was celebrated and consummated, she and the sister who testified on her behalf went to great lengths to let the ecclesiastical judges know she was unwilling to have sexual relations with Angelo on her wedding night. It was her sister Marietta, however, who generously offered the graphic details. Her description of Camilla and Angelo's first night together is both imaginative and humorous, yet the testimony also forces the reader to reflect on the feelings of a teenage bride anticipating sexual relations with the unwanted stranger her parents had chosen. Marietta explained Camilla's attempt to evade Angelo's advances on their wedding night:

> My sister asked me for a sewing needle. With it and some thin thread she sewed the nightgown together, so that Angelo could not have sex with her. The morning after I saw my sister, her nightgown was still sewn together, and thus I knew that she had not consented to have sex. She did not consent for many nights, and it was a great effort to have her go to bed with him. On this matter my mother is informed.[12]

Marietta added that the couple were together only a few months and that they truly hated one another. Indeed, Angelo and Camilla had hardly lived together as husband and wife, and Camilla's confession of prostitution called out for some adjustment on the part of the Church. The story of being sold by her father for 400 ducats and her unwillingness to consummate the union added compelling evidence that the bride had not consented to the marriage. Consent was a fundamental requisite if the union was to be valid. The judges granted the annulment.[13]

Camilla's story raises an important issue: Was divorce impossible in Catholic areas of sixteenth- and seventeenth-century Europe? In the eyes of God and under the laws of the Church it was, for the sacrament of marriage was a permanent spiritual union. However, if the concept of annulment—that a valid marriage never took place—were substituted for that of divorce, the practical results were the same. Annulment, like divorce, offered supplicants like Camilla Belloto the possibility of a remarriage. Her case, and the others discussed in this chapter, suggest there was a degree of consensus in sixteenth- and seventeenth-century Venice that some marriage ties should be broken, and that they could be struck from the record by creating a discourse that did not ostensibly transgress the laws of God as defined and defended by the Church. The boundaries that Church laws and reforms drew around marriage rites played an important part in shaping that discourse. They created a structural context for invalidating marriage. Yet the narratives of supplicants and witnesses also played an important role in sustaining acceptable justifications. Their subtexts both reflected and shaped popular values, offering us deeper cultural insights into the history of marriage, family, and sexuality.

WHEN THEOLOGIANS met at Trent in 1563, they reiterated the twelfth-century decree that marriage was both a natural contract and a sacrament.[14] However, a promise of matrimony followed by sexual intercourse was no longer considered sufficient, for late medieval courts throughout western Europe had been flooded with breach of promise suits and questions of when and how an agreement became binding.[15] There was also the long-standing problem of clandestine marriage, a practice that had pervaded the European landscape. Children ignored the wishes of their parents, celebrating the rites of marriage in private in order to avoid the destinies that had been mapped out for them. Parents from all social ranks, but particularly from the upper classes, where endogamy preserved and enhanced power and status, were pressuring the Church to prevent clandestine marriage, and the issue was vigorously debated at Trent.[16] French and Spanish prelates argued for a more public celebration of marriage, and the former further demanded that a valid marriage require parental approval. In contrast, many Italian prelates, including the Venetian Patriarch Giovanni Trevisan, were not as concerned with clandestine marriage, defending the medieval canon law that only the mutual consent of the partners was necessary to make a valid union. Venice issued no formal instructions to its representatives at Trent, allowing them to vote their conscience.

The *Tametsi* decree that resulted from the Council debates was a compromise. The consent of the partners to the marriage had to be made public, with an announcement of the banns three times in the local community. Partners were required to marry before the bride's parish priest (or the groom's, if the former was not available) with two or three witnesses present. The priest performed the rite, asking partners to voice consent in their own words, while the couple actually served as the ministers of the sacrament. The priest then gave his blessing to the union; it was the form that confirmed the natural contract of marriage. Next, the marriage had to be registered. Finally, the union had to be consummated, making the couple "one flesh." If these conditions were not met, the church did not consider the marriage valid.

Catholic reformers did not agree to make parental consent a requirement of marriage, a decision of great importance. It implied that forging marriage ties was not exclusively a private, family affair, based on property arrangements that were registered before a notary.[17] Instead, the *Tametsi* decree placed the Church in control of both contract and sacrament, which became inseparable. Reformers strongly discouraged clandestine marriage, declaring it a mortal sin, and it became harder to form such private unions. Nonetheless, the practice did not disappear, for the prohibition was only as effective as its enforcement. Thus, at times unions were still formed by simply reciting vows before a parish priest, either in church or at home, and the banns were not necessarily published ahead of time.

Secular authorities in Europe had more interest in abolishing clandestine marriage than the Church did. The French and Spanish monarchies were swift to enact legislation against it, while the Republic of Venice worked at a slower pace, perhaps because the duty to register the marriages and births of the Venetian patriciate and the *cittadini* was already assigned to the Avogaria di Comun. There were no special provisions to register the marriages of ordinary people until 1663, when the Senate enacted legislation to ensure that the exchange of vows was performed publicly and the union was registered. Until then, marriages were registered in the parishes where the celebration was performed, a strict requirement of the Church. Both secular and ecclesiastical authorities frowned on clandestine marriages but ultimately recognized them as legitimate.[18]

The impact of the *Tametsi* decree went beyond clandestine marriage, however, a strategy betrothed couples used to avoid an arranged match. Among ordinary people in Venice, the Tridentine rules released to parishioners encouraged them to request the annulment of vows already taken. Individuals devised strategies to have their marriages declared invalid, dismantling the unions parents, guardians, benefactors, or ex-lovers had arranged for them. Moreover, the narratives of the Patriarchal Court indicate that the doctrinal requirements of mutual consent followed by copulation were still important factors in demonstrating the validity of the marriage contract, in addition to the procedures of celebration outlined at the Council of Trent. The *Tametsi* decree ultimately came down on the side of free choice.

Support of free choice went beyond the Council of Trent. Early modern legal theorists also agreed that parental coercion was incompatible with the free consent of partners required in marriage. They followed on the heels of both medieval theologians and canonists who insisted that if either bride or groom had been induced to consent to marriage by force or fear from any party, the contract was invalid.[19] The Venetian legal authority Marco Ferro still cited this position as part of Venetian practice in the nineteenth century: "a marriage contracted out of fear is *ipso jure* null."[20] Whether or not the marriage was consummated was further, important evidence of mutual consent and thus a key criterion in deciding its validity. Clearly, from the testimonies in the cases brought before Venice's ecclesiastical court, supplicants and witnesses were aware of the issues of consent and consummation, whether transmitted by the narrow circle of lawyers who specialized in marital litigation or by word of mouth in the community.[21] Thus, they cooperated in constructing similar narratives in order to reach their goals.

The concerted actions of supplicants, witnesses, and procurators in obliterating the picture of a consensual union make the investigations of the ecclesiastical court formulaic. There is a built-in structure to the cases, shaped by legal theory. The stories of supplicants and witnesses are replete with unspoken secrets and contrived lies, with "fictions" in the sense that the narratives were constructed. When there were only a few reasons that would nullify a marriage, many stories of a couple's domestic history likely remained untold. Instead, the storytellers privileged the scripts that the culture found plausible and acceptable, and made characterizations that promised to bring about the desired outcome of the case.[22]

What is significant about the Venetian narratives, besides the concerted action of litigants and witnesses, is the justifications the story-tellers and their representatives believed could convince the judges that the marriages were invalid. An argument based on "incompatibility" would not meet the legal criteria for a marital dissolution. An annulment could not be won on grounds of estrangement, irreconcilable differences, lack of love, physical unattractiveness, or bad breath. Yet all these reasons appear in the sources. "Invalid" was the legal construction the case hinged on; it provided an acceptable way out for both the supplicants and the judges who heard their pleas. But in fact the underlying discourse was about the unsuitability of a union that had not cohered or sustained the values perceived to uphold the fabric of society. The best marriages were those that provided financial security, safeguarded honor, and ensured community stability.[23] When they suffered serious deficiencies in these areas, there was some community consensus that they could be dissolved.

The performative dimension of the narratives presented to examiners is also significant and merits close scrutiny. What kinds of scripts and characterizations did women use to persuade the judges to annul a marriage? Stories of coercion by threats of violence or disinheritance were among the most common. Violent anger and the threat of physical harm were compelling factors in proving that marriages were products of coercion. Camilla Belloto's narrative adhered to contemporary legal definitions of a forced marriage contract and the rules regarding what constituted coercion.[24] Harsh words or a few blows were not enough to persuade theorists and the ecclesiastical judges who applied the law that a marriage contract had been compelled. Threats of serious violence and death, however, presented convincing examples of coercion, for *grave* fear ("grave" signifying "very serious"), it was argued, was incompatible with free choice.[25]

Like Camilla Belloto, Vittoria Cesana used the threat of physical harm to prove that her marriage to the Venetian nobleman Giovanni Battista Barbaro was coerced, and thus invalid. Her father, Antonio, she claimed, had put a knife to her throat and threatened to kill her. When the vicar heard her petition, Vittoria stated:

I would like, and I seek from the court, the annulment of the asserted marriage made in appearance between me and the Illustrious Giovanni Battista Barbaro. It took place against my will by force of my father. [When Vittoria's father announced the betrothal, she said] I began to cry when I heard this, and to say I did not want Signor Barbaro for a husband. It was not my wish nor my consent. I never would have married him, because when I was at our villa in Zumiana, I had promised someone from Padua, whose name I do not remember.[26]

Clearly Vittoria had revealed her affections for another, whose name she would not disclose, feigning forgetfulness. Asked how her father had coerced her, Vittoria replied:

He grabbed my arm and took me to a room, pushing the door with his hand so that it was only partially closed. There in the room he pulled out a knife from a table drawer, and holding it in hand, he took me by the shoulder and said, "Look, if you do not promise me you'll marry Barbaro, I'll kill you." Also grabbing me by the throat, he uttered the same threats with the same words and with the same knife in hand. And fearing he would kill me with that knife, I told him I would obey, with my voice, but not with my heart, and because of the great fear I had that he would kill me. But the marriage never derived from my will or consent. . . . Then he took me to another room in my brother's house where the priest was waiting with the said gentleman, Giovanni Battista Barbaro, and other people whom I do not remember because I was feeling a great deal of pain and confusion. I said yes with my voice alone to the priest's question of whether I accepted Giovanni Battista, fearing my father would kill me. I cried continuously because I did not want [Barbaro], and I only said yes out of fear of dying. The marriage never was, and never will be, a real one.

Vittoria's father, accompanying her to her brother's house, had rounded up a priest she did not know, which clearly violated the Tridentine rules on marriage. Vittoria's case reveals that some priests did not adhere strictly to their pastoral duties, even though theologians at Trent had warned that a cleric who performed a marriage outside his parish could be suspended.[27] Perhaps the priest found by Vittoria's father was motivated by the belief that paternal authority should override the will of children, because there was no consensus over parental consent to marriage, either in Venice or in the rest of Catholic Europe. It is also important to remember that in Venice, parish priests were chosen from among property-holding parishioners, who might influence priestly behavior. Perhaps Vittoria's father simply offered this priest money or favors to satisfy his wishes. That Vittoria's father went outside the parish to find a priest to perform the marriage rites also suggests that his own parish priest might have objected to his scheme, standing by the rules outlined in the *Tametsi* decree.

In building her case, it was important for Vittoria to claim that her discontent with the union was public knowledge. She told the examiner that she had complained to everyone, including her spouse:

> Telling him that he was not my husband, I refused to go to bed with Giovanni Battista, but I had to, because my father, my mother, and even my sisters wanted me to. I only stayed with Barbaro three days and three nights, always by force, because I continuously made him understand that he was not my husband, that I was forced to marry him because of my father's violence. After those three days Barbaro, feeling my aversion for him, left my house and never returned. I have not had any news of him. I do not know where he is, and I am happy about that because he was not my husband, and he never will be. This marriage should be declared null because it was coerced, against my will and with oppression.

In this case, the supplicant's brother, mother, and sisters did not oppose the father's decision, so prior to the marriage the unhappy young woman turned for help outside her family, hoping to reverse her situation. Vittoria sought aide from the same friends after the marriage as well, when she built her case for an annulment. It was Vittoria's servant and two noblemen, Theodoro Minio and Antonio Boldù, whose testimony convincingly corroborated her story.[28]

Theodoro Minio, the *compare* (close friend) of Vittoria's father, Antonio, had accompanied the distraught young women to her father's door. He had urged him to reconsider and had tried to dissuade him from forcing the arranged marriage. "Signora Vittoria confided in me because she had become attached to another person, and they had even exchanged words about marrying." Theodoro had spoken to Antonio on Vittoria's behalf, without betraying her confidences. According to Theodoro, Antonio responded, "My daughter had better follow my ways because I am her father, and I do not want to lose out on this favorable match."

Vittoria persisted in seeking help from her friends. Theodoro told the vicar that Vittoria begged him and another friend, Antonio Boldù, to intervene on her behalf and prevent the marriage. Theodoro continued:

> Her father was in a room talking to his wife. The two of us approached him when he was alone, without his wife, asking if it was true that he had arranged the marriage between Barbaro and his daughter. He said yes, and then we begged him to consider his daughter's feelings, as she had not been given the opportunity to participate in making the match and was very unhappy about the negotiations he was conducting. But because he was her father, he was sure that he was doing this for her own good. We left Antonio but continued to talk to Vittoria about the matter.[29]

Theodoro confessed that he and Antonio Boldù had eavesdropped on Antonio Cesana and his daughter, Vittoria, peering through a keyhole (a device often used by witnesses in their depositions to explain how they were invisible observers), and had witnessed the knife scene. "Seeing that the young girl was completely afraid and confused, we left immediately, not wanting to remain any more or to intrude in others' business." Their departure suggests, oddly, that they did not fear for Vittoria's safety. Perhaps the knife scene was concocted to make the story of coercion more credible. More interesting is the friend's expression of concern for Vittoria's feelings. In this case, generational differences did not stand in the way of the father's friends consoling and supporting Vittoria.

Antonio Boldù was questioned immediately after his cousin Theodoro. The testimony of this *compare* of Antonio Cesana was shorter than his cousin's. Nonetheless, he confirmed that Vittoria did not want Barbaro, information he derived from an important source, the women servants he chatted with at *casa* Centana. But Boldù remarked that Barbaro loved Vittoria, and had courted her and desired her as a wife.

Vittoria, with the aid of her lawyer, Paolo Gentili, and the two noblemen who testified in her favor, had made a persuasive case that she had been violently forced into marriage. Her husband, perhaps to defend his honor, had hired a procurator, the nobleman Giovanni Contarini. But though Barbaro's procurator tried to minimize the thrust of Vittoria's argument, he produced no statement for his client, nor did he provide witnesses. In reality, Barbaro had already left the marriage. The court granted Vittoria an annulment. She had not married of her own free will. Moreover, the marriage had not followed the official proceedings specified at Trent, and thus was invalid.[30]

Threats of violence did not come exclusively from fathers. They could be delivered by a guardian or, as in Magdalena Filosi's story, by her mother's lover.[31] In 1620 Magdalena's mother and her live-in partner, Iseppo Ciurano, forced her to marry a weaver, Anzolo Faniente, whose surname suggests he was unemployed (*fa niente* literally means "to do nothing"). In this case both spouses sought an annulment. They complained that Anzolo's parents, fearing Iseppo's violent rage, persuaded him to marry Magdalena.

Although some parents and guardians behaved irresponsibly by giving girls or young women to abusive or unsuitable spouses and then not offering assistance, others were more caring and, upon discovering serious problems, attempted to remedy past mistakes. We cannot be certain whether the stories were true or fabricated to sway the court. Yet it is striking in these annulment cases to see that women's ties (whether emotionally positive or negative) with their natal families often endured after marriage. Parents who recognized the flaws in their choice of partners, who changed their minds or strategies, or who simply conceded that the marriage had failed came forward and testified in their daughters' favor.

In Paolina Pirron's case her entire family was willing to end the marriage they had persuaded her to make. Paolina, a tailor's daughter, was married at age sixteen and requested an annulment fifteen years later.[32] She claimed she married Lorenzo Comelli in fear of her father's rancor, and out of general deference to her parent's authority.

> I seek an annulment because the marriage was never part of my spirit, nor would I ever have chosen Lorenzo voluntarily as a husband, but when forced into the ceremony, I said yes to the priest, out of fear and because of my father's force. [He] forced me not only with his words but also with threats and with violence to say yes with only my voice that I would be happy to take Lorenzo as my husband. [Asked about her father's threats, Paolina explained,] They were that if I did not consent to take Lorenzo as my husband, he would have thrown me out of the house and would not want me to be his daughter anymore. Be-

yond this piece of roguery one or two times, I don't exactly re-member, I ran away from home and went to stay with my cousin Paolina nearby. At the time I lived in the neighborhood of San Felise. But I was not certain I could save myself in my cousin's house from the threats and violence of my father. My mother and father came to get me, and took me away by force. They continued to offend me with threats and with blows, continu-ously being violent with me and coercing me to take Lorenzo as my husband. Finally, one day about sixteen years ago—I don't remember the exact day—my father came home spontaneously with a priest, the Piovan of San Felise. Although I do not re-member the exact day, the marriage took place the same day I was threatened and thrashed as [my father] had done once be-fore. And that morning again he threatened to throw me out of the house and to disown me as his daughter. In the afternoon, after the noon meal, he forced me to say yes to the priest. I con-sented only with words, not with my heart, nor with my true consent. Truly not then, nor now.[33]

Again in violation of the *Tametsi* decree, a priest outside the bride's parish had been persuaded to carry out the will of a forceful father. Two days later Paolina continued her testimony. This time the central subject was her wedding night. At least in this case, the maiden about to have her first sexual experience was given no gentle preparation. It is plausible that with unwilling brides and forceful grooms the expe-rience was painful, and that families exhibited a certain callousness and clumsiness about the conjugal duty.

The first night of my asserted marriage with Lorenzo, my father forced me with violence to enter the bedroom. He shut me in the room. I resisted getting into bed with Lorenzo. He was ex-tremely violent, dragging me and throwing me on the bed. He did this three or four times, as I left the bed. He threw a chest on top of me and he struggled to get me on the bed. But then I was still dressed, never wanting to take my clothes off and consum-mate the marriage with him. I told him I was forced to marry him, and that he was not, nor would he ever be, my husband, even with all the violence he had committed to consummate the marriage.

The next morning Lorenzo, in bed with me and undressed,

but very angry and tired, did not say a word to me. And I, having cried and still crying, took my maiden dress off and remained in my undergarments in bed, in deep despair and continuously crying and resisting sexual intercourse, as I had done all the night before. Because of the importunity and violence of my father and mother, who the entire next day wanted to eat me alive [a metaphor for "kill me"] and made a big commotion about the house, I was miserable and afraid, always protesting against my father and mother that Lorenzo was not my husband. . . . The second night, as violent as the first, I was ragged from the violence I had experienced. Having slept with my maiden clothing, I was forced to undress and to go to bed with Lorenzo. My father threatened me, saying if I did not consummate the marriage the second night I had gone to bed with Lorenzo, he would crucify me. Thus, having experienced more violence, I got into bed with Lorenzo without my clothes on, but crying and lamenting. And it was that night that the marriage was violently consummated, as I shouted and lamented a bit with fear that if my father and mother heard me, as they were near my room, they would have mistreated me the next morning.

Paolina lived with Lorenzo for only three months. She was careful to emphasize that she did not manifest free will to marry, crying often about her unhappy circumstances. She finally fled her husband and returned home. Her parents finally understood she did not want this man, and they agreed to take her in. Her in-laws and husband agreed. Thus, they were all willing to seek an annulment from the Patriarchal Court.

Paolina's father, mother, mother in-law, and husband deposed on her behalf. Her father, Giovanni, admitted he had coerced her to marry, and he expressed his regrets.[34] A neighbor and a former apprentice corroborated his statement.[35] Paolina's mother, Pasqueta, testified that her young daughter feared both her parents. Pasqueta also maintained that she and her husband had forced Paolina to marry. Her testimony offers important insights into parenting, and the emotional exchange between a stern mother and a timid daughter.

She lived under our obedience, and it is true that she feared us. She feared me more than my husband because as a woman I was always at home, and I governed her with great fear and I was also angrier than my husband in governing her. I remember these things quite well as Paolina's mother. I don't know if others knew about this because I did not go to others' houses. . . . My husband thought he was a good young man. . . . We threatened her because we knew the girl was timid and feared us, and that she would do what we said. . . . The morning after, my daughter did not tell me anything, out of respect, and I did not ask her anything, but from her face I understood that she had cried all night. . . . Paolina never told me anything about the days she slept with him at my house and at his.[36]

Lorenzo's mother, careful to defend her son's integrity, also testified that Paolina never loved Lorenzo but was predisposed to another man.

Paolina said she was not happy with my son Lorenzo because he could not dress her in silk the way she wanted. I don't know anything about her fears. During the three months she lived at my house, they were always fighting. Although he loved her, she did not love him. She was in love with a Michelin, who lived at her father's house. I know this because I witnessed Michelin and Paolina on many occasions during the three months she lived at my house.[37]

Lorenzo himself testified that his wife relented to consummate the marriage only on the second night of their union, and that he thought she was in love with another.

The day I went to her house to marry her, she cried continuously, and she said she was not happy to take me as her husband. If she married me, she said, it was because of the threats and blows from her father and mother; so she said and complained publicly. Paolina cried the entire wedding day. The first night she slept with me because her father and mother violently forced her, taking her to my bed. That night she did not want to consent to consummating the marriage. On the contrary, she was violent. With all that, the marriage was not consummated. But since her parents wanted to beat her and throw her out of the house, the second night when they put her in bed forcefully, I violently forced her to consummate the marriage. She called to the devil to take her away, saying that all that she did, she did because she was forced, and that she was never my wife. Paolina and

I were only together for three months, always in conflict and in war night and day, since she was always firm and resolute that I was not her husband and that she had done what she had done because her parents had forced her. One morning she fled from my house and went to her parent's house, and from that moment on, she did not return to me. I believe it was because she was in love with someone else.[38]

It was unusual for a husband to concur with his wife's legal position and, moreover, to admit he had been forceful with her. Lorenzo clearly wanted the annulment petition to be successful, and thus his testimony was in harmony with the other depositions in the case. The testimonies of Pasqueta, Paolina, and Lorenzo all revolved around degrees of fear. *Reverential fear,* in canon law the trepidation in a parent–child relationship, was not considered serious enough to sway a resolute person to marry. However, *grave fear* was, and it invalidated the marriage, as did acts resulting from physical force. Paolina won her case. The judges annulled the marriage.[39]

The threat of disinheritance was another motive that supplicants used to explain how they were coerced into marriage. Mothers or other female guardians were more often accused of making these threats than were male guardians, and it was more often daughters who attempted to override their mothers' arrangements. If it could be demonstrated that a parent or guardian had threatened disinheritance and that the daughter was without recourse, that was sufficient cause to have the marriage judged invalid. A case in point is Arcangela Ceraione, who requested that her marriage to the goldsmith Bernardino Gisbè be annulled in 1620.[40] Arcangela claimed through her procurator, Giovanni Rossi, that Bernardino was not to her liking, but her mother, Arcangelas's only means of financial support and the sole provider of a dowry, constrained her to marry against her wishes. Her mother, Domina Antonia, was

fierce, resentful, and prone to following through with threats. Thus, her daughter was extremely fearful of her. [Antonia] . . . threatened her, not just to hit her, as she did, but also to throw her out of the house and abandon her altogether. . . . If Arcangela said "no" before the priest, Antonia would have killed her or thrown her out of the house.[41]

Stern mothers like Domina Antonia were common elements in the stories of unwanted, arranged marriage. The repeated submission of evidence of this kind to the ecclesiastical examiners suggests that Venetian mothers were strong figures of family authority, commanding reverential fear from their children.

On Fat Thursday 1620, Arcangela married Bernardino Gisbè. The date was ironic: Carnival was a time for fun, but this wedding, virtually a sham, was not a joyous occasion. Besides maintaining that her mother forced her into marriage, Arcangela emphasized that she did not want to consummate the marriage on her wedding night, making so much noise in resisting her new husband that many [neighbors?] ran to her aid.[42] The argument that Arcangela had not consented to the union with Bernardino but had been forced into marriage satisfied the judges, and she received an annulment in 1621.[43]

Eight years later, in another case, Isabetta Damiani engaged a lawyer, Francesco Lazaroni, and petitioned to annul her vows to Iseppo Sansoni, a musician.[44] Lazaroni argued that Isabetta's uncle, the barber Favio Montagna, forced her to marry the man of his choice. As her guardian and her legal representative, Favio administered the resources earmarked for her dowry as well as her inheritance. Thus he controlled whether Isabetta would marry and whom. The annulment petition read:

> Favio Montagna, a barber-surgeon, Isabetta's uncle, was her only and absolute guardian and procurator. She had neither father nor mother at the time of her marriage, and she revered her uncle as a father. Favio Montagna had the entire management of her dotal assets and other inherited wealth with all the documentation, so that she could not marry [without his consent], being poor, young, and an orphan.[45]

Isabetta was in love with Stefano Bosselli, a bronze caster. Although she married Iseppo Sansoni, the couple separated after only ten days. The marriage, it seems, was seriously troubled from the very beginning, for nine days after the marriage, the Avogaria di Comun issued a restraining order against Sansoni.

> I, Monte Mezzan, infantryman [*fante*], have an order from the Illustrious *Signor Avogador* Gradenigo dated the 28 of this month [of August] for *Domino* Iseppo Sansoni, musician, who lives in

San Vio in the houses of Da Mulla, who upon a penalty of prison, jail, or banishment, to be chosen by judicial authorities, must not in any way, not even through people who intervene on his behalf, offend, or molest with words or deeds, Madonna Isabetta Damiani [the daughter of Francesco], his wife, nor remove anything from her house that is part of her dowry.[46]

Nine and a half years later, Isabetta approached the Patriarchal Court. Again it seems plausible that she wished to rewed. Sansoni opposed the annulment. Although the formal outcome of the case is unknown, Isabetta's will, preserved elsewhere, reveals that she remarried a wine merchant, to whom she left all her worldly goods.[47] Either Sansoni had died or Isabetta had won the annulment.

In contrast, Cornelia Calzago's case in 1597, based on financial coercion, failed to obtain the desired results. The supplicant blamed her widowed mother for her ill-fated marriage to Giovanni Francesco Fisaro,[48] but her confessed behavior does not seem likely to have produced a winning story. Cornelia had a lover, a Signor Bartholamio Polchari, whom she met secretly at her uncle Zuanne Pisani's house. Her mother tried to break the liaison, which would have tainted the family honor, by arranging a marriage in secret with Giovanni Francesco. Cornelia told the court that she submitted because her mother threatened to beat her and to throw her out of the house. Still hopeful that she could wed her lover, Cornelia tried to undo the marriage her mother had arranged, filing for annulment with the Patriarchal Court. Her mother, however, still controlled the purse strings and, with them, the course of Cornelia's married life. In response to Cornelia's appeal before the Patriarchal Court, she procured her own ecclesiastical lawyer and, by way of compromise, offered to help Cornelia obtain a separation in order to divert her from the annulment, and probably from her lover. The ecclesiastical judge ruled that Cornelia's marriage was valid, possibly because he did not approve of her relationship with Bartholamio Polchari.[49]

In another losing case, presented by the lawyer Giovanni Pagnonum in 1628, Joannetta Hortolani argued that her mother forced her to marry Francesco, the son of a carpenter at the Arsenal. Francesco was poor and willing to accept Joannetta with a meager dowry. Joannetta had left Francesco after fourteen months of marriage. She did not speak of what she had been doing since, although eighteen years had passed since they had exchanged vows before the parish priest. Now thirty-three years of age, Joannetta was hopeful the Patriarchal Court would find the marriage invalid. The statement that Pagnonum presented to the court on her behalf explained how she had come to the decision to approach the court.

> Although she married against her wishes and free choice, she has always firmly believed that her marriage is valid, good, and could not be dissolved. Until the last feast day, when she spoke with some people about her situation and she was told that according to canon law and the opinions of theologians and canonists, the marriage could be found invalid, provided she could prove the way it was arranged. She wanted to consult with the ecclesiastical doctors and thus she introduced her petition for the annulment in the Patriarchal Court.[50]

That Joannetta found out about the possibility of annulment only after eighteen years of marriage is an interesting comment. It might indicate that there were limits to the gossip networks in Venice, or that cultural mores were changing. It might also signify that she was simply not telling the truth. She had married according to the rites of celebration required at Trent, a strong argument that the marriage was valid regardless of her unwillingness to continue the relationship. More important, her statement draws attention to the importance of ecclesiastical lawyers as transmitters of canon law and as the intermediaries between unhappy spouses and the Patriarchal Court. Joannetta hoped her vows would be annulled.

Like Paolina's story, Joannetta's was largely determined by a strong maternal figure. When Joannetta was thirteen, she was happily betrothed to a sailor, Zuanne Calafaro, with her father's consent. It was agreed that Joannetta was still too young to marry, and while the engaged couple waited, Joannetta's father promised to put together a dowry. Unfortunately, Joannetta's father died two years later, while Zuanne was out of the city on a ten-month sea voyage. Her mother, Angela, spent the savings meant for the dowry and then forced Joannetta to marry Francisco. The petition read:

> Madonna Angela pressured [Joannetta] day and night, persuading her to marry Francesco, who had visited the house frequently. And every time [Joannetta] saw him, not being able to stand him,

she escaped to the neighbors' houses, here and there, staying until he left. At the neighbors' she cried continuously and lamented with everyone that she was engaged to Zuanne, who would soon return from a voyage. Her mother was forcing her to marry Francesco against her free consent and will. Thus she fled and was desperate, not knowing what to do so that she would be left alone.[51]

Perhaps Madonna Angela felt such great financial pressure that she believed the best thing for her daughter was to arrange a marriage of convenience, irrespective of the virtues and vices of the designated groom.

But after the Council of Trent, daughters like Joannetta went to court, presumably with the encouragement of lawyers who realized the usefulness of the *Tametsi* decree, arguing that they had been dealt an injustice. In her deposition Joannetta used the common refrain in annulment cases: she said yes to the parish priest with her voice but not with her heart, an assertion that was difficult to demonstrate or deny. Nonetheless, the statement was articulate:

> Married October 3, 1610, in the church of San Pietro di Castello and questioned repeatedly by the priest, Pre Anzolo di Michieli, she did not respond until the third time, out of fear of her mother, and she was very troubled, responding yes with her voice but not with her heart. The priest was astonished, and [defensively] he said, "I wouldn't marry this couple, if I had not been commanded to do so, seeing her to be so reluctant."[52]

It was an admission that he had not performed his pastoral duty but had bent to the strong will of an authoritarian mother. Here is further evidence of the influential roles that Venetian mothers played both in family and society.

Joannetta produced nine witnesses, mostly widows from her neighborhood who knew her at the time of her courtship with Zuanne Calafaro. Just as if this were a street performance of the commedia dell'arte, there was a chorus of sympathy for the woman who had lost her true love and had been forced to marry a poor slob. The women's testimonies focused on the love Joannetta and Zuanne had felt for one another, and the unsuitability of her husband, Francesco.[53] The first witness was Zuanne Calafaro's sister in-law. Dona Clementia, forty-two, the widow of a carpenter who had worked at the Arsenal where Francesco was employed, confirmed Joannetta's husband "only earned sixteen *soldi* per day." This was not enough to support both Joannetta and himself. Dona Clementia also confirmed that Joannetta's mother had spent the inheritance her husband had left their daughter, and then had threatened to scratch out Joannetta's eyes if she did not marry Francesco. The second witness, Lucieta, fifty, the widow of a wool weaver, came from the neighborhood of Joannetta's youth. Although uncertain how much time had passed, guessing twenty-four or twenty-five years, Lucieta explained that she knew Joannetta when the girl lived with her and her family under the columns in Zielo at Castello.

> I would hear when I visited my mother that this Zuanne Calafaro made love with Zanetta (Joannetta), that he loved her, and she was in love with him. I heard this from Zanetta, too. [Of Joannetta's mother, Lucieta remarked that] she was not a judicious woman. Valentino was a man who saved things to put away for his daughter Zanetta's dowry. . . . I know these things because I heard them in the presence of other women who were in my mother's house, but I do not remember precisely who they were. These things I have said were public knowledge in the whole neighborhood.

Witness number three, Lucretia, a forty-two-year-old widow, gathered some of her information in a similar fashion, standing on her balcony and listening to the neighbor women chat. But she had also observed the drama between Joannetta and Zuanne.

> They took walks in front of my house, and Joannetta invited me to come and see her betrothed, and so I would go and observe their glances at one another. . . . He was very poor, and dirty. In truth I would not have given him a cat as a wife, as he did not even have shoes on his feet.

Lucretia had also heard that when Zuanne Calafaro returned to find Joannetta married, he suffered greatly. The fifth witness was the only man called to testify. Santo Francate was a carpenter and coworker with Francesco at the Arsenal. He refused to say whether Joannetta and Zuanne had made love, "because I mind my own business."

Joannetta did not produce any other evidence, and despite the chorus of solidarity her request was denied.[54] In this case the judges were not moved by the supplicant's arguments that she had loved one man and was unjustly wed to another. Instead they followed the logic of ecclesiastical law. Joannetta and Zuanne had never been joined in wedlock. Further, Joannetta herself had raised the doubts of her adjudicators by admitting she had voiced assent to marry Francesco at the ceremony, conducted before a parish priest and witnesses. Any voluntary gesture potentially rendered a promise binding.[55] Thus, Joannetta's marriage was valid according to Church law. Still, the sentiments of the petitioner and her witnesses are important to note. They clearly privileged love and affection over parental arrangements in choosing marriage partners.

In another disinheritance story, the noblewoman Helena Corner refused to recognize Giovanni Badoer as her husband, requesting an annulment in 1596.[56] The evidence she produced was compelling. Helena and Giovanni were married in 1585, at ages sixteen and forty, respectively. It was an unusually large age gap. Her lawyer argued before the court that she never would have married Giovanni if not for her mother's iron will and financial control. Now that her mother was deceased and Helena was a woman of independent means, she was free to seek an annulment. She, her lawyer, and the kin who testified on her behalf went to great lengths to prove that the marriage was a product of the financial ambitions of her mother. Perhaps equally important, Helena's lawyer portrayed Giovanni as unfit to be a husband because of mental deficiency: "full of fury, crazy, mentally inept, and incapable of having intercourse with women." Helena's aunts, uncles, and cousins all came forward to support this claim. They blamed the ill-contrived liaison on the sternness of Helena's mother.[57] After her marriage a stepbrother tried to help Helena escape on a ship to Candia, but the voyage never took place. Instead, with her stepbrother's help, Helena took refuge in an asylum for aristocratic women, the Monasterio di Sant' Anna, but eventually her mother forced her to return to Giovanni. It was only after her mother passed away that she turned to the ecclesiastical court, which annulled her marriage on grounds that Giovanni was impotent.[58] It is clear from this case and others that strong-willed mothers were a common theme in the petitions for annulment. This gives us further perspective on the power of Venetian women in their own families and within their social circles. They could, and did, greatly influence the destinies of their daughters, who gave them both respect and the reverential fear given to fathers. Venetian mothers exercised considerable control over daughters, especially if their husbands were absent or deceased, and that control was not always well received.

What evidence were female supplicants supplying their adjudicators in hopes of convincing them that they had resisted forced marriage? Language, gesture, and facial expressions were all-important components of storytelling and, in this case, of constructing a sense of self. The supplicants often made reference to their gestures, facial expressions, and emotions when they recounted their histories of courtship, marriage rites, and the wedding night. Their primary aim was to demonstrate their emotional unwillingness to marry, despite having voiced consent.

Magdalena de Francisus's story, which came under review in 1625, describes some of the emotions and gestures of brides subject to violent intimidation.[59] Magdalena was only thirteen when her father, Giovanni Battista Toscani, arranged her marriage to Alvise Buonamico. Alvise, it seems, did not take the vows seriously. Banished by the Venetian Republic, he left for Genoa, abandoning his bride on their wedding day. Did he take her dowry with him? He told her parents he would return for her in two years, but he never kept his promise. Illicitly, he had taken another wife. Magdalena insisted during the ecclesiastical investigation that she had shed tears in protest, but her father responded with threats to mistreat and beat her. Tears as evidence of intimidation probably became a critical issue in the case. Giovanni Battista's behavior, it was claimed, frightened his wife, his children, and everyone else in his house. Magdalena's mother intervened to restrain her husband, but this only intensified his rage, and he threatened to beat his wife as well. When Giovanni Battista summoned the priest, he told Magdalena she must consent or he would beat her. Magdalena cried all the while the priest performed the ceremony, and thereafter she always told her family and neighbors that she was forced to take Alvise against her will, for fear of her father. Her supportive mother came forward to corroborate Magdalena's story.[60] The marriage contract was pronounced invalid, because it was motivated by *grave fear* rather than voluntary consent.[61]

Many early modern legal theorists argued that even if the child were overwhelmed by parental authority and obeyed from "reverential fear" (fear deriving from deep respect), the marriage was nevertheless valid. *Reverential fear* was judged slight, especially in the case of "naturally timid" children, because it could not move the will or reduce the voluntariness of the act. However, physical compulsion, or threats of injury (causing serious or *grave fear*) or disinheritance, pointed to real coercion and invalidated the marriage contract.[62]

At the age of twenty-five, Paolina Businelli sought to annul her marriage of ten years.[63] Her husband, on the other hand, wished to remain married, a factor that may have made Paolina's case more difficult. The unhappy wife declared that her cousin and legal guardian, Alessandro, arranged the marriage to Girolamo Cernotta without Paolina's knowledge and forced her to marry him when she was only fifteen. She claimed that when she first saw her betrothed, she did not like him, and refused to sign the marriage contract. However, Alessandro held the authority to administer her assets. Paolina stated that although she did not agree with his orders, she obeyed him because of her *natural timidness* and *extreme reverence*. When she stood before the priest, she demonstrated her dislike of Girolamo by a change in facial color, from red to pale, and in expression, from happy to melancholy. She responded weakly to the priest after the third request, and she cried so that others could witness her unhappiness.

Paolina was even more reluctant when it came to matters of sex. She claimed she refused to sleep in the same bed with Girolamo on her wedding night, but then agreed when Alessandro's wife and the wife's sister obtained Girolamo's assurance that he would not touch her. Girolamo complied the first night, but on the second he wished to have "sexual commerce." Paolina leaped from the marriage bed and insisted on sleeping with her cousin Camilla. She resolved not to return to Girolamo. He was not her husband, she said, because she had not consented to the marriage. She claimed that her husband and cousins had decided to have a priest exorcise her so that she would be willing to have sex. When her husband made further sexual advances, she ran away. Eventually he forced her "with great violence." Paolina returned to Alessandro's house, protesting that she would go to any convent rather than stay with her husband. She ran away from Girolamo seven times. Finally she went to the church of the Jesuits and asked the clerics to annul her marriage. They promised to study the case and suggested that meanwhile she stay at the *soccorso*, a refuge for women in troubled marriages. But her cousin Alessandro forced her to return to Girolamo, from whom she attempted to hide. To keep her, she claimed, Girolamo locked the balconies and doors and kept the keys, but she still managed to escape. Girolomo denied the allegations. The outcome of the ecclesiastical inquiry into Paolina's situation is unknown.

Women's claims of sweet innocence or reluctance were insufficient by themselves to win positive judgments. However, extenuating circumstances, such as whether or not the couple had children, were likely factored in. Arsilia Pegorin is a case in point. In 1593, at the age of twenty-nine, she sought to annul her arranged marriage to the barber-surgeon Bernardino Struppiolo after sixteen years and the birth of two children.[64] Her procurator, Domino Ventura Chiarelli, declared that, at thirteen, she was "timid, ashamed, and unknowing yet, due to her tender age, the difference between good and bad." Arsilia, an orphan, had been under the care of her maternal grandmother, Madonna Andriana, and her maternal aunts, Madonna Catterina and Madonna Meneghina. Arsilia recalled that the women were "mean, conceited, cruel, and frightening," especially her grandmother, "who hit her frequently, without reason." Her grandmother forced her to marry Bernardino, a widower who was much older, by intimidating her with "threats, fears, and punches." She escaped three times from Bernardino, "going as a free woman wherever she wanted." Twice she was compelled to return after violent coercion from Clarissimo Signor Benetto Contarino, a patrician who was her husband's friend. After six years of marriage she abandoned her husband, but was forced to return when her aunt beat her. The last time she had not returned to her husband and two sons, ages fourteen and fifteen. She had been living on her own for a year. Arsilia admitted that her husband treated her well, but that she had not chosen him. Instead, she wanted to marry Zaccharia the merchant.

After having run away three times, she decided to consult with a lawyer about obtaining an annulment. Her whole argument rested on the fact that she was young and inexperienced in the ways of the world. She stated that she had been deceived into marrying this man of a "mature age." Nor was the celebration of the marriage published in advance. Arsilia did not see the groom until the day of the wedding, when her grandmother and aunts dressed her in white and announced they were marrying her off. She claimed she had not known what she was doing and had innocently responded to the priest, not realizing what this meant, "as I was a girl and did not know the importance of the word 'yes.'" After the wedding dinner she immediately went to her husband's house and consummated the marriage. "I did not want to.

Actually, he had a knife in hand." She produced seven witnesses to sustain the assertion that her grandmother and aunts had forced her to marry.[65] However, after sixteen years of marriage, two children, and three attempts to leave her husband and children, Arsilia may have appeared to be unruly and unreasonable. Her narrative may even have fallen in line with contemporary notions of women's alleged physical and mental weakness, their irresponsibility and ignorance. Her conduct breached acceptable cultural norms. The court probably was not going to legitimize the breakup of her family. The request was denied.[66]

The cases under examination here provide good examples of how the attitudes and priorities of women, irrespective of social class, changed over the course of their life cycles. It is striking that almost all the women seeking to dissolve their marriage ties had reached a mature age. Married in their teens, they usually petitioned the court in their twenties or early thirties. Most often the authority figures who allegedly forced them into marriage were deceased, freeing them to reflect on the past and attempt to change their lives. Mature women like Camilla Belloto and Magdalena Filosi came before the court protesting that they had been too young to willingly give their own consent in marriage. Now emancipated from parental authority, they looked to the ecclesiastical court to help them remake their lives as mature adults.

The language of complaint these women expressed in their court depositions undoubtedly came from the terminology of canon law. *Great fear, knives at their throats, saying "yes" with one's voice but not with one's heart* embellished most of the stories. Unsurprisingly, we find the same language of complaint in stories from women forced to take religious vows. Sister Chrestina, who fled convent life after the death of her father and brother, discloses some of the same elements we find in our annulment scripts. Sister Chrestina decided to bond with a man, in this case a man who happened to be a canon lawyer and who could help her with her court case. No doubt he had supplied her with the legal language of complaint, and a narrative to go along with it: Sister Chrestina claimed that her father had forced her to enter the convent at age eleven by threatening her with a knife.[67] In another case, Sister Laura Querini, trying to break her religious ties, stated, "I professed with my mouth, but not with my heart."[68]

Besides the ecclesiastical courts, women's lamentations against parental authority and their hopes for a refashioning of self were familiar themes of neighborhood gossip. Moreover, they had found their way into both the theater of comical farce acted out in the Venetian *campi*, which people of all social stations could hear and see, and the literary debates of the period. It is well worth surveying these other cultural venues before we listen more attentively to the women's complaints about arranged marriages in court.

The urban landscape in Venice featured theater, especially during the pre-Lenten season of Carnival. The years between 1570 and 1630 were a golden age for the commedia dell'arte, and Venice was a primary center for the open-air staging of improvised comical farce. The comic improvisations of human dilemmas offered cathartic release for both aristocrats and commoners. The *commedie*, and operas such as Orazio Vecchi's *Happy but Penniless* (1597) and Adriano Banchieri's *The Madness of Old Age* (1598),[69] revolved around familiar domestic scenarios: secretly married maidens; dissatisfied wives; widows seeking new marriage bonds; avaricious old fathers insisting on loathsome, arranged marriages; unhappy daughters who feigned obedience and plotted with their lovers and loyal servants to escape the hateful fates their fathers had designed for them. Serving maids and male servants played a central role in these comedies; they aided their mistresses and masters by carrying messages, making appointments, providing serenades, procuring ladders, concocting disguises, intercepting dowries, eavesdropping, tale-telling, spying, bargaining, and covering up secret trysts.

The themes of the commedia dell'arte and the depositions for the Patriarchal Court coincided when servants and youth committed to their own individual desires conspired against older men to thwart neatly arranged marriages based on class and wealth. In the comedies, as a rule, the clever and resourceful youth were the victors. For example, the Venetian *Magnifico* Pantalone retracts his order that his daughter marry a rich old man and instead allows her to unite with the young lover she prefers.[70] In the resolution of this conflict, the comedy writers and actors no doubt fulfilled a fantasy for many in the audience, but in real life the liberty to side openly with the younger generation came only after much discussion, and it continued to be contested.

During the 1540s and 1550s in Venice, comic practice elicited an argument that divided according to popular and aristocratic points of view. Ordinary people expressed a preference for less respectable subject matter than aristocrats would tolerate. Writers such as Parabosco

(1524–1557) were left with the difficult task of trying to address both popular and aristocratic mores. Should happy endings be achieved through approved marriages, where partners turn out to belong to the same class, so as to avoid the criticism that accompanied plots in which liaisons broke social barriers or defied parental authority? Or should these endings favor the more popular desires to cross class boundaries? The argument was a familiar one. The Venetian patriciate, like other European elites, was attentive to keeping its ranks pure. But recalcitrant children had resorted to clandestine marriages and other mésalliances, and had found refuge in the ecclesiastical sphere, where their unions were recognized. The *Tametsi* decree of Trent did not resolve these conflicts in social reality. Thus, the arguments over comic practices that preceded the court cases by almost a half century continued to resonate in the voices of the young people who rebelled and exerted pressure on the Curia to grant them annulments.

The stories in our ecclesiastical investigations and the farcical dramas of the commedia dell'arte share common ground in other ways. Both reveal that everyone was an eavesdropper in the drama of life, providing services to brides or grooms in distress. Did the comedies serve as models for the court storytellers? Did the amateur nobles and professional commoners who acted in the public squares serve to coach the supplicants and witnesses who appear in our court cases? The connections between the tales that actors supplied their audiences and those of viewers who went to court are certainly plausible but hard to document.

The literary backdrop to the court cases probably has more limited social resonance than open-air theater; it may have touched only those who could read or who had the opportunity to listen to someone else read. But three women polemicists from Venice—Moderata Fonte, Lucrezia Marinella, and Arcangela Tarabotti—wrote on women's problems during the late sixteenth and early seventeenth centuries.[71] Tarabotti (1604–1652), condemned to a monastery by the tyranny of her father, in particular protested the way daughters were farmed out to religious institutions or ill-suited husbands in the selfish interests of their parents. Among her works were *Monastic Hell*, *The Purgatory of Poorly Married Women*, and *Paternal Tyranny*. *Paternal Tyranny*, also titled *Simplicity Deceived*, published shortly before her death, denounced the abuses of paternal power. It was immediately attacked and placed on the Index of Banned Books. Otherwise, Tarabotti's points of view found sympathy among feminist writers such as Lucrezia Marinella. Her work was also in harmony with a host of French feminists writing between 1595 and 1655. In Venice she counted among her sympathizers the two daughters of the French ambassador, who were living in her convent.[72] Moreover, women in Venice abhorred being forced to take vows, and some even tried to renounce them and start new lives.[73] The disgruntled married women in our court cases present the secular parallel; they rejected arranged marriage. The literary discussions of the period point to this changing climate, in which women more willingly dissented against the plans their parents had made for them.

The annulment cases in the Venetian Patriarchal Court illuminate what some women found wrong with the husbands their parents or guardians had chosen for them. One of the objections women voiced in court, as well as in comical farce, was dramatic differences in age. Historical demographers tell us there was a significant age gap between husbands and wives in early modern Italy, particularly in upper-class households. The average age at marriage for men was more than thirty, and for women it was fifteen.[74] The examples in the Venetian ecclesiastical investigations modify the notion that early marriage for women was specific to the upper classes. Moreover, although the age difference may have been attractive to parents seeking sons-in-law who could support their daughters, the requests for annulment make it clear that it was abhorrent to some of these women, especially in the years after marriage. Aging husbands also help to explain the long delays in some cases between wedding and annulment. Angela de Fais, the daughter of Pietro, a master weaver, requested an annulment in 1586, against her husband's wishes.[75] Her father and her uncle, "selfish, frightful people," forced her with threats and fear to marry Bartholomeo de Albertis, a man who delivered wine for a living. She was not more than twenty at the time she filed for the annulment; her husband was nearly thirty years her senior.[76] With both her father and uncle now deceased, Angela gathered a host of women to defame the men's characters in court. She also sustained that her husband suffered from impotence, another problem younger women might have with aging husbands. In the case of Camilla Belloto, reviewed earlier, Camilla underlined not only her youth—she was only thirteen or fourteen when her father proposed Angelo—but also her husband's physical appearance. She described him as "a man with a very ugly face and bad habits." Witnesses concurred. Her sister described Angelo as "ugly and unkempt." Her mother found him "ugly" and with "rough manners." Her distant relative, Jacobo, described Angelo as having a "big, disfigured eye."[77]

Looks, virility, and age were all concerns of younger women marrying older men. It is apparent not only in the Venetian court cases, but in contemporary theater as well. In particular, the age gap at marriage was a central theme of erudite comedy and the commedia dell'arte. Playwright Andrea Calmo (1510–1571), reputedly the son of a Venetian fisherman or gondolier, clearly of humble origins and writing for audiences of his own class, created a comic victim who was unsuitably in love. Calmo himself acted in this role, a mature Venetian merchant who lost his dignity in senile passion.[78] Yet another Venetian writer from the artisanal class, Gigio Giancarli, also directed comic assaults at the figure of an old man in love, and in his comedy *Zingana*, the young Angelica, who is planning an elopement with the man of her choice, appeals for sympathy to the women in the audience. Later, Adriano Banchieri (1568–1634) would set the old man-young woman theme to music in *The Madness of Old Age*, published in Venice in 1598.[79] And the actress Isabella Andreini took up the cause of women in the age gap discussion:

> The profanation of our charms in continually uniting us to imbecile old men has been a great enemy of gallantry; for they are a class despised by the whole wide empire of lovers. This strange alliance between youth and old age, which avarice has suggested to our fathers, permits many abuses. It causes separations and is the opportunity of elegant and dissolute abbés who are always on the watch for such incompatible marriages. Girls do not willingly accept the rewards of such marriages; or when accepted, they hate the austerity demanded by spectacled husbands.—The voice of Isabella, in the Commedia dell'Arte.[80]

One of the first women to act publicly on stage, Andreini wrote her feelings about arranged marriage in her personal letters. Her "On Marrying a Daughter" is the story of a father announcing to his daughter that he has arranged her marriage, the pain she feels, and the father's lack of empathy.[81]

The discussion of age at marriage during the sixteenth century extended beyond comedy to treatises and rhyme. A few erudite women writers, among them Moderata Fonte, touched on this theme in their spirited debate about the merits of women over men. Fonte (1555–ca. 1598), from the prestigious class of original citizens in Venice, presented some of these ideas in *Il merito delle donne*, a fictitious dialogue carried on in a domestic setting among seven women. The women represented all stages of the female adult life cycle, both young and old and of single, married, and widowed status. One of the themes of the work is the drawbacks of marriage. In this context one of the characters, Virginia, brings up the subject of age by asking the newly married Cornelia, "Do you want us to love the elderly, to the exclusion of younger or older men?" Cornelia replies:

> I'm not saying that, because you all know that a bird in the hand of a boy and a young woman in the hand of an old man will never be well together. Old men are as astute as mature ones, on the contrary they exceed them, but in all the rest they are lacking much, for their merry years have passed and with them their every attractiveness and elegance.[82]

Another objection women expressed in the ecclesiastical court was to unwanted sexual relations. Isabella Floriani testified that her father chose a grammar teacher, Ambrosio Mazzoni, because he was willing to marry her without a dowry. Isabella lamented that Ambrosio had forced himself on her at the tender age of seven. "The said Messer Ambrosio, on the pretense of teaching her, violated the honor of Isabella." Though Ambrosio's alleged behavior with a prepubescent female was criminal, apparently it went unnoted. Nor did Isabella comment on the unlikeliness of finding another husband because she had lost her virginity. Isabella married Ambrosio when she was fourteen or fifteen.[83] Although she opposed the marriage, she bowed to her father's will. She insisted that little or no dowry was a strong incentive for her father to give her away, despite the questionable moral character of the prospective groom. Ambrosio, however, wished to remain married. He denied all of Isabella's allegations and the court took his side, denying the annulment request. The only other recourse Isabella might consider was a separation.[84]

Disparities in social class also triggered objections to marriage. Upper-class women were loath to marry down, but some women also feared marrying up. Vittoria Cesana testified that she would have rather died than marry the man her father chose, the noble Giovanni Battista Barbaro.

I, Vittoria Cesana, learning of the agreement my father had made to wed me to the nobleman Giovanni Battista Barbaro, made it understood that his efforts were all in vain, because I was resolved to not want him for many reasons, and I would have preferred to kill myself rather than consent.[85]

The nobleman Theodoro Minio, Vittoria's friend and confidant and the *compare* of her brother-in-law, offered further explanation of the distressed woman's objections. He told the vicar, "She was very surprised that her father wanted to wed her to nobles, certain that with the passing of time she would have experienced troubles, as she was not their equal."[86]

Interestingly, it was most often women who took their cases to court. Surely it was harder for a man to persuasively argue that he was coerced, or that he "said yes with his voice but not with his heart." But perhaps of greater significance, there was more at stake for the groom of an arranged marriage than for the bride. The groom acquired a dowry, presumably to his satisfaction. Moreover, his marriage signified that his parents had chosen him to carry on the family line, and with it the family estate. No doubt the bride's attractiveness and compatibility interested him, but to disobey his parents potentially entailed significant loss. It is also plausible that parents gave their sons more veto power before a marriage agreement was drawn up, so as to avoid failed relationships. Nonetheless, disappointments were always possible later in life, and some husbands did agree to dissolve marriage ties, allowing their wives to initiate petitions in the Venetian Patriarchal Court. But this was much rarer, for a wife's petition for annulment was injurious to her husband's honor. Men took offense at being abandoned, and they were seriously concerned about their reputations as both husbands and men.

Ultimately, unmarried daughters were a financial liability that marriage could remove. Parents thus may have been more unwilling to permit them any veto power. And because brides had fewer options than grooms, they may have been more likely to seek annulments in later years. It is clear in most of the cases presented above that women expressed preferences for relationships with men other than those their parents or guardians had chosen for them. Whether or not the narratives in the ecclesiastical inquiries were stretched to give drama and credibility to the pleas, they were based on the situations of women who were unwilling to live out the arrangements made during their teens and who took some initiative to reconstruct their lives.[87]

Rebellion against parental authority was not aimed just at fathers. Mothers as well bore the brunt of their children's discontent over arranged marriages. Mothers as well as fathers exercised authority, motivated by practical considerations. Daughters, on the other hand, were concerned with the age, appearance, and social station of a prospective mate. Moreover, their preferences were often for attractive, young men and for romantic love. Mature women, we also learn, did not necessarily perceive their marriages as final, for the activities of the Patriarchal Court promised hope of a way out. Further, hope crossed generational lines: some parents also acknowledged failed marriages and attempted to help their children through the Patriarchal Court. They were supported by community members who served as character witnesses during the ecclesiastical investigations.

To conclude, evidence abounds from a variety of sources to sustain women's aversion to both arranged marriage and forced monachization. The commedia dell'arte raised these issues in jest, and a feminist literary climate took them up in earnest. But it was the *Tametsi* decree, promulgated at the Council of Trent in 1563, that raised the hopes of wives and husbands who were unhappily living out the arrangements their parents or guardians had made for them. In defining what constituted a valid marriage, it also inadvertently offered templates for invalid unions. Married couples and ecclesiastical lawyers seized the opportunity in the decades following Trent, flooding the Patriarchal Court with annulment suits. Coercion, the legal argument that offered the possibility of an annulment, became a dominant trope in Venetian marital litigation. It originated with canonists and theorists. Procurators and lawyers transmitted it to supplicants, their kinsmen, and neighbors, who in turn spread the rules by word of mouth. At the same time, word of the activities of the Patriarchal Court moved through the neighborhoods when notaries made visits to take depositions. Gossip was a critical means of disseminating information, and it was widely recognized in Venice as the prerogative of women.[88] Coercion as defined by canon law gave the stories in the ecclesiastical investigations their structure and framework, and members of the Venetian community at large supplied the language and color of the narratives presented to the court. Successful stories and characterizations both reflected and shaped contemporary cultural norms, attitudes, and values. Thus, whereas the Patriarchal Court in Venice served as the ultimate authority on the validity of a marriage contract, it was actually the spouses and their families, in collaboration (if not collusion) with the community, who regulated failed marriage. Unfortunately, the records of the Patriarchal Court do not offer evidence of the balance between law and emotion that went into the judges' decisions, but it is notable that the court was a grand receptacle of local gossip, and thus it is legitimate to reflect on how creative agency—gossip, secrets, and lies—not only affected the application of canon law but also helped to shape Venetian legal culture.

"It did not seem to be that he was satisfying me the way he ought to."

BEDTIME STORIES

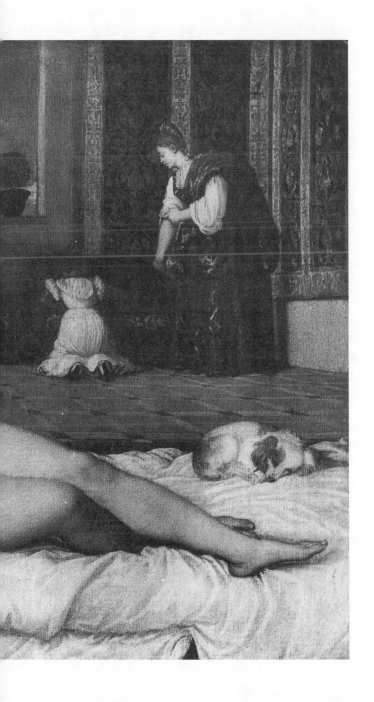

A MARRIAGE NOT CONSUMMATED, according to canon law, was not valid. Sexual impotence that prevented consummation was legitimate grounds for dissolving the union, and was thus an important component of some annulment cases.[1] In the Venetian ecclesiastical investigations the term "impotence" was applied to women as well as men. It signified the incapability to have the sexual relations necessary for reproduction, in a woman's case because her vaginal opening was too narrow to accommodate the insertion of a penis. Impotent men reputedly suffered from erectile dysfunction and premature ejaculation. Because it offered hope of breaking marriage ties, provided the presiding adjudicators could be persuaded by a credible story, impotence, like the discourse on forced unions, was another trope in the ecclesiastical investigations conducted in the Patriarchal Court.

Who chose to develop a discourse about intimacy? To substantiate the claim, the supplicant needed to have access to the experts, who included physicians, midwives, and clerics. All played important roles in regulating sexuality in the Venetian community and also held critical positions of power in the marriage disputes played out in the Patriarchal Court. Together with servants, kin, and neighbors of the litigants, they offered imaginative discourses on conjugal responsibilities and on notions of bad or unsatisfying sex.

The four ecclesiastical investigations that follow exemplify the discourse of impotence as it unfolded in late Renaissance Venice. Their scenarios offer us much more than presumed instances of sexual dysfunction. In reading these texts, we have the opportunity to reflect on how they both mirrored and shaped attitudes surrounding marital intimacy and sexual agency. The narrators inadvertently reveal how information about sex and reproduction was transmitted in family and community. They also disclose, somewhat deliberately, the kinds of sexual behavior and values that fell within canonical norms, even if they did not entirely live up to them, and the individuals who wielded power over sexual be-

---

Previous spread: Titian (c. 1488–1576). *Venus of Urbino* (1538/1539). Florence, Galleria degli Uffizi. Photo: Alinari/Art Resource, New York. Wife or Courtesan? Despite the signifiers of marriage—two wedding chests to store the bride's trousseau, the myrtle plant, and the bouquet of roses—it is unclear whether Venus's sexual gaze is bridal. Was the sexual empowerment of women confined to courtesans, or also appropriate to sixteenth-century married women? See Goffen (1997: 146–148).

havior—parish priests and high prelates, ecclesiastical lawyers, midwives, and physicians. Finally, despite deliberate references to acceptable norms of sexual behavior, the stories suggest a different reality, one less bound by church canons or social convention.[2] Litigants and witnesses from both the professional and the neighborhood communities drew from their own cultural repertoire and used their best creative resources to spin out tales that masked or minimized digressions from the rules of sexual behavior. Their testimonies revealed their own priorities. So, for example, proving virility in the case of males, or the desire to bear children in the case of females, took precedence over confessing adulterous relationships to ecclesiastical authorities. The stories did not always satisfy the adjudicating examiners. At times we can only guess why, for every script carried its own subtext(s). Moreover, the written record leaves no trace of the emotional interaction between examiners and their subjects. Still, these problematic texts open up for readers the world of sexual intimacy in late Renaissance Venice, connecting the legal language of complaint with popular Venetian culture.

"Long, Short, Fat, Thin, Vigorous, or Soft as Putty?"

In the late autumn of 1590, Camilla Benzoni, a young woman from the Venetian upper class, finally decided, after suffering in silence, to end her union of three years and seven months with *Domino* Gasparo Centani. She told the Patriarchal Court that Gasparo was suffering from impotence and had never consummated their marriage.[3] If Camilla could convince the court that Gasparo was permanently incapable of copulating, then the union could be declared null and void.[4] On the other hand, if medical experts determined that he was suffering a temporary setback but was capable of having sexual intercourse, the ecclesiastical authorities would compel the couple to remain together for at least three years and to try again to consummate, and thus validate, the union. A sexual dysfunction that prevented consummation beyond three years of cohabitation was grounds for annulment. By contrast, a consummated marriage was permanent and could never be broken as a result of a subsequent sexual dysfunction.[5]

The young woman approached the Patriarchal Court from a high social vantage point. Camilla's deceased father, the *Magnifico Domino* Giorgio Benzoni, had been a Venetian citizen.[6] Though citizens did not have the social standing of patricians, as a constitutional, hereditary elite they nonetheless carried important political and social weight in Venetian society. Camilla also availed herself of the support of her stepbrother, Alessandro Busellino, in whom she had long confided her marital difficulties. It was Alessandro who procured a lawyer to prepare for litigation.

Camilla told her story to the patriarchal vicar Desiderio Guido, doctor of Roman and canon law, at his residence in San Geremia the week before Christmas, 1590.[7]

> I thought I was married. I don't know, that is I believed I was married to *Signore* Gasparo Centani. I lived with Gasparo for two consecutive months, and the two of us slept in the same bed, except when we were away or when I was ill for a month. When I first settled into Gasparo's house, I slept with his stepmother for three or four nights because Gasparo had gone off to purchase grain and other staples. He slept with me the first night he returned, and attempted to have sex with me and to do what husbands do with their wives, but he did not do anything. And he said he would confess his failure to perform to my father the next day, besides telling me he was sorry that he could not do what was necessary.

Camilla was not opting for a forced union story. She portrayed herself as an obedient daughter. So the vicar had to determine what was behind the impediment. He asked Camilla whether she was reluctant to have sex with her husband. She recalled her husband making several attempts to consummate the marriage on the wedding night.

> His penis was erect, and he tried to do the normal thing, but it tired and fell, accomplishing nothing, nor did he spill any seed, and that same first night he tried to have sex with me several times, and each time his penis did not succeed. Nor did I refuse him or put up any sort of resistance, but rather showed the appropriate modesty. Yet his penis performed the same way each time, without spilling seed. . . . I have heard from others that a man cannot enter a woman without the woman experiencing some pain or feeling.

A limp penis, failed penetration, spilling semen outside the womb, all were important elements in narratives designed to demonstrate that the marriage could not be consummated. Camilla feigned innocence, showing the appropriate modesty that was expected of women during this period, but by the time of this deposition she used explicit sexual language and appears to be sexually aware. In her testimony she was careful to emphasize that she had cooperated with her family's choosing Gasparo and had been willing to perform her conjugal duty in the marriage bed, again fulfilling expectations of women of her time. But there was another unspoken factor that may have had a role in this couple's troubled marriage bed. Although lack of privacy was certainly not unusual for the times, the presence of Gasparo's stepmother may have been a source of discomfort to both spouses.

For the first month of the marriage, Gasparo tried nightly to finalize the union, but was consistently unable to penetrate Camilla.

> After the first night Gasparo tried to have sex, but he couldn't put his penis into my vagina. He spilled his seed outside of me, and on those first nights in the first months, and more than one time each night, he tried the same way, and he was never able to know me carnally. He always spilled his seed outside, and I think he became weary of doing nothing else in those five or six months. When my husband's penis became erect, he was only able to keep it up for three *miserere*. [The first word of the fifty-second psalm. The figurative meaning is associated with weariness. In this context Camilla seems to have used the reference to signify a brief moment.]

After the wedding night, Gasparo made a point of telling Camilla that the bedsheets were washed, an attempt to keep up appearances before the servants and guests. Laundered sheets were an important part of the unspoken but visible ritual that confirmed the consummation of marriage before family and community. Thus servants were endowed with both intimate knowledge and power, and they could be called to marriage court to testify. More important, they could manipulate the community news web through their gossip. Beyond their roles as news carriers or rumor starters, female servants commonly conveyed information about marital intimacy to novice brides. If serious problems arose on the wedding night, some young maidens who held their servant women in trust would retreat to their beds to escape having sex with their new husbands.

After Camilla's testimony, the vicar began to demonstrate his knowledge of sexual intimacy and the potential problems in lovemaking that sometimes trouble new partners. He asked Camilla if she had felt any pain or had rejected her husband's advances by pushing him away with her hands. She replied,

> He did not hurt me because he moved around from here to there as it was comfortable for him, but he did not cause any pain in my vaginal canal. I did not push him away with my hands. The truth is his penis was erect but not such that it convinced me he could consummate the marriage, because when his member touched me, it did not have the force needed to enter. I am a virgin.

Then the vicar, demonstrating the knowledge that foreplay was an important prelude to successful intercourse, asked whether Camilla and her husband were affectionate with one another, touching, kissing, and doing what husbands and wives do. Camilla assured him they were, again maintaining the modesty expected of a virginal bride but also once again belying her sexual innocence.

> I did not hesitate to give my husband all the caresses appropriate to the decorum of marriage, as he gave to me, and it is true that he was more affectionate with me than I was with him because it did not seem to me that he was satisfying me the way he ought to.

The response of this unhappy wife indicates that it was not only the examiner who took into account the emotional and physical needs of the female in achieving a happy sex life. Camilla's words reveal that both the examiner and the examinee shared an important assumption: that women were entitled to sexual satisfaction.[8] Perhaps this stance was not entirely foreign to ecclesiastical judges and lawyers, either. Though not many theologians would go so far, Giovanni Delfino, in *De matrimonii et caelibatu* (1553), suggested that sex within marriage could be aimed at pleasure and enjoyment without risking sin.[9] Indeed, it appears that the ecclesiastical examiner was doing his part in furnishing advice on how to achieve a successful sex life.

As a new and unhappy bride, Camilla had gotten sexual information from local women. Not believing Gasparo's claim that she needed to weigh more to become pregnant, she asked "knowledgeable women" in the neighborhood how a woman became pregnant. "And they told me what they thought, so that I understood better my sexual relationship with my husband, that is, that my husband was incapable of impregnating me." In her education about sex and reproduction, Camilla, like other Venetian women, took advice from females of different social stations, including kin, servants, and neighbors, as well as midwives.

The vicar expressed curiosity as to why Camilla had kept silent so long, not confiding in servants or kin. Camilla explained that she feared negative consequences from her husband. It was not an unreasonable fear: husbands could retaliate against wives who injured their honor by accusing them of sexual deficiencies or abandonment. Accusations of impotence were a formidable weapon women could launch against notions of male honor, but they had to be sure they had protection against the ire and humiliation such accusations potentially invited.

One Christmas, however, Camilla finally confessed to her priest, Don Clemente Teatino, with as much modesty as she could muster. Don Clemente assured her he would study the case, but cautioned that dissolving a marriage was serious business. Shortly thereafter, at Carnival, Camilla confided in her stepbrother, telling him the marriage has not been consummated. Alessandro promised to consult some experts. He found out that an annulment case would not be considered unless the couple were barren for three years, although an ecclesiastical judge could shorten the waiting time before a case would be reviewed. Camilla decided to suffer her pain in silence, fearing some negative reaction from her husband. She told her examiner that she continued to be ready to consummate her marriage. Yet again, her words revealed an unspoken assumption: that women, too, had sexual desires and that they were entitled to satisfaction.

> I would ask my husband not to tease me, and he would reply,
> "Do you think I was always this way? I've had sex with other
> women." He claimed his impotence was new, and he wanted to
> tell his father so that he could see a physician. He then did see
> some physicians, who prescribed baths, but as it was wintertime,
> the moment was inopportune.

There was probably no shortage of remedies for impotence available from apothecaries. In the commercial hub of Venice, the demand for medicinal plants from the eastern Mediterranean was met within the city's maritime empire. The Republic ruled Crete and Cyprus, and had trading relations with Constantinople, Syria, and Egypt, all important fonts of medicinal herbs, liquors, and minerals. During the mid-sixteenth century, the physician Pietro Andrea Mattioli urged the Venetian Senate to procure these products, with positive results. Venice became a major center of botanical study, with new information quickly disseminated by the Venetian presses, including Mattioli's 1548 commentary on the state of materia medica. Moreover, the pharmacies, under state supervision, became highly developed. In 1565 pharmacists established their own guild, the Collegio degli Speziali, with a membership of seventy-one district pharmacies. That number rose to one hundred by 1617, when the city's population was 142,000. Word went around to physicians starting up practice in late sixteenth-century Venice that they needed to know only two things to be a success: how to make women fertile and how to get along with pharmacists.[10] Thus, by the late sixteenth century, a variety of medicinal cures, herbal potions, aphrodisiacs, and lotions were available to remedy male sexual dysfunction.[11]

The historian Guido Ruggiero relates the 1591 case of Apollonia, a healer accused of love magic, who told her Venetian inquisitors her remedy for impotence.

> The technique that I used for unbinding those who cannot have intercourse with their wives is as follows: for some, I have them put under the bed the blade of the plow, that is, the metal with which one plows the field; for others I have them put [there] the hoe and the shovel which are used for burying the dead; for others I have them take a ring with which a young virgin was married and which has been placed in holy water, then they must urinate through this ring.[12]

Urinating through a ring was sympathetic magic, just as "knotting" referred to making men impotent. Inquisitors, in turn, reported their thoughts on impotence and its cures to the Holy See. In 1580 the papal nuncio in Venice, Alberto Bolognetti, wrote, "These incantations produced truly diabolical results, as with those who, being at first unable to consummate their marriages, freed themselves from impotence by urinating in the immediate surroundings of a tomb or on the door of a church."[13]

In Italy, England, and France alike, clerics, political theorists, physicians, and midwives espoused the belief that magic both caused and cured impotence.[14] Reginald Scot's *The Discoverie of Witchcraft* (1584) introduced popular audiences to the terrors of sterility that were brought on by incantation. The basis of Scot's work had already been officially canonized in the *Malleus Maleficarum*. His remedy for men "bewitched in the privie members" was to break the smoke of the tooth of a dead man, to anoint oneself with the gall of a crow, to spit in one's own bosom, and to piss through a wedding ring.[15] Similarly in England, Jane Sharp's text on midwifery, published in 1671, after the author had been in practice for thirty years, stated:

> There is barrenness by enchantment, when a man cannot lye with his wife by reason of some charm that hath disabled him; the French in such a case advise a man to thread the needle *Noutr C'equilliette*, as much as to say, to piss through his wife's wedding ring and not to spill a drop and then he shall be perfectly cured.[16]

Late Renaissance Italians had no shortage of remedies for impotence. They included ingesting various foods, among them red chickpeas, chestnuts, pistachios, pine nuts, ragwort, cinnamon, cubebs, sugar, testicles of quail, oil from the inner bark of storax and from the elder tree, large-winged ants, musk, and amber from the Orient. Many of the advice manuals that offered these remedies were published in Venice and probably were purchased by herb dealers, and buyers and sellers of medicinals, spices, chemicals, and drugs.[17]

Gasparo sought medical advice for his impotence, but Camilla reached a point where she was no longer willing to save her marriage. When the vicar asked whether she was prepared to respect the court's decision, her response suggested that something beyond sexual dysfunction made her averse to remaining in the marriage. She replied,

> I have no intention of returning [to him]. I cannot believe justice would require this. I would not return, and I would not trust him for all the world. If the court decides he is my husband, I will not stay with him one hour because of the dishonor he feels about me leaving him. He could do me harm.

Whether or not Gasparo would resort to violence, it was a clever answer, for potential physical danger was more likely to persuade the judge to release Camilla from Gasparo's house. Still, her answer also reveals that she no longer wished to be married to him.

Lorenzo Lotto (c. 1480–1556). *Venus and Cupid*, (c. 1520). Metropolitan Museum of Art, New York. Gift of Mrs. Charles Wrightsman, in honor of Marietta Tree, 1986 (1986.138). Cupid shoots through a marriage wreath, linking the function of the bridal Venus to reproduction.

But Camilla had to furnish the vicar with an acceptable reason for leaving her husband. She referred to the advice given her by another of her confessors, Don Bernardo, who told her that by not consummating the marriage, she and her husband were living in sin. It was this, she said, that compelled her to take leave on Thursday, the day of Santa Cecilia. "I seek from justice an annulment because I am still a virgin and have been with my husband for three years and six months." Camilla's case, thus, rested on the assertion that Gasparo had not, and could not, consummate the marriage. It seems her confessor had grounded her well in the laws that invalidated the marriage contract.

On December 19, 1590, the day after Camilla's interrogation, the vicar questioned Gasparo.[18] Not surprisingly, the husband offered a very different version of the married couple's sexual history. Maintaining his feelings of male pride and his notion of honor, he emphasized that he was fully capable of intercourse. It was his wife who was reluctant.

In forty-two or forty-three months I always lived with my wife and slept in the same bed with her, save for a few nights when either she or I was out of town. [When the vicar asked whether they had copulated, Gasparo replied affirmatively, and to the questions of how often and in what way, he said] I don't remember the number of times. I didn't count. But I can say that in four or five months, with the exception of the fifteen or twenty days that we slept apart when she was at the Villa, and during the days of her menses, every night I had sex with her and often once or twice a night. After that period of time, not as frequently, but I continued until last June, and I would have had a lot more sex with her if she had not been so stubborn with me and if she had consented, but for all that I begged her, she would no longer consent.

The vicar then questioned why Camilla might have been a reluctant sexual partner. Gasparo responded,

I don't know where else it could come from but from the little love that she felt for me. Her heart was elsewhere . . . not with her husband, so that neither begging nor swearing from the first day we were not able to have a satisfying exchange of words, of kisses, of caresses, and other similar things that occur in a marriage.

Was Gasparo suggesting Camilla loved someone else? Or had the first encounter of their arranged marriage revealed some innate incompatibility? On this the written record sheds no light. Nonetheless, Gasparo was stating that love and affection were considered an important part of a marriage, beyond its economic utility or its potential social and political benefits. Camilla and the ecclesiastical examiner appear to have taken the same position. Affection was the glue that held the marriage alliance together; without it, emotional sterility prevented bonding. According to a common belief, lack of love could cause physical sterility.

The vicar continued by probing the couple's sexual behavior, asking Gasparo whether he had penetrated Camilla, "transforming her from virgin to woman and spilling his seed into her 'natural vessel.'" Gasparo replied, "Yes, but I cannot certify whether that made her a woman." He continued to lament that she pushed him away and grabbed his throat. "I was forced to withdraw or do the best I could." It is interesting here to note the idea that, as in the story of Adam and Eve, it took a man "to make" a woman. Defloration was the decisive event transforming maiden into woman.

The vicar showed no reluctance to describe sexual acts in detail, asking, "Did your wife agree to receive your penis, for it is usual to lead the woman with pleasure to coitus." Gasparo responded,

> I cannot be certain, but from some of her gestures I believe so. Yet many times afterward I asked her, and she replied that it was not true that she had orgasm[19] or was brought to orgasm, but that those movements she made were because I hurt her and she could not suffer. And many times I asked her if I had put my penis into her and she replied "thou didst, thou was there."[20]

The vicar had his doubts, replying, "These are common things that are easy to know, when the penis tears the hymen and spills its seed. You could be certain of what happened between you and your wife, whether you had coitus with your wife or not."

But Gasparo insisted he was not certain.

> But I will say that, given the signs of blood that my women servants saw after the wedding night, and the change of sheets, and the immediate washing of the dirty ones, that my wife became a woman. These are the only certainties I can offer. But I repeat, she was so reluctant to satisfy my wishes and to meet her obligations that I was almost always annoyed by her strangeness, and I did the best I could. I always spilled my seed within her, except for five or six times when my penis accidentally slipped out, in which case she lamented at length.

This also seems to be a contrived answer. Why would Camilla have complained? Because she was frustrated or, more acceptably for canonical norms, because the attempt to achieve conception was aborted? Nor did Gasparo's answer satisfy the vicar. He took the occasion to educate Gasparo.

> Although blood and other spots in similar cases are signs of consummation, that the penis entered the woman, it is doubtful that in attempting to break the hymen only a little blood would be spilt without the penis truly penetrating. Thus clarify if during

the sexual act with your wife you put your penis into her. Say yes or no. Because we know from many instances that if it were true that you tore her hymen in the process of continuous intercourse, her vaginal passage would be ready to easily receive a man's penis.

Gasparo concluded,

I said, and I say, my penis entered her, and if in the course of time it tore her hymen and made it easier to enter, the woman has always been difficult with me and has not been willing to accommodate me, and I can only judge that this is because she does not love me very much. And I believe her vaginal passage is blocked, and thus my penis cannot enter far enough so that the seed can be received in the womb.

The vicar was not about to let Gasparo get away with this last assertion, which contradicted earlier remarks.

Having said that you put your penis into the woman and spilled your seed is different from saying the woman's passage is blocked. And it is evidence of poor aptitude that your penis could not enter and spill seed, because as everyone knows, when the penis is potent and erect and tears the first cloisters of the vagina, it enters and spills seed. Otherwise, in the case of those who are not strong, or are frigid, or have some other defect, although the penis becomes erect and makes impact with the surface of the vagina, it cannot tear the hymen, enter, and spill seed. So, think about what I have said, particularly about your penis, whether it is long or short, fat or thin, and vigorous in its operations.

One can only imagine the feelings that ran through Gasparo at that moment when required to elaborate on his endowment. His answer was judicious.

I believe my penis is well proportioned, neither too long nor too short, neither too fat nor too thin. As for its robustness, in all the time I was with my wife, I not only had to pass and tear the pubic cloister, but also to plunge in and persist until the act was completed. It is true that when I poked with my penis, she pushed me away, and I had other unsatisfying experiences with her as well.

The question of how or in what way Gasparo was physically endowed was not a lighthearted one. Giovanni Marinello's sixteenth-century medical treatise lists a very short or a very long penis as one of the causes of sterility. Others included medical problems involving the brain, liver, stomach, kidneys, or gallbladder; incompatible blood, phlegm, black bile, or yellow bile between husband and wife; and sperm that was incapable of generating. The last condition could be a result of too much heat, cold, humidity, or aridness. It could also happen if the penis was in the vagina too long, or as a result of premature ejaculation.[21] Like Marinello, the English midwife Jane Sharp commented on the importance of penile size to the process of conception. In her book, she declared, "If the Yard be of a moderate size, not too long, nor too short, it is good as the Tongue is, but if the Yard be too long, the spirits in the seed flee away; if it be too short, it cannot carry the seed home to the place it should do."[22]

The vicar asked Gasparo if he ever had a physician examine his genitals during his marriage to determine whether he was potent or not. Gasparo assured him he had, at the request of Camilla's stepbrother, Alessandro Busellino. He consulted a midwife and a physician, both of whom found no problems. The vicar asked Gasparo why he had consulted these people, and Gasparo replied,

> To respond to Alessandro's doubts. I did this after my wife left me. It took place in the cloisters of the Padri Tollentini, well after I had married. The first five months of our marriage I had sex with her. Then I grew tired, and for a few days I had great difficulty consummating the marriage act. I did not realize that this was due to my having had sex so frequently over a long period of time. I doubt that this lack of strength was due to having been bewitched, though it is true I complained to my wife that I thought some woman had done me some harm. Thus I resolved to visit the Excellent Messer Benetto Flagini, and I told him about my weakness, and he confirmed my suspicion that some woman had bewitched me. He prescribed some medication to be taken orally and some baths if I needed them, but I did not finish the cure because I returned to my pristine self quickly. I got the medication at the Apothecary Dalla Cerva at San Pantalon. That was the only medication I used.

Fears of being dishonored by his wife presumably led Gasparo to refrain from contesting Camilla's request for an annulment. "Not because

I admit to being impotent but because I do not want to take back a woman who left me." It is possible that Camilla knew Gasparo would be so offended by her accusation that he would let her go, though this is not what she would tell the judge. If Gasparo's description of the couple's sexual relations were true, it suggests Camilla was uncomfortable with his lovemaking, and this was something the examiner could discern for himself.

Still, the task remained for Camilla to prove Gasparo had not penetrated her, that the marriage had not been consummated and thus was invalid. For this it was necessary to call in the experts. Camilla asked two midwives to confirm before a notary of the Patriarchal Court that they had examined her and that she was still a virgin. When the notary visited their homes, *Dona* Bona, the wife of a textile worker, and *Dona* Catherina, the wife of a goldsmith, came forward on Camilla's behalf. Of note, Catherina had been called as Gasparo's witness, but she took Camilla's side. We cannot know if that was due to her convictions, the result of a better offer, or stern persuasion from Camilla's stepbrother. Bona explained,

> I looked diligently to see whether [Camilla's] vagina had been forced [open]. I considered the matter at length and touched [it] with my hands. In my judgment, and based on my experience in similar cases, there was no sign that Camilla had had sexual relations with a man, for her vagina was closed and the passage was very narrow. I swear by my experience in these matters that this is true. . . . I think that Camilla is a virgin.[23]

The second midwife, Catherina, offered similar conclusions.

> I examined her with every convenience, having her lie down on the bed and wetting my fingers to see if I could feel a place to enter, and I testify in good conscience and owing to my experience as a midwife and having seen women with similar conditions that Camilla has not had sex, nor is her hymen broken. Her opening is closed.[24]

Gasparo contradicted the testimonies of the midwives, asserting that they had been deceived or were acting under the influence of his adversaries. This was no time to appear chaste or considerate of women; he boasted that he had had sex with other women and had impregnated them. He complained that the midwives had "been grossly deceived. She [Camilla] made herself seem narrow. That is the usual thing

women do. . . . The midwives let me know they did not want to tes-
tify on my behalf." At this point, Gasparo, too, wanted the annulment.
But he insisted that this was because of Camilla's shortcomings, not his.
He told the vicar,

> I am only interested in my own honor, also for assurance of my
> life. This woman has made her dishonorable behavior public and
> notorious in all the city. So, Your Illustriousness, I will comply
> with all that justice requires, but I do not intend to pay any of the
> expenses.

Gasparo was determined to disprove the accusation of impotence.
Several months passed between his first deposition and his presentation
of evidence to restore his reputation. In the interim the patriarch
Lorenzo Priuli appointed a new vicar to replace Desiderio Guido.
Thus, Gasparo's final arguments in August 1591 were reviewed by *Domino* Giovanni Mocenigo, doctor of Roman and canon law, who came
to his post from Cyprus. Gasparo insisted without any sign of self-con-
sciousness that he had had sexual relations with other women prior to
marrying, including virgin young girls, and had even contracted a sexually transmitted disease, from which he was cured. His father, one of
the governors at the Ospedale degli Incurabili in Venice, was once
asked to take in an infant Gasparo had fathered. Moreover, Gasparo
claimed, Camilla thought she was pregnant on numerous occasions.

This time Gasparo had several midwives depose to support his assertions.[25] One of them said she was not surprised he had trouble en-
tering his wife because she had a low pubic bone. Though the testimony still affirmed that Camilla had not been penetrated, the fault was
transferred from him to her. The patriarchal judges, however, were not
easily duped by the contradictory testimonies of the midwives. Moreover, if there was even a possibility that the couple was healthy and fertile, then accusations of impotence would not convince them to dissolve the marriage, even though the couple had been together for the
requisite three years before approaching the court.

The verdict for Camilla and Gasparo, signed by the vicar Giovanni
Mocenigo, *Auditore Generale*, came in September 1591.[26] He had determined that the couple were legitimately married, but that the union had
not been consummated. The pair were ordered to resume cohabitation
and to try once again to have intercourse. There was to be a year's trial
period before the case would be reconsidered. In all likelihood, based on

how these cases were handled, the couple would not receive an annulment unless it was determined, by midwives for Camilla or physicians for Gasparo, that one of them suffered some permanent affliction that prevented sexual relations. Given the way the investigation had unfolded, this was unlikely. Though the midwives had argued that Camilla was still a virgin, they had not offered any convincing evidence that she was incapable of sex. Moreover, Gasparo offered ample evidence that he was capable, though perhaps not with Camilla. Ill feelings ran strong between the couple, hardly the circumstances under which to cultivate a satisfying intimate relationship. Both partners were held responsible by the Patriarchal Court to fulfill their conjugal duties. But the court seemed to function more like a marriage and family counseling office than a tribunal, working to help the young couple in their difficulties. In this particular case the first vicar, Desiderio Guido, had tried to make Gasparo more sensitive to his wife's sexual needs and emotions, in the hopes that the marriage would eventually work out. Whether it was bad sex, no sex, or some other problem or desire that made Camilla try to leave Gasparo, we will never know. The case was never reconsidered.

"I Left Because I Still Don't Know What He Is. He Isn't a Man for a Woman"

These were the opening remarks of Lucretia Balatini. What a tantalizing first statement. What did she mean by "He isn't a man for a woman"? That he was impotent, or had different sexual desires? If the latter, sodomy was a grave offense, tried in the secular courts and punishable by death.[27] The word "sodomy," generally expressed as *contra natura*, was never actually uttered in this ecclesiastical case, but it lingered, suggestively, in the shadows.

With her father's encouragement, Balatini took her case to the Patriarch Giovanni Trevisan in March 1584.[28] The twenty-two-year-old daughter of a Venetian boatman wished to have her marriage vow to the weaver Francesco Revedin annulled on grounds of impotence. Trevisan had his vicar, Antonio Tomasini, examine the supplicant at the vicarial residence in San Geremia.

I married Francesco seven years ago, when I was a maiden, and in the first three years I lived with him, he wasn't able to consummate the union. I remained a maiden, until a man who frequented my house took my virginity, with the consent of my husband. I had a son with this man. Throughout this time I lived with my husband, until two months ago. My husband continued to try and consummate our marriage, but he never succeeded. My husband's shortcoming is that when he wants to consummate the marriage, his member stands up, but when he tries, it immediately goes limp and spurts out seed, which spills on the sheets and on my thighs. He has never been able to penetrate me.

What husband would consent to his wife having sex with another man? One who was worried about keeping up appearances when there was no child on the way after a lengthy period of married life? Did the weaver allow his wife to bed another man to cover his embarrassing problem of impotence, or his inclinations to have sex with men? Perhaps. However, it is equally plausible that Lucretia had an adulterous affair, bore a child out of wedlock, and sought the annulment in order to legitimize her status and refashion her complicated family life. She admitted having had sex with various men, but she claimed it was not of her own volition; rather, her husband had prostituted her for his own support. Another trope? It certainly came up over and over again in women's tales of broken marriage, though indeed selling sex to subsist may have been the only recourse for some women with limited or no economic resources and no family support. Was Lucretia telling the truth? That was the perplexing matter the judge had to decide, basing his verdict on demonstrable evidence as well as on the credibility of the supplicant and her witnesses.

Lucretia's attempt to prove her allegations against Francesco rested on the testimony of her neighbors, in whom she had confided on numerous occasions. Among them were Matteo de Castro and Aquilina Moschini, elderly folks who rented lodgings from her husband.[29] Lucretia stated,

The first three years of our marriage I complained to several people, as well as to my husband and other people I am close to, that he was impotent in consummating the marriage, as he still is. . . . If he had penetrated me, there would have been some sign. I would have gotten pregnant, as new brides ordinarily do during the first years of marriage. I became pregnant ["got big"] immediately after I had sex with Antonio Boccaletto.

Lucretia tried to use to her advantage the prevalent tradition that having children was an important part of being married. Childlessness was a heavy social and emotional burden for both marriage partners. Lucretia was attempting to play on the sympathy of the ecclesiastical examiner, using her desire for children to minimize her adulterous relationship with Antonio. Moreover, what is particularly significant about Lucretia's argument is that the barren marriage was not *her* fault. Normally, if there had been sexual relations, culpability for childlessness was assigned to the wife, even though this cultural construct was not consistent with sixteenth-century knowledge of human physiology. Males were credited with creating new life, whereas females simply provided vessels for the growth of the fetus.[30] Lucretia was attempting a less conventional argument: that Francesco did not fulfill the conjugal duty of performing sex for procreation, and this failure to perform was justification for her adulterous affair.

Lucretia gave the vicar a little more background, sketching her marital history.

> I tried to leave him three years ago, when I became pregnant with Antonio's child. My father, however, wouldn't let me pursue the case in the Patriarchal Court. He wanted me to continue to try to see if my husband was potent. But after three years, being young and desiring children, and to avoid sinning, which is why one marries in the first place, I left him last Christmas with his consent, as he recognized his impotence, and he voluntarily returned my dowry.

Lucretia was contrite about her sin of extramarital sex, but her call for redemption—to be released from Francesco in order to marry Antonio—pushed beyond canonical boundaries. It was a bold move. Francesco had apparently been willing to let his wife go and live with Antonio Boccaletto. Lucretia testified that when she complained of his impotence, "He replied that I could leave and do as I pleased." But Francesco had a completely different story, which he told the vicar the month following Lucretia's deposition.[31] He affirmed his potence and suggested that the barren marriage was the result of Lucretia's shortcomings, and perhaps even machinations.

> For seven years I have consummated my matrimony with her, and she has been with me almost every night. While we con-

summated the marriage, many times she had orgasm before I did, and sometimes we had orgasm together. I don't know if she was a maiden, because I was a sexually inexperienced male, and I did not know what a woman was, no less how to consummate a marriage. My wife taught me all the different ways to have sex, side by side, and with her legs on my back.

Francesco's vague but suggestive remarks could be used against Lucretia, for according to the canons of the Church, there was only one way to have sex, and that was in the missionary position. Moreover, Francesco's remarks about Lucretia having had orgasms was important in making his case that the couple was trying to make a baby. Early modern manuals describing reproduction regarded female orgasm as necessary for procreation, for only in this way would female seed be released.[32] Theologians, following Aristotle or Galen, believed female seed existed, and that its release coincided with orgasm.[33] Giovanni Marinello's sixteenth-century treatise on sterility explains that couples who really wanted to have children tied the husband's testicles loosely. When the woman was about to have orgasm, she untied the testicles so that they had simultaneous orgasm, mixing their "seeds" together.[34]

The adjudicating vicar asked Francesco how he knew he had consummated the marriage. The response attempts to lay the blame for barrenness on both Lucieta's reluctance to have sex and her encouragement of coitus interruptus.

> I knew I had consummated the marriage when my wife and I were joined, I spilled my seed in her vessel, and many times I felt her spill her seed on my member, which was in her vessel, and many times she did not want to consummate the marriage when I initiated. She withdrew when I was about to spill my seed, and she made me spill it outside of her. Because she claims I have not taken her virginity, nor consummated the marriage, I volunteer to have myself examined, because what she says is not true. Moreover, I'll have the weaver Antonio Boccaletto, who has had something to do with her carnally, testify that she was not a virgin.

Furthermore, Francesco complained that once his wife had had an affair with Antonio, she began to complain that he was not a man and that she wanted to leave him in order to marry Antonio, an eligible widower.

In his deposition Francesco lamented that Lucretia had gossiped with neighbors about their sexual relationship. She told them he had hurt—literally "broken"—his penis having sex. Francesco denied giving his wife permission to have a sexual relationship with Antonio Boccaletto and insisted she left him to be with Antonio, telling her lover she could have the marriage dissolved or could even have her husband die. Francesco maintained that Antonio told several people that Lucretia was not a virgin when he started having sexual relations with her.[35]

In May, Lucretia and her father appointed an ecclesiastical lawyer, the Reverend *Domino* Basilio Sidineus. Meanwhile, the Patriarchal Court ordered that Francesco, who was defending himself, be examined by two physicians to determine his sexual capabilities. On June 2, 1584, the first physician, Francesco Battalea, reported the results.[36] The doctor described the husband as having a slight frame and confirmed that Francesco had testicles and ejaculated without difficulty. A second doctor, Hermolaus de Hermolais, confirmed the same but raised the possibility that Francesco could lose his erection—something, he explained, that happened even to men with robust bodies. There was no way of knowing this without the patient actually giving a live performance.[37]

The following July the two elderly renters who lived in Lucretia and Francesco's house were called to testify on Lucretia's behalf. Matteo de Castro, a sixty-year-old Bellunese immigrant, confirmed that Lucretia had complained to him of her husband's impotence.

> I know of these things because Lucretia told me, and in the presence sometimes of my wife, and other women, whose names I can't remember at the moment. She told me many times, over perhaps six years. I do not know if Francesco is impotent; that is God's will. I do not know if Francesco is a man or not with regard to impregnation. I know from Lucretia that Antonio Boccaletto impregnated her. My wife and some other women told me that Lucretia was a virgin when Antonio had her, but Lucretia did not tell me this.[38]

Dona Aquilina verified her husband's testimony.

> I know, having been in the house for three years, that Antonio Boccaletto had sex with Lucretia, she got pregnant, and she had

a baby boy. I know this because the child completely resembled Antonio Boccaleto, and that I can swear. . . . She told me many times that Boccaletto had taken her virginity, but Boccaletto never told me this.[39]

A third witness, *Dona* Marieta, who knew Antonio Boccaletto, spoke on Lucretia's behalf. Marieta explained during the interrogation that all her knowledge came from Lucretia or the neighbors.

As for getting pregnant, I was with my first husband eleven years and never got pregnant. For four years now Boccaletto has been telling me that Lucretia would be willing to end her marriage if he would take her as a wife, and that if he had sinned, he wanted to repent. He doubted he would be forced to marry her. He did not tell me precisely if he knew he had taken her virginity. . . . And when I questioned Lucretia, together with another woman who visited my house, we understood that she did not know what a man was. Catherina told Lucretia's father and mother that they should not allow her to remain with her husband because he was impotent . . . it is certainly true that after Lucretia gave birth, she said it would be better to separate and to live in fear of God than live this way. And I sent her to *Padre Maestro* Perin de Fran, my confessor, to see if he could make her remain with her husband, mortified, and to live in fear of God, but she did not want to stay with him.[40]

Marieta's remarks are interesting. The woman was careful to underline that she knew Lucretia was living in sin. Out of concern for her friend's soul, she had urged Lucretia to seek the counsel of a priest. It is what the examiner would want to hear. However, we also learn that Lucretia preferred sinning to an unhappy marriage, and that she took the steps, though not without a price, to change her life circumstances, despite the Church's teachings.

We are left without a verdict for Lucretia's case. It hardly seems plausible that she obtained an annulment. Perhaps the investigation was suspended, if the judge concluded she had committed adultery. Of course it was her hope to sustain that a marriage with an impotent husband had never taken place, so that she would be guilty of the lesser sin of sex outside of marriage, but not of adultery. Moreover, she would be free to make a marriage with Antonio that was legitimate before

God and the Venetian community. It presented, possibly, a way out for a woman who had exercised sexual freedom and had not felt compelled to be demure about it.

A Midwives' Tale

On November 24, 1583, Giovanni Francisci, a young carpenter at the Venetian Arsenal, petitioned the Patriarchal Court for an annulment.[41] His wife, Lucieta Paduani, he claimed, was unable to have sex. As was standard procedure in such circumstances, several midwives were asked to examine Lucieta in order to substantiate the claims of Giovanni — called Zuanne in Venetian dialect.

The following April, *Dona* Marietta, a practicing midwife who was the widow of *Domini* Filacaipo, reported to the court the results of her tactile examination of Lucieta.

> A few days ago, I don't remember how many, I examined Lucieta together with another midwife, who lives at Santa Sofia in the environs of San Piero de Castelo. I don't know her name. Then, in a house at the Bridge of the Arch I saw the daughter of a midwife who lives in the neighborhood of Zan Bragola. I don't know her name. In my judgment this young woman is not capable of having sexual relations with a man, because her vagina is so closed that when I tried with great effort to stick my small finger inside, I was not able to penetrate her. In good conscience I do not believe a man could have sexual relations with her.[42]

A closed vaginal passage leading to the womb, according to Marinello's manual on women's illnesses, caused sterility.[43] The midwife was suggesting that Lucieta could never have children, a serious pronouncement.

After *Dona* Marietta testified, Catherina, the midwife who had accompanied her furnished contradictory evidence.

> I saw the young girl's vagina. . . . She couldn't be more than fourteen or fifteen. But she is a woman in her vagina. Half of my finger entered her. In my judgment her virginity was taken from her, because half my finger entered her, and with respect to what I saw, she can have sexual relations with a man. Another time,

together with the same *comare*, in the home of a lawyer on the Bridge of the Arch, I examined the girl, and similarly I found her deflowered.[44]

Yet a third midwife, *Dona* Magdalena Scuda, had visited Lucieta in the house of the same lawyer, the Excellent Pamphilo Corner, at the Bridge of the Arch, in a well-lighted room. In May 1584 she testified.

I examined the daughter of midwife Paula of Zuanebragola. She is a girl of about sixteen, it seems to me. I made her lie down on the bed, and I examined her vagina. I have never in my life seen a woman's vagina like hers. At the entrance of the vagina there is an opening just like other women's, but the opening is filled with flesh, so much so that I do not know how she can urinate. Having seen her this way, I did not touch her further. It seemed superfluous, seeing her so filled with flesh. In my judgment she is a virgin, and it does not appear that a man could have sexual relations with her. Nor can one see that her flesh has been torn. After I examined her, I called her mother, and I showed her the girl, who was lying on the bed, and I told her, "Madonna, look at that, and do not lament at what I am about to tell you. Even you can see." She [the mother] stretched the girl back so that I could show her the skin of the vagina and demonstrate that she was a virgin. At least that is what I think.[45]

Zuanne continued to sustain the case that Lucieta was incapable of having sex by calling on the expertise of a physician who had examined the girl when she was twelve or thirteen years old. When deposed, the physician, Paolo Litigato, explained,

Her mother, who is called midwife, told me that she would appreciate my opinion about the ability of this girl to conjoin with her husband, or to see if there was some impediment that made her incapable. So I looked at her discreet parts, and I found them ordinary, but it is true that I judged that her pubic bone, as doctors call it, known vulgarly as *pettenecchio*, was depressed. But that doesn't prevent reproduction. But if she were ever to get to the point of giving birth, I wanted to consider further the work that would be involved. So I looked at her vulval orifice in her discreet parts. That is, the entrance where the virile member must pass to carry the seed to the womb. And so I also asked my colleague, and in my judgment this girl could conjoin with a man, and this is what I told him. I simply looked at the girl, as I said, but I did not touch her internally. I did not put my finger into her vagina.[46]

Lucieta's mother had more than one cause for concern. The first regarded her daughter's health. But the second, if the midwives and the physician were correct, was that her daughter would be excluded from the marriage market. It was important to dispute Zuanne's accusations. Thus Lucieta's mother mounted a defense of her daughter by gathering witnesses who would testify that it was Zuanne that was impotent. She was well equipped to do this, for she herself was a midwife with the expert connections necessary to make a compelling case in court. The investigation thus evolved into a contest over which of the two spouses was failing to perform, and experts were called in.

The Patriarch's vicar ordered a medical examination to evaluate Zuanne's potency. The physician, Belisario Gadaldono, issued a sworn statement. Having "examined his genitals, and diligently considered the form and proportion of the virile member and the testicles, I judge him able and potent to have sexual relations with women."[47]

On June 14, 1584, a friend, Lucia Paduana, testified on Lucieta's behalf. The forty-year-old Lucia, from the artisanal class, was related to Lucieta's mother. Lucieta's mother had assisted Lucia with the birth of her own four children. She was a close confidante, she explained, even hosting the engagement of Lucieta and Zuanne in her home. She remarked that at the time, no one questioned whether Zuanne was potent; rather, they inquired about the quality of the man, if he led a bad life or not. "I heard from my *comare*, Lucieta's mother, and from another woman whose name I do not know, that the said woman put her hand on Zuanne's penis and found it to be 'as soft as putty.' "[48]

On November 14, 1584, *Dona* Helena, a thirty-year-old immigrant from Brescia, gave the court her assessment of Zuanne, based on having lived with Lucieta's mother and having been privy to inside information.[49]

It was said that Zuanne had two wives before Lucieta. With the first, Catherina, he could not have sex, and she, too, wanted to go to the Patriarch and dissolve the marriage, but she died of the contagion before she could. Following the contagion, Zuanne took Orseta as his wife. I heard it said that Orseta had sex with other men because Zuanne could not, and she contracted syphilis. Orseta died, and Zuanne married Lucieta . . . . we discovered that the girl was still a virgin, and her mother began to complain. But the girl did not talk about it. She was ashamed. The [couple] had been together two or three months.

Helena proceeded to testify that she and Lucieta's mother had put Zuanne's virility to the test one playful evening during Carnival. Zuanne was eager to prove his virility to the women who had accused him of not being a man. She explained,

It was I who was in Lucieta's house the evening of Carnival. Lucieta was sewing. Zuanne said it was not the right moment to sew. He began to murmur, as one says, that he wanted to sleep with me. We said he was not a man. I told him if he wanted to sleep with me, I wanted it [his penis] in hand, to see for myself. So we began to play, and we proceeded over one [storage] chest and another. And I put my hand down below, and I took his member in hand—however, over his pants—and I found him like a measly thread of soft linen (*lesigno de lin tenero*). We played for more than an hour, and I made a lot of effort, and I threw Zuanne on the breast of Lucieta's mother. She also put her hand on his member and found it in the same state.

More than a year later, in November 1585, yet another witness came forward for Lucieta. *Dona* Laura, the sixty-year-old wife of Petri Cebibi Alborantis, supported herself by making handkerchiefs and women's hats.[50] Her first husband was Zuanne's best man when Zuanne married his first wife, who was Laura's close friend. Laura testified that Zuanne's first wife had told her that she slept with Zuanne and his mother and his sister-in-law all in the same bed. She inferred that they all knew Zuanne could not copulate with his wife. Thus, the whole line of testimonies on Lucieta's behalf, from her mother and other midwives, revolved around dredging up witnesses who knew Zuanne was impotent.

Midwives were one of the primary sources of information about sexuality and reproduction in the neighborhood community. They were frequently called to court, for example, to testify in infanticide trials, in the deflowering of virgins, and in physical examinations that required evaluation of female maladies.[51] It was of fundamental importance, then, to control the power of midwives, and a number of individuals and institutions tried to do so. To begin, in the case of the ecclesiastical investigations, litigants wanted the support of midwives for their claims. At the same time, however, the Church was interested in regulating the work and opinions of midwives as a means of regulating female sexual behavior. Particularly after the Council of Trent, the Church became more invested in making the midwife a regulator of sexual morality. Pope Paul V's *Rituale Romanorum* in 1614 called for bishops to supervise the work of midwives during their pastoral visits.[52] The Venetian state, recognizing the important role midwives played in maintaining social order in the sexual arena, pursued a policy of control by the early seventeenth century. In 1624 the public health magistracy obliged new midwives to take a state qualifying exam and to register.[53] All this said, it is evident that midwives could be recruited by the litigating parties in the marriage court. Though unrecorded, this activity no doubt came with other benefits, such as favors or even payment, making midwives a powerful group in the Venetian community and important actresses in the Venetian marriage wars. Their power was based not only on technical expertise about sex and reproduction but also on their knowledge of sexual commerce in the community. Their testimonies could make or break honor by pronouncing virginity or exposing defloration. They helped determine who was marriageable and who was not. Like other witnesses they, too, could be bought, corrupted, and threatened. No wonder Church and state wished to regulate them. No wonder physicians wished to disqualify them.

Coworkers, neighbors, and friends could also be called upon for support in the marriage disputes. Lucieta and her mother availed themselves of the stories their allies were willing to tell. Giovanni Domenico, a twenty-year-old Brescian Arsenal worker from the Val di Sabbia, testified on November 29, 1585.

> I heard . . . that Zuanne's penis couldn't get stiff, and that he couldn't have sexual relations with a woman. I know that Catherina and her husband both slept with his mother during the early months of marriage because it was said that Zuanne could not consummate the marriage. . . . It was said that while his wife lived with him, Zuanne made an effort but could not consummate the marriage. I heard from this Catherina and her mother that he got

on her and rubbed, and he spilled his seed outside her vagina, between her thighs, but that he could not have sexual relations the way others do.[54]

The description of making love between her thighs suggests sexual relations between men. Perhaps it hints at the kind of sex Zuanne preferred, or perhaps Giovanni deliberately invoked this idea to support Lucieta's case. Helena Calafati, a poor widow, had heard, as had Giovanni, that Zuanne's first wife, Catherina, had gone before the Patriarchal vicar.[55]

After Catherina's death Zuanne took another wife, Orseta. Orseta had lived with a number of men, including Iseppo, the brother-in-law of one of the witnesses, *Don* Nicolò.[56] When Iseppo died, Orseta went to live with Nicolò for four years. Then she married Zuanne. Orseta's experience suggests that marriage, the convent, and domestic service were not the only options women chose in order to subsist. Cohabitation, even if it meant sinning, was a means of survival.

Using Orseta and other women for evidence, Zuanne's witnesses belied his alleged impotence. *Domino* Aloisio Debento, a draper, claimed that Zuanne's second wife, Orseta, had actually had a child that subsequently died.[57] *Dona* Angela, the widow of Joannis Petri Boara Calderarij, a thirty-year-old worker who made sails at the Arsenal, came forward and openly admitted that she had had sex with Zuanne four times.

> One Sunday morning after I returned from Mass, I ran into Zuanne, who said he wanted to have a drink with me. I responded, "Invite me, and I will drink." He said, "Come on up if you want a drink." So I went, and I remained and lunched with him, and I stayed the whole day with him in his house. Although he went out a while, he returned that evening, and we dined together and then we both slept in the same bed. I stayed the entire night with him, and Zuanne had sex with me four times. As far as I saw and felt, he is a man able to have sex with women. He never had sex with me again after that night. When I went to his house that Sunday, no one was home. I have never been in his house again.[58]

Yet another woman, Julia, a thirty-five-year-old silk weaver and daughter of a field worker, claimed Zuanne wanted to marry her as soon as he could dissolve his marriage with Lucieta, and that she, too, had had sex with him.

> And I swear by the Virgin Mary, the Saints, and the Evangelists that he said if he got away from his wife Lucieta, with whom he is now, that he would take me as his wife, and this was in the presence of Mattheo the carpenter, and Mattheo's wife, Lucieta. Next year it will be two years [since he said this], and under these promises he came to me and wanted to sleep with me. What could I do? . . . and so I settled for his having sex with me, as he did, and so he had sex with me for six or eight days, but during the day. One night the following month he came to my house and slept with me and had sex with me. To tell you the truth, Zuanne is able to have sex with women because he has had sex with others. For this reason I know he is able. It is true that the first time Zuanne wanted to have sex with me, he could not. I do not know the cause of this. I believe because he was too eager because he loved me. I'd say he was dying for me. But that very day, an hour or two later, he returned and had sex with me, and he was able to, just like other men.[59]

Julia, Zuanne's neighbor for about seven years, openly admitted to her interrogator that she wanted him to win the case.

Zuanne, thus, had produced testimony to attest to his sexual capacities. In this case, thus, although Lucieta and her mother had used their influence in the neighborhood community to put Zuanne's virility in question, ultimately the arguments of the unhappy husband prevailed. Zuanne was granted an annulment, though he was obliged to share the expenses of the court case with Lucieta. The verdict, dated May 16, 1586, confirmed the fear of Lucieta's mother: her daughter was judged "impotent."[60] It would no doubt hinder or ruin her chances of remarrying.

"I Can't Stand the Smell of Him"

On April 5, 1619, *Dona* Felicità engaged a lawyer and approached the Patriarchal Court for an annulment. She had been married to a merchant, *Domini* Matheo Fada, for only fifteen months.[61] Matheo, Felicità claimed in her deposition, was ailing and unable to have sex. Her husband hired a lawyer and opposed the annulment, maintaining that his illness had been only temporary and that all of her claims as to his being chronically ill were untrue. But in her deposition Felicità stated that her husband had told many people over the span of eight years that he had gonorrhea, contracted while in the fleet of San Marco. If she knew gonorrhea was a sexually transmitted disease, she concealed it. Instead, she told the vicar she thought the illness was the result of Matheo's drinking a lot of wine. "He urinated putrid, viscous, rotten matter," she said.

When Matheo married *Madonna* Felicità, he had this ailment, she claimed, and it made him weak and prevented him from having sex. He was not able to consummate the marriage. Felicità continued by stating that Matheo had hidden his infirmity from her kin because, had they known, they most certainly would not have consented to the marriage. When Felicità discovered the illness, she told her husband that he should never have married her, or any other woman, and that she had been ruined. She claimed he responded that she was mad, and that all men were like that.

After being with him for thirty-five days, Felicità could not stand the smell of him, and she complained to her relatives. She also worried that he would infect her. Thus, she left him and returned to her parents. Felicità's parents consulted a physician, who told them Matheo's illness was at an advanced stage and was incurable.

Matheo denied all of Felicita's allegations.[62] He said he allowed a French physician, *Signore* Carlo Sirios, to medicate him, and after a few days he was cured. By the late summer the husband produced an arsenal of witnesses to support his stance, among them his sister Cornelia, his brother-in-law Julius, and Julius's friend Alessandro.[63] Cornelia knew from both her mother-in-law and her husband that Matheo had had a medical problem but had been cured. Julius was actually witness to the malady, but he also swore that he knew his brother in-law's sexual history prior to marriage.

> Matheo had a woman for five years, and if he could not have sex with her, he would not have stayed with her. Thus, I swear it is not true that he did not have sex with his wife. And I had spoken with the other woman, who is now dead, and she told me he had difficulty urinating but that they had sex. I slept with my brother in-law many nights when we were on a trip last year, returning

from Pisa. I never noticed any stench, and I saw his shirts, and I even saw him naked. I never saw any sign that he smelled. It's true that his wife left him, but I do not know the reason why. And my [other] brother-in-law Alessandro told me Felicità's relatives made Matheo see five physicians, and they said he could be cured.

On August 31, 1619, the examiner called Alessandro Marinonus, who confirmed what Julius had said.

The case lay dormant through the end of 1619. Then, at the beginning of the next year, it took a peculiar turn. Felicità retreated from arguments for annulment that focused on Matheo's medical condition and turned instead to another old standby in the discourse on breaking marriage ties, coercion. In a supplemental statement dated January 29, 1620, Felicità lamented that her mother had forced her into the marriage.[64] For this claim, unlike the other, the unhappy wife could gather testimonies of support.

Felicità explained that her mother, Lucieta, had hastily arranged the marriage with the help of relatives. Her father, Anastasio, was away in Constantinople. The family in Venice thought Matheo was a good match for Felicità. They had obtained good reports about him: that he was a man of good quality, disciplined, and well situated financially with lands in Codevigo, a district of Piove di Sacco in the Diocese of Padua. Felicità told the vicar that she begged her mother, saying something like "I heard you are making a match for me with Matheo the draper. Don't do that. I don't want him under any circumstances. I'd rather drown than marry him. "

Lucieta, Felicità maintained, had a terribly angry nature. When she heard her daughter was refusing Matheo, she began to shout and to threaten her. Insisting that he was a good match, she threatened that if Felicità refused, she would be without a husband for the rest of her life and would never see her mother again. At these words Felicità began to cry so hard that the entire household heard her and felt bad about her mother forcing her to marry against her will. Felicità's lawyer described her in the acceptable legal fashion of the day as a girl "young, timid, sad, and very obedient to her mother."[65] Ultimately, the lawyer concluded, Felicità had married against her will, evidenced by the fact that both before and after the marriage she was melancholic.

In February 1620, the month following Felicità's second presentation, her mother supplied the Patriarchal Court with a statement in which she confirmed that she had forced the marriage but that she did not know of Matheo's illness.

> I did not know Matheo was indisposed. If I had known, I would not have permitted him to marry my daughter. . . . After my daughter was married for 22 days she sent Fra Antonio Comin, her uncle, to me with word to come and get her. She lamented that she would throw herself off a balcony over Matheo's illness. The following Saturday I sent my brother Andrea to pick up a citation from the *Monsignore* Patriarch. My aunt, *Madonna* Lucretia de Bernardin Cocco, and her servant accompanied me to remove Felicità from her house. We brought her to my house, where she has been ever since. She told us many times that she left him because she could not tolerate the stench.[66]

Lucieta pointed out that although Felicità was unhappy after the marriage, she did not tell her why, out of fear. Felicità's sister was careful to confirm her mother's words about coercion in her testimony.[67] She explained that they were said in anger, that her sister did not want Matheo, and that she was timid, afraid, and obedient. "It's true that our mother is *terribile*, and she wants things her way, so we fear her because of her nature."

The following June, Felicità was questioned. She recounted,

> I was married for fourteen months to Matheo Fada. Now I do not know where he is, but he is a draper. I stayed with him about eleven days. . . . I did not volunteer to marry him. I did not like him. He wasn't for me. He was inferior to my condition. [Asked why she married him, she answered] Because my mother wanted it. . . . At the time my father was in Constantinople, and we received news that he had died. My mother was approached by a woman cousin, by an aunt on Matheo's side. First I said I did not want him, but she hit me . . . and she said I would live a bad life if I did not accept him. . . . I never loved him, nor did I have any inclination toward him.[68]

Later, when Felicità's father returned to Venice, he apparently was very distressed by the match his wife had made. Felicità reported, "When he found out what my mother had done, he said if I do not get free from this marriage, he wants to kill his son in-law, and cut my mother's throat, as it was she who wanted me to marry him." The hastily arranged match to someone of an inappropriate social class had occurred at a time of family instability.

When asked if she slept in the same bed with him once married, and if they had consummated the marriage, Felicità began to waffle. She replied "partly yes and partly no," meaning they slept together but did not successfully consummate the marriage. The examiner persisted, retorting, "You can understand if the marriage was consummated or not." Felicità, posing as innocent and inexperienced, insisted, "But I did not see anything." Next the examiner asked whether Matheo was infirm, and Felicità said she had heard from others that her husband had gonorrhea, but she did not know if that prevented him from having sex. When further questioned, she added that she had not known he was infirm.

> I heard that he purged himself, but I did not see if he was cured. After I left him, I never slept with him again. I did go with him the first night, but only because my mother made me. And yes, we had sex three or four times.

Now the examiner had caught her in a seeming contradiction. "But you said you did not see any sign that the marriage was consummated, and now you say you copulated three or four times." Felicità began to get nervous. "I said I did not see any sign, and I beg you, I did not know if I consummated the marriage or not." The examiner remained firm, trying to extract the truth. "I warn you that you are obliged to go with Matheo and have sex with him, as is convenient with a husband and wife. You have not told us that you took him because you were forced. Nor were you done any violence and for that you would not be his wife." Felicità vehemently insisted, "I tell you that I did not willingly take him, and rather than have sex with him, I want to go all dressed up to the Devil's house, and this I beg you with resolve."

After the interrogation it appears that someone, no doubt her lawyer, discovered that Felicità had not followed the prescription that could satisfy ecclesiastical examiners. She was prompted to furnish the court with an addendum. There is some added testimony, dated July 17, 1620, written in a different hand.[69] Felicità states, "If in my deposition made a few days ago there were some dubious words about whether the marriage had been consummated or not, I declare that while Matheo Fada tried to have sex with me, he was never able to penetrate my vagina because when he pushed, his member went soft, and he did not ever know how to consummate the marriage, and as a sign of this I never saw any blood, and this I affirm with my sworn statement." Abandoning the script lines that went with the discourse on coercion, already familiar to us in the previous chapter, Felicità once again returned to the script on impotence.

By this time the old refrain was familiar. A soft member, failed penetration, clean sheets. Felicità's "afterthought" did not convince the court. Nor did her deposition. Matheo had denied her accusations and affirmed his willingness to remain in the marriage. The court ordered the bride to return to her husband and give the marriage a chance for another three years, after which the accusations of impotence could be reevaluated.[70]

BREAKING MARRIAGE TIES was not a simple matter. Though canon law dictated the themes for bedtime stories, ultimately the credibility of the witnesses and the attitudes of the judges had weight in the final outcome of the cases. The judges were duty bound to preserve marriage ties, unless there were serious reasons to dissolve these unions. They were also concerned that sex result in reproduction. Thus, they made serious efforts to help young couples achieve satisfying marital intimacy, taking into account the needs of both husbands and wives.

Priests also listened to the lamentations of husbands and wives about the marriage bed. Wives in particular, our documents reveal, sought advice on sexual matters from their confessors. Parish priests raised these issues in the confessional as part of their pastoral duties, serving as an important outlet for the anxieties of spouses. The counsel of priests in difficult marriages might prepare the way for the marriage court. Other studies have shown that Catholic churchmen had great influence over what went on in the marriage bed, instructing women to refuse sodomy and even intercourse on certain holy days. Women were also instructed to decide for themselves whether or not a husbandly command was unchaste. Church authority was intended to supersede the patriarchal authority of husbands[71] while still ensuring that marriages remained intact.

But preserving marriage ties at all costs was not the aim of young people who were tracked for marriage, often by their parents, relatives, or guardians. Some of them were adventurous, willing to rebel against the system of arranged marriage. They found specialists who could aid

them with their scripts for court: lawyers who specialized in marital litigation, priests, physicians, and midwives, as well as neighbors and kin.
Nor did they fear testifying in court.

These bedtime stories suggest that not all women were passive
pawns in the marriage market. Some did not accept marriage with
men of a lesser station. Some did not accept insensitive or sexually
inept men. The women in these Church investigations expressed a
sense of entitlement—to a satisfying marriage, to a satisfying sex life,
and to having children. Moreover, they exhibited a capacity for creative
agency by going to court, gathering witnesses, and mounting and mar-
shaling evidence in their favor. Though they feigned sexual innocence
in order to underline their pristine virginity, they were hardly demure.
Moreover, they were well informed from a variety of sources in the
Venetian community about sex and reproduction.

Men, too, demonstrated their sense of entitlement in these cases,
though it is less surprising for their sex. They upheld a double standard, which permitted men and forbade women to exercise sexual lib-
erties. The more sex men could demonstrate they performed, the better, and performance took precedence over morality in all of these
cases. Sexual relations with a prostitute and spawning illegitimate children were preferable to suffering from the reputation of impotence.
Whereas husbands might be willing to collude with wives in annulment cases based on lack of mutual consent, they were not willing to
admit to impotence to get out of a marriage. Too powerful a violation
of their sense of identity and honor, an admission of impotence affected their status in the community. Thus a woman who disclosed a
man's impotence, or a woman who fabricated his impotence, availed
herself of a powerful weapon. Lucieta, her mother, and the other midwives knew this. Camilla knew this, too, and feared her husband would
strike back. These women launched their legal offenses with the
knowledge that they had contingent support and protection. There
was indeed a double standard, but some women, the ones who reached
out for help from the Patriarchal Court, knew how to use it to their
own advantage.

"I pleased the Illustrissimo by granting him my practice."

CONCUBINES AND COURTESANS
IN THE COURTS

"FAREWELL MY CONCUBINE" might be the refrain a patrician lover sang to his old flame when the candle had lost its flicker, or he had finally succumbed to family pressure to renounce a long-standing, illicit affair. At times fathers and brothers demanded such renunciations. When a son or brother who was not selected to marry appeared to be reneging on his commitment to remain single, simulating marriage with his concubine, the joint family venture became vulnerable to inheritance disputes or dissipation of the patrimony. Thus, father and/or brothers exhorted the family member gone astray to pawn his concubine off on a man of lesser status. From a male patrician perspective, the honor of the wayward woman was restored through legitimate marriage while the interests of the *fraterna* remained intact. Concubines, however, did not always willingly go away. Moreover, they so resented being conveniently discarded and shuffled around by their noble lovers that they sought the aid of the Patriarchal Court. Their cases afford us the opportunity to study modes of cohabitation outside the legal, conjugal bond.[1] They also cast light on the sexual activity of both married and unmarried patrician males.[2]

LAURA BELFANTE had lived with the nobleman Andrea Dolfin for a long time.[3] They had one child and she was expecting another when Dolfin, under pressure from his brothers, arranged a marriage for her. Insisting that Laura take a husband, Dolfin arranged a union, when she was eight months pregnant with his child, with the farmworker Andrea Goleno, who would appreciate the dowry. Two weeks later Laura left her new husband, acquired a lawyer, and sought an annulment, arguing she had never wanted Goleno. She was unsuccessful.[4] The court may have bowed to pressure from the Dolfin family, and Laura's pregnancy weighed in favor of marriage, in this case with the farmworker.

Isabella Cigala, however, a widow who cared for the daughter of Daniel Dolfin, was more successful in breaking her marriage ties. Daniel and Isabella had had an intimate relationship before the noble-

---

Previous spread: Titian (c. 1488–1576). *Danae and the Shower of Gold* (1546). Naples, Gallerie Nazionali di Capodimonte. Photo: Alinari/Art Resource. Cupid has already struck Danae and Jupiter in this erotic painting. Does Jupiter, hidden from the viewer, purchase this beautiful woman by showering her with gold, or, captivated by the power of love, does Danae freely grant him her favors?

man decided to marry his lover off to Adriano Fostinello. Isabella came before the Patriarchal Court in 1617, complaining that she had never wanted Adriano.

> From the time I entered the Dolfin house to govern that child until my marriage, I had had my own house for two years. That is, the Signor Illustrissimo Daniel Dolfin had given me a house in Venice in the Calle dei Cortellati in the middle of the Giudecca, where I had pleased the Illustrissimo by granting him my "practice" [sexual services], although I had a house that I went to occasionally, where my possessions were but I did not sleep there. I only went to look after my possessions. And I had the keys to this house. I only went there when Signor Dolfin asked me to.[5]

The vicar asked Isabella why she did not want to live with Adriano like a Christian wife. She answered that she had never considered him her husband.

> The Illustrious Dolfin gave him to me against my will, and forced me to sleep with him, locking me in a bedroom until I consummated the marriage. But I don't know how that happened because I also escaped from the bed that very same night. I wasn't in bed with him even an hour because he had such bad breath. I couldn't stand to be near him.

The vicar noted her deposition did not claim Dolfin violently forced her to marry Adriano. Moreover, if she had bowed to Dolfin then, why didn't she wish to stay with Adriano now? She responded, "He could not support me." She also repeatedly claimed that she was repelled by Adriano's bad breath. The vicar replied, "Falsely, some women believe they can annul [a marriage] because of bad breath. But God has joined you in matrimony, through your consent, and you will live with your husband so long as the Divine Majesty pleases."

To better judge the situation, the vicar summoned the servants of Daniel Dolfin to testify. They confirmed that Isabella had lived with him for two years and that he had had sex with her for a long time, feeding her and paying her expenses. But one male servant explained that after having had sex with her for two years, Dolfin decided he wanted to live in the grace of God, and that this was a good reason to end the relationship. How could the vicar argue with that? Dolfin himself testified before the vicar, explaining he had married Isabella off to remove himself from sin. He confirmed that she did not want Fostinello, that he had forced her to marry the man and to consummate the union. The morning after Isabella's wedding night, Dolfin's women servants told him she had escaped from the marriage bed and slept in another room. Dolfin added that all of his servants knew what had transpired that night. The nobleman's testimony sufficed to fulfill the arguments for annulment, and it was granted on grounds that Isabella had not consented freely to the marriage.[6]

Vicenza Dandolo was even more successful than Isabella, for she both obtained an annulment from the man who was forced upon her and kept the upper-class partner of her choice. She severed her marital ties with the weaver Iseppo Samitarij in 1561,[7] claiming that her guardian, the nobleman Piero Capello, had arranged the marriage without her consent. After being orphaned at thirteen or fourteen, Vicenza was taken by Capello, who knew her parents. He and his brothers had divided their estate, and Capello was living independently. When it came time to marry off Vicenza, Capello gave her a dowry of 500 ducats. In this case the nobleman did not insist that his ward stay married. When he realized how unhappy Vicenza was, he financed her attempt to dissolve the marriage. The two eventually established a permanent relationship, and in 1580 Vicenza filed a property suit against Piero Capello's (male) relatives in the Venetian Giudici di Petizion,[8] a secular tribunal, to gain part of his estate. Her petition indicated that the priest at Santa Eufemia had performed the marriage rites for Vicenza and Piero in 1565, while the bride was expecting her first child. The alleged marriage took place on the Giudecca, an island on the margins of Venice, removed from the public eye. Piero apparently kept the union and his two children with Vicenza from his family, and the siblings were attempting to protect their patrimony from claims stemming from a clandestine marriage.

This case clearly casts more light on the lifestyles of Venetian noblemen who were not allowed by their families to marry officially or to carry on the interests of the lineage. Moreover, some of the women with whom they had long-term relationships were not prepared to renounce the investment they had made in the union. Some obviously preferred to be the lovers of scions of the nobility rather than the wives of commoners, and they took their cases to the courts.

If He Had Cherished His Honor,
I Wouldn't Be in This Place

Though marriage in late Renaissance Venice promised women a better life than if they lived independently, in reality it did not always fulfill expectations of security, nor did it always preserve honor. Bad marriages forced women to make poor choices. Some refused to avail themselves of the city's asylums, viewing them as institutions of control rather than of protection,[9] and turned instead to prostitution. If they had the attributes and the requisite connections, some became courtesans. Neither fate was glamorous, but it was a means, albeit a poor one, of survival. Life was a series of difficult choices for all women, whether honest or wayward, who were not adequately protected by kin. As the next case will show, even wayward wives found ways to use the Church, the state, and the community to ensure their well-being.

On June 17, 1579, a Venetian wine merchant denounced his wife as an adulteress.[10] Petitioning the State Prosecutors (Avogaria di Comun) to mete out justice he wrote,

> Illustrious State Prosecutors:
>
> My great misery and calamity give me, Zuane Bonifacio Facini, the courage to appear before you. I'm sure that when you have the truth, you will alleviate [me]. . . . I have been married for about seven years, with Zuana, the daughter of Zuane Bagolin, who was a cobbler. This has brought on my calamity, as this sorry, wicked woman has never had good attributes, but has always led an infamous and dishonest life. While she lived in my home for fourteen months, she never lacked anything, and after my treating her as an honorable wife, she still decided one night, around one in the morning, to run away. She took advantage of the fact that I was in another room with my brother, talking business, and when I came out looking for her, I found that she had fled without my knowing. But then friends and others convinced me to take her in once again. I did not want to, but I consented, as the State Prosecutor Venier was about to penalize me. So I took her back, believing that this wicked woman would remedy her errors and behave well. But all was in vain, as she returned to her previous vomitlike ways and ran off once again, this second time. With whom she ran away I don't know,

as I was out of the house, doing my business. When she returned, she could not enter the house because I had locked the door. I ask that this infamous and shameful woman remain in a public place. She is a public prostitute. I say these things with tears in my eyes, also hopeful that the Majesty of God will one day, after so many unhappy ones, relieve my misery and affliction. I ask you to make your verdict an example, fitting of the case, and that you find a punishment that will be an example to other greedy women that want to satisfy all of their appetites and that marry not to get married but to be married in name only, thinking they can get better ahead this way than perhaps if they were not married.

Humbly,
Zuane Bonifacio Facini

Three days later, State Prosecutor Marco Venier began to interrogate the neighborhood witnesses Zuane had selected. The interrogations lasted into the summer. The first witness, Balthasar di Venezia, said, "I heard she ran away, but I don't know with whom." The second, a cobbler in the parish of San Canciano, revealed that several gentlemen frequented the husband and wife's house. The third witness, whose name was Guardo, tried to describe the wife's excursions with her patrician lover. He said,

> I have heard rumors that she ran away. . . . She went out one Carnival with that gentleman and stayed out all night. I know because I was with Zuane, and we found her at her father's house in San Agostìn. When Zuane found her, he beat her and said foul things and said she was not worthy of him.

The witness appeared to be alluding to the wife's extramarital sexual relations but was hesitant to come out and affirm anything. The next witness, a carpenter named Pietro Taso, reported a conversation he had had with Zuane after he complained that his wife had run away. "She is beautiful, but she is a beautiful *poltronzona* [someone who feigns incapability but is actually lazy]."

A boatman, Rocco, was the next to depose. He testified that a Messer Palao had picked up Zuana, whom he enjoyed while they rowed to the theater. *Dona* Maria, the wife of a Bergamasc cobbler in the neighborhood of San Canciano, provided even more damning testimony about Zuana and her sister Adriana. She claimed that "she never wanted to do good by him. She even beat her husband. . . . I saw these things because the balconies of my house are next to theirs, and after midnight I would hear [him] . . . screaming 'They're killing me, they're killing me.' " Another woman from the neighboring parish of San Tomà, *Dona* Marina Justi, also declared that Zuana was a public courtesan.

Many of the witnesses the State Prosecutor interrogated described Zuana's return to her husband after four years, her knocking at the door and asking him to open up, and his refusal. A fruit vendor testified that four years before, when he was still a young boy delivering goods to people's homes, he had witnessed men passing Zuana's house all day long, with her husband's knowledge. Presumably her husband was making appointments for the men to have sex with his wife.

The last witness for Zuane was Giovanni Maria, a gondolier whose daily routine had given him snapshots of Zuana's evening adventures. He had frequently rowed her, he said, in the noble company of Messer Palao and Zuane Contarini, and Zuane Nani.

In August 1579, a month after this preliminary interrogation of witnesses for the husband, State Prosecutor Marco Venier assigned the case to the criminal sector of the Signori di Notte (Night Watchmen). Valier also gave Zuana permission to leave her husband because he was not feeding her or providing adequate support. She and her husband were ordered to appear before arbitrators. They each selected two, as was the custom. The arbitrators unanimously agreed to order Zuane to insure the dowry. Zuana, of course, agreed. Not wanting to return to her husband, she gathered her things and went to live with her sister and brother in-law.

Zuane Facini was crestfallen at the arbitrators' decision, for he had been forced to agree to terms that put him at a financial disadvantage. He submitted a statement, dated August 31, expressing his bitterness over insuring the dowry he claimed he had never had. He tried to override this decision by implying that his wife was a discarded courtesan now guilty of adultery. This strategy could solve his financial troubles, for, if convicted, Zuana would lose her dowry. He lamented that he was supposed to have received 2,000 ducats as Zuana's dowry, but had been deceived into agreeing to a 1,000-ducat dowry and into giving her the authority to confiscate his possessions for that sum. He continued,

That sentence was enough to send me begging to live, which she does not have to do. I do not know a better expedient than to resort to the good justice of the Signori and file against Zuana according to fair law, since I found she is adulterous and also a public prostititute by reputation. The Signori di Notte must see the truth of these things and have her return the assets I have lost as a result of the sentence described.

Zuana was called before the criminal sector of the Signori di Notte to respond to her husband's allegations on September 24, 1579. She told the two Venetian patricians that her husband "sent gentlemen and others to the house," including "the *Magnifico* Marco Zane, the son of Marin, and Messer Zuane, the spice merchant who lives on the Fontego dei Tedeschi in Sant'Agostìn, Zorzi Contarini, and Zuane Moro." She testified in further detail as to her husband's role in prostituting her.

He sent them up to the house and invited them to do every vile thing to me. He himself put me to bed. He even gave them the key so they could come into the house. When one night Messer Zuane Moro came, I locked myself in a room, and he said "Open up." And I replied, "I'll only open up for one person," because I had seen Moro with fifty men in the company of my husband, and I did not want to open the door. He said, "Open up, it's me alone." I never wanted to open the door. I had a bad night, fretting, until I saw Messer Zuane Moro leave the house. When he left, and the servant saw this, she told me I could open the door. I immediately started screaming at my husband, telling him it wasn't enough just to have him nagging and betraying me. He replied he knew nothing about it, and that he would do whatever he liked, and he nagged me every day, offering me up, and he would have sent me fifty men a day .... and so he nagged me day and night, saying that I should make that gentleman happy. I ask you to examine Messer Zuane, son of Christoforo Locadelli, the draper who lives on the island in the house of Messer Zuane Donà; Gabriel the fruit vendor, who lives in San Barnaba; Maria, the wife of Bortolo, because she knows about my husband sending men to me; and *Magnifico* Moro, who had sex with me. I never wanted to consent.

But after granting permission for Zuana to live apart from her husband and with her sister and brother-in-law, the interrogators discovered she was actually living with a merchant. Zuana attempted to defend her actions.

> It's been said I am committing adultery, having left my husband and not leading an honest life. I don't have any other way to feed myself, and he [my husband] is not the type of man who will support me. Rather, he wants to live off of me. . . . As a woman who does not have the ability to live without some supplement, and constrained by need, I settled for living with this merchant, not having any other options. He is an honorable man. My husband, instead, would send me two or three men if the occasion presented itself, and he consumed all I had, and he even sent prostitutes to the house. If he had cherished his honor, he would not have reduced me to the place where I am.

Zuana, thus, was cohabiting with a merchant who treated her well, even if that meant adultery, because her husband was not honorable or good to her. She said this openly to her adjudicators.

Sorting through the contradictory statements of this husband and wife and outlining the possible realities they suggest is a thorny business. It seems clear that a Venetian noble, Zorzi Contarini, ready to discard his lover, had married Zuana off to Zuane. Zuane claimed he was coerced into this arrangement. No doubt the promise of a 2,000-ducat dowry—a handsome sum—was enticing. Perhaps he was bought. Perhaps also his social superior had enticed him and then duped him, if it is true that the gentleman never came forward with the promised payment. Zorzi Contarini did not stop seeing Zuana. It seems likely he married her off to appease his brothers, something that one of the witnesses suggested during the ecclesiastical investigation that followed the secular case. The duped, fortune-hunting husband sought to put his investment-gone-awry to another use, prostituting a woman he viewed as compromised in the first place by her initial relationship with the gentleman. Perhaps he did receive the dowry payment and still chose to subsist by offering up his wife's sexual services. Zuane might have compensated for his earning potential by making a profitable marriage, or alternatively making his marriage into a profit-earning adventure. There was no shortage of wealthy, single patrician males, excluded from the endogamous marriage market of the Venetian ruling class, to fuel the city's sex industry. How many other husbands married to put wayward women to work? How many other wayward women married to assuage the nervous kin of their patrician lovers? What Zuane may not have counted on was that Zuana's patrician patron and other lovers within Venice's governing elite were willing to protect her against a rapacious husband.

Thus far, our sorting out of Zuane and Zuana's contradictory statements has privileged male points of view. But the picture looks different from female angles of vision. Supposing Zuana had been a gentleman's mistress prior to marrying Zuane, she had, for whatever reasons, learned to survive by making her services available to noblemen. She was a courtesan, not a common prostitute. It may have been appealing to her that this marriage with Zuane would grant her entry into a life of legitimacy, with the promise of a substantial dowry on which she could fall back. Or, as literary scholar Margaret Rosenthal has maintained, "A Venetian courtesan's reputation and social standing were made more secure if she were married, or more importantly, if she were protected by Venetian patricians."[11] Yet it may also have been painful to be excluded from the circles of patrician males. Moreover, she may have been forced to bow to the will of her gentleman friend. She no longer wished to see him, despite his persistence. Was this a result of her anger over the horrible mismatch he had made for her? She did not bargain on becoming a common prostitute, sharing her mattress with the hordes of men, commoners and nobles alike, that her husband corralled. No doubt her husband's entrepreneurial spirit taxed her health and psyche, not to mention her overall well-being. It would have been a short-lived endeavor. Clearly, even for a courtesan, this was a step down in lifestyle. Rather than a caring gentleman lover, she had a ruthless husband, and she had to give over the fruits of her labors.

Once Zuana fled from her husband, refusing to work for him and trying to reclaim her dowry, Zuane pulled out the last card he had, according to Venetian law: he accused Zuana of adultery. If Zuane were the victor in this case, Zuana would be compelled by law to forfeit the dowry. The marriage was a farce from the beginning. The ultimate question in this case was who would get to keep, at least on paper, the gentleman's alleged gift of 2,000 ducats. Zuane was not an honest husband, and Zuana did not come to her marriage bed as a virtuous wife, but rather as a courtesan of the Venetian nobility. Who was really on trial, an adulterous wife or a pandering husband? In this case the state came down on Zuana's side. The Signori di Notte absolved Zuana on October 30, 1579. Though hardly an innocent matron, Zuana moved deftly through the Venetian system of justice, with the aid of her patrician friends.

The marriage was not over yet, at least not in the eyes of the Church, but Zuana was ready to sever her ties and would use Zuane's pandering as ammunition. Here, too, it is possible that she acted under the guidance and support of patrician friends. Zorzi Contarini may have meant well in betrothing her to Zuane, but the latter had not lived up to his part of the bargain in providing an honorable existence for Zuana. Thus in 1582 Zuana took her case to the Patriarchal Court, where she asked for a separation. Zuane sought to keep the marriage together, presumably still hoping to hold on to the dowry.

Zuana's maid, Maria, began the round of depositions. The forty-four-year-old wife of a mirror maker from Castelfranco contributed to her household economy by sewing and washing for others. She had testified for Zuana once before, when the latter was insuring her dowry at the office of the Giudici del Procurator. Maria confirmed that Zuane had sent men to the house to have sex with his wife, against her will, but she denied that Zuana was an adulteress. Maria also gave some background: that Zorzi Contarini had given Zuana in matrimony to Zuane, and that Zuane had wanted Contarini to sleep with his wife. The next witness was Jacobo de Avantio, the bodyguard of Zuana's patrician benefactor, Zorzi Contarini. He confirmed that Contarini went out with Zuana frequently.

Zuana also brought in the commoners her husband had allowed to have sex with her. In February 1583 the merchant Giovanni Maria Mascharini, probably embarrassed, admitted he had had sex with Zuana

> ... because Messer Zuane the ruffian sent me to her house and wanted me to have sex with her. Otherwise he would have denied me his friendship. And he put me into bed with her. Zuana did not want to consent, but she had to. She had to be patient because this is what her husband wanted. And he not only brought me into the house, but others as well. I know he brought in Messer Zuan Moro, because his wife was furious about it. . . . The next day she told me that Messer Zuan Moro had blown out the candles and wanted to force her to his will, but she did

not want to consent and she hid in the wine cellar and saved herself. For this reason Messer Zuane her husband was furious, saying [Moro] was a gentleman and that she should service him. Zuane told me that Moro loved his wife and he urged [Moro] to frequent his wife.

Zuane also selected witnesses to depose before the chancellery of Patriarch Giovanni Trevisan, to testify that he was a good and honorable person. In a rare instance, Pietro Grigio, a merchant, admitted that he had been coached by the man he was asked to represent.

Zuane sought me out, telling me these words: "Messer Piero, would you do me a favor and come be examined about my situation, as I have been slandered by my wife, who says I am a drunk, that I frequent taverns and eat in them, and that I am a gambler?" I haven't seen much of Zuane, but I do not know him to be this way.

All of Zuane's witnesses assured the examiners for the Patriarchal Court that he was a good man, but the patriarch was interested in knowing how he made his living. He was a merchant in name, but he had no shop once he was married. So how did he make his living?

Unfortunately the records of the ecclesiastical investigation stop here, so we will never know if the case reached a conclusion, or if some life circumstance prevented its completion. Patriarch Giovanni Trevisan would have wanted to ascertain whether Zuane had fulfilled his responsibilities as a provider. He was familiar with the case as it had developed before secular authorities, for a copy of those proceedings was with his files. Considering Zuana's successful results with the Avogaria di Comun and the Signori di Notte al Criminal, she had a strong chance of receiving the formal permission for a separation of bed and board.

It is not so much the incompleteness of the Church investigation that is striking, but that neither the ecclesiastical record nor the secular proceedings included formal testimony from Zuana's noble benefactor or his friends. Only the lower-class neighbors and the servant were called before the courts. Yet we know in this case that the supplicant had at least one noble in her camp, and though it cannot be demonstrated through the written record, that fact is more than likely to have influenced the outcome of this case. In fact, the noble benefactors were specifically forbidden by law to support or defend courtesans in public. In 1543, Venetian authorities had passed the following ruling:

> In view of the many advantages enjoyed by such persons of a low and abject order . . . none of our noblemen or anyone else of whatever order may personally or by proxy or at the behest of others plead or intercede on behalf of any infamous person, said person having been brought to court by the aforementioned Office of Public Health, under penalty of a fine of 100 ducats and two years' banishment from our Supreme Council; if not a nobleman, the same two years' banishment from Venice and from the district [will be enforced].[12]

The decree was meant to safeguard the honor of Venetian patricians and their families. It afforded a degree of privacy as well to courtesans, prostitutes, and concubines. But apart from the laws of the state, patricians were people as well, holding ties of affection with illicit partners and using their influential connections to protect them. And courtesans, prostitutes, and concubines, at least the ones who took their cases to court, learned how to work through the administrative routes and judicial procedures that could help them change their adverse circumstances. Those who wed, understood as well the power of challenging their husbands' honor before the community and the courts. This tactic was vital, for, as Chapter Six will show in detail, they were not prepared to relinquish their dowries.

"I know you like to have fun. Now I forbid you to go out of the house, if you do, I'll give you plenty."

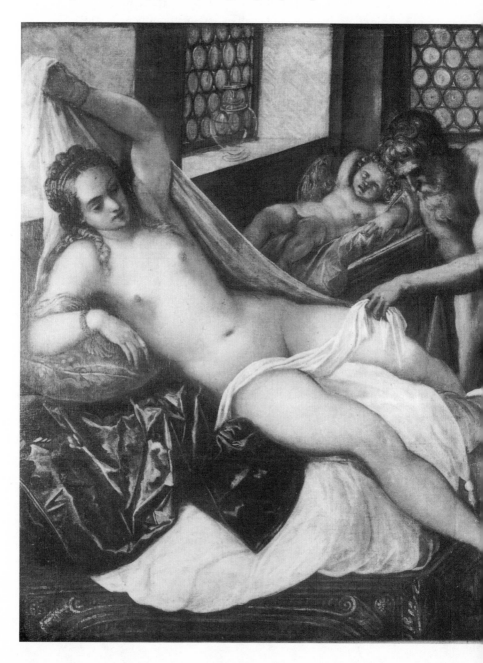

TALES OF VIOLENCE, HUNGER, AND BETRAYAL

IN 1584, Pasquetta Peregrini decided to change her unhappy domestic circumstances. No longer willing to live with Romano Cavatia, her husband of four years, she initiated proceedings for a separation in the Patriarchal Court.[1] Like many other women who left their husbands, Pasquetta retreated for the duration of the ecclesiastical investigation to a place that would preserve her honor and safety, the convent of San Maffei on the island of Murano. A month later she moved to another refuge, the convent of Sant'Andrea.[2] There, in June 1584, two months after she had left her husband, Pasquetta told her story to the notary who had come to record her deposition.[3]

Pasquetta painted a bleak picture of her life with her husband. She claimed she had never wanted Romano, a manuscript illuminator. She would have preferred a religious vocation, but her parents and relatives had constrained her to marry.[4] This part of the testimony fits into the familiar discourse on forced unions, and her complaints are commonly found in wives' justifications for separation. The Church sanctioned separations only when by mutual agreement husband and wife expressed a preference for religious vocations; when either spouse committed adultery; or in instances of extreme cruelty, when life and limb were in severe danger.[5] The last reason is the most common one supplied to the Venetian Patriarchal Court.

Pasquetta lamented that the marriage had quickly turned sour. Her husband had gagged and beat her; had denied her sufficient food; had demanded anal sex (a criminal offense); had been unfaithful; had squandered her modest dowry of 300 ducats; and had pledged her pearls, rings, and dresses, symbols of status among married Venetian women. She packed up four old blouses and a dress,[6] and fled their house in the Venetian parish of San Moisè to the island of Murano, accompanied by her sister-in-law Isabella, the unhappy bride of her husband's brother.

Fed up with their dreary living standards, the two sisters-in-law had

---

Previous spread: Jacobo Tintoretto (c. 1518–1594). *Venus, Vulcan, and Mars* (c. 1550). Alte Pinakothek, Munich. Photo: Alinari/Art Resource, New York. In the domestic setting of a Venetian palace, with prismatic windows and a Murano glass vase, the drama of an adulterous wife caught in the act is played out through classical myth. Venus attempts to cover herself with a sheet, while her husband Vulcan peers beneath the covering and her lover Mars, scarcely hidden, crouches under a table. Cupid feigns sleep while enjoying the marital conflict he has created.

decided to abandon their husbands. The night of Saint Job, around 3 A.M., they hailed a passing boatman and asked to be taken to Murano. It was perhaps a twenty-minute journey by rowboat, but the psychological distance by sixteenth-century standards was significant. On Murano, Isabella pleaded with a woman whom she claimed she did not know to give refuge to Pasquetta. The woman agreed, and Pasquetta stayed for eight days, until her mother came to her aid.

Isabella had made separate plans: she remained with people she knew in Venice, at the house of Andrea Castello, a weaver in the parish of San Canciano.[7] Eventually her husband, Antonio Cavatia, left the marriage to become a soldier, and he abandoned Isabella to support herself through domestic service. Though there is no evidence that Isabella filed for a separation in the ecclesiastical court, typical of many women, she did take measures in the Venetian tribunals to protect her dowry. Later, she would testify before the patriarchal vicar on Pasquetta's behalf.

It is surprising to learn how much latitude to make choices of serious consequence these two Venetian women from the artisanal class had. Isabella testified that before their departure, she and her sister-in-law had procured a lawyer, Zan Jacomo Gradenigo.[8] Pasquetta pointed out in her testimony that she and Isabella had made the decision to leave their homes independently. Surely the flight from irate husbands in the early hours of the morning risked their honor as well as their safety. Yet the actions of these two unhappy wives demonstrate how women who sought personal satisfaction found ways to change their life circumstances. It cannot be assumed, moreover, that their behavior invited disapproval, for the fact remains that they found help at every step along the way: the Muranese woman whose identity remains unknown, the religious institutions that sheltered Pasquetta, Pasquetta's own parents, some of her in-laws, and, ultimately, the Venetian statutes and courts that protected her property. There was a consensus within the Venetian community that a wife had reason to leave her husband if his neglect and inappropriate behavior threatened her welfare.

Nor were battered wives alone when taking their cases to court. Kinsmen and neighbors could build or destroy the honor of accused husbands, and were therefore an important resource for wives who made use of the power of public exposure. First, a series of witnesses who had frequented Pasquetta and Romano's house testified on her behalf. Two of Romano's in-laws expressed disapproval of his irresponsible management of money. The first was his brother's wife, Isabella, who confirmed that Romano had gambled away Pasquetta's clothing and pearls. The second was his sister's husband, Giovanni Meneghetti. With his own grudge to bear, Giovanni complained that Romano had taken not only Pasquetta's pearls but those of his own wife as well. He went on to confirm that Romano severely beat Pasquetta.[9] Romano's apprentice, Jacobo Vassalino, also came forward as a character witness against the misbehaving husband. He complained that his master still owed him wages and that he, too, had borne the brunt of violent blows.[10] If the personal grievances of these intimate visitors to Romano's house cast some doubt on the validity of their testimonies, those doubts were cleared by the next series of witnesses, members of the community who described Romano's abusive and irresponsible behavior. A Florentine gold vendor, Benvenuto Doni, testified that Pasquetta had complained to him of her husband's misbehavior.[11] Other neighbors stated that Pasquetta and Isabella had left because they were going hungry as a result of their husbands' gambling debts.[12]

Whether the accusations of these witnesses were true or false, they carry significant weight. First, they constitute an important index of community standards, standards that Romano had violated by failing to provide adequately for Pasquetta and by placing her physical welfare in jeopardy. Second, they reflect the community anxiety that resulted from domestic discord. Domestic quarrels were disruptive because they were public affairs, and neighbors did not hesitate to come to the distressed wife's aid. Finally, criticism by witnesses is an example of the kind of control the Venetian community could exert over misbehaving husbands. Opinions of both men and women converged in open disapproval. It was important for both sexes that a husband materially support his wife in a fashion commensurate with her social class. Support included food, clothing, and, for the upper classes, jewels and servants as well. There was an explicit expression of disapproval over any husband's taking back, selling, or gambling away the gifts of clothing and jewelry that he had made to his wife.[13] Discipline was permitted, but causing physical harm crossed the boundaries of accepted norms. Love and affection were occasionally mentioned, but material support seems to stand out as the most important criterion for a good husband to meet.

Natal kin could also be an important source of support for a mistreated wife. Some studies, particularly of the upper classes, tend to characterize the relationship between parents and a married daughter as distant.[14] This was certainly not the case for Pasquetta. In fact, she had had her mother's help for some time, and would have her father's support in this case as well. Her mother, Borthola, had been taking her sacks of food, flasks of wine, oil, and wood three or four times a week throughout her marriage.[15] Borthola also made efforts to protect her daughter's valuables. A gold vendor who testified on Pasquetta's behalf remarked that Borthola had come to his shop questioning what had happened to her daughter's gold buttons. She saw to it that the gold vendor was examined by officials from the Uffizcio del Petizione, a Venetian tribunal that handled property disputes.[16] There is thus good reason to believe that Pasquetta's parents, aware of her serious troubles, encouraged her to break the marriage ties.

Indeed, the alliance between parents and daughter is explicit in Pasquetta's case. When she summoned her mother to Murano, the latter quickly made arrangements to hide her in the convent of San Maffei, deceiving the nun by saying that her daughter, who was nineteen, was not yet married. Accompanied by a servant, Pasquetta's mother visited her frequently. She also arranged for her daughter to be transferred to the convent of Sant'Andrea, a *hospitio*, or place of refuge; Pasquetta's father would pay all her expenses. Romano attempted to see his wife at the convent, but the abbess refused his request. He told his ecclesiastical examiner during the court investigation,

> I discovered my wife was at the *ospedale* of the Convent of Sant'
> Andrea. I went there, after speaking with the *monsignore vicario* at
> San Andrea, and I spoke to the abbess, who would not let me see
> my wife.[17]

This was probably yet another protective measure, for in the case of this violent husband there was sound reason to fear that Romano could harm his wife. It is entirely plausible that Pasquetta's mother decided to reveal her daughter's difficult situation to the abbess of Sant'Andrea.

When Pasquetta was safely tucked away, her father took legal action against Romano in both the ecclesiastical and the secular courts in Venice. He chose a procurator[18] to present his daughter's case before Patriarch Giovanni Trevisan and his vicar Antonio Tomasini, after witnesses had been interviewed in their homes by a notary from the Curia. Romano, too, had a procurator, who argued against the separation. To protect his daughter's financial resources, Pasquetta's father also aided her in obtaining a favorable judgment from the Giudici del Procurator, insuring her dowry against Romano's potential insolvency.

It is clear that Pasquetta's natal family had some stake in protecting the dowry as well, likely a combination of guarding their investment and concern for their daughter's financial security.

Thus, women like Pasquetta could avail themselves of sympathetic kinsmen and neighbors to change their domestic circumstances. Her parents were willing to admit the failure of her marriage, and worked to protect both her welfare and her financial interests. The sentiments within the closed circles of family life often remain masked behind more public concerns, such as the preservation of status. Pasquetta's case affords the opportunity to study women who were not necessarily bound by the patriarchal interests that governed families of the ruling class. In addition, it offers a window from which to view the ties of affection and support that surrounded more fortunate women. Mothers and fathers took an active role in protecting their daughters' welfare, even after marriage.

Whereas the women who enjoyed the material, practical, and emotional support of their natal families in these separation proceedings held a distinct advantage over those who did not, married women, irrespective of social class, could call on other members of the local community to aid them in their efforts.[19] The ability to manipulate gossip was important to the success of women seeking to change their marital status without the help of natal kin.[20] They needed witnesses for the ecclesiastical tribunal who would portray them in a sympathetic light and at the same time cast serious doubts on their husbands' reputations.[21] A case in point is Cecelia Bressan, whose marital problems resembled Pasquetta Peregrini's.[22] Cecelia's husband, Orazio, a shoemaker from the hamlet of Piove de Sacco, did not provide the basic necessities for his wife. He beat her; he threatened to kill her; and he wasted her dowry away. In 1580, Cecelia's parents helped her file for a separation. They maintained that Orazio's violent behavior toward his wife was "public knowledge," a common assertion in these Church investigations and obviously an important part of the legal terminology. They brought forth five witnesses from the vicinity of Cecelia's home to confirm that Orazio spent more money than he earned; that he said vile things to his wife which threatened her honor, such as calling her "whore"; and that he beat her. One neighbor, Cornelia Venosa, a sixty-year-old widow, testified that Cecelia had miscarried twice as a result of Orazio's beatings.[23] Another neighbor, the spice merchant Battista da Venezia, stated that the community was aware of the couple's marital problems, that Orazio had attempted to kill his wife, and that he had heard that Cecelia had taken refuge in a (woman) friend's house.[24]

Orazio defended himself with only one witness, a friend who denied any knowledge of his violent behavior.[25]

The evaluations of neighbors were also of critical aid to Paola da Venezia, who had asked to be separated from the fuller Jacobo Furlano after three and a half years of marriage.[26] Her description of her domestic situation mirrors those of Pasquetta and Cecilia. Paola testified that her husband had beat her and had consumed her dowry of 137 ducats. Instead of going home to eat with his wife, "as did every good Christian," Jacobo continually ate in taverns and got drunk. Then he returned home and beat his wife. He spoke to Paola with cruelty, as if she were a prostitute, and did not provide food for her. The neighbors took pity on her and fed her. Jacobo, Paola maintained, led a bad life of taverns, prostitutes, and gambling. He lived without fear of God and had not confessed for years. Her husband, she said finally, did not show signs of loving her. On the contrary, she thought her life was in danger, and ultimately left Jacobo because he had threatened to poison her. Poisoning, it seems, was the sixteenth- and seventeenth-century trope for life-threatening circumstances in these cases. It was often invoked as a reason to separate from a spouse.[27]

Jacobo's violent behavior aroused deep sympathy for the mistreated wife among the neighbors, who vividly discussed Paola's departure from her husband. When the notary from the Curia came to take depositions, the testimonies from neighbors in the parish of Santa Margarita became pivotal to her case. Giovanni, a cloth merchant who lived below the couple, testified that Jacobo came home late at night, inebriated, and beat Paola.[28] When he arrived home, the misbehaving husband slammed the door and yelled. He beat Paola on the back, said Giovanni, who had seen her bruises. Andriana da Venezia, who lived in the same building, saw Jacobo take Paola's belongings little by little to pay his gambling debts. Andriana said her mother gave her and her siblings a little less to eat in order to feed Paola. The family saw Paola's bruises. Andriana and her family tried to exert some control: they told Jacobo to leave his poor wife alone.[29] Jacoba, another neighbor, remarked that Paola went hungry, and that Paola's mother had given her a little money to see to it that her daughter did not starve. Maddalena, the wife of the wool weaver who rented Jacobo a room, also witnessed the latter beating his wife. Besides expressing sympathy for Paola, the woman openly criticized Jacobo's behavior. Her husband, she testified, had shouted with disapproval that Jacobo should not treat his wife that way.[30] Two other neighbors defamed Jacobo's moral character, stating that he slept with a prostitute. Santo, a fuller, stated that he had seen Jacobo sleep with Marietta, a public prostitute in San Barnaba. Santina, the widow of a wool weaver, recited the common litany of flaws attributed to bad husbands by the community. First, she named another prostitute in San Barnaba that Jacobo reputedly slept with, Camilla. Second, Santina added that she had heard Jacobo say he wanted to poison his wife. Third, she emphasized that the husband led a bad life and was a blasphemer. The only thing missing was the accusation that Jacobo did not confess. True or inflated, Santina's testimony together with the others demonstrates that there was some attempt by neighbors in Paola's building to regulate Jacobo's misconduct.

Aid from Paola's family is less explicit but no less useful in this case than in that of Pasquetta Peregrini. We find Paola's mother disseminating knowledge of her daughter's mistreatment to potential witnesses, men and women who eventually corroborated Paola's case. It was in one sense an appeal to the community to aid her daughter; and in another, an effective weapon against her son-in-law. A neighbor, Jacoba, the wife of Giovanni Organeotti from Santa Margarita, testified that Paola's mother, Fiorenza, gave her money to feed her unfortunate daughter.[31] Geronimo di Arborio, a customs official, testified that Fiorenza, who was a midwife, had complained to his wife about the terrible life that her daughter had. The couple had taken pity on Paola, and Geronimo employed the unfortunate Paola to care for his pregnant wife.[32]

Whereas urban women from the popular orders took advantage of the hearsay of neighbors, sometimes even manipulating it themselves, women in the upper ranges of Venetian society may not have had the same options. The privacy of their large palaces or country villas may have hidden their husband's behavior from neighbors. However, they could rely on their servants for critical testimony about their married lives.[33] On the one hand, this could put the servant in a precarious position relative to the master. On the other, harboring family secrets potentially gave the servant some leverage. Servants could spread rumors around the neighborhood, even if the injured wife could not. The Venetian noblewoman Isabetta Bembo, who requested a separation in 1623 after six years of marriage,[34] called on her women servants to confirm that her husband, Francesco Priuli, had mistreated her. They were not reticent to speak up. One by one the women, ages fifteen to forty-four, came forward to relate that Francesco had doled out bread to his wife, had kept another woman in the house, and had given his wife syphilis. In addition to the servants, several neighbors in Isabetta's parish, San Giacomo del Orio, verified these assertions, and a doctor came forward to testify that Isabetta was diseased.

The testimony from servants as well as neighbors was also critical in the case of Faustina Gradenigo, a noblewoman who filed for separation from her second husband, Carlo de Cappo, on grounds of mistreatment and adultery.[35] When the notary went to the house of nobleman Marco Bembo to take down the distressed wife's deposition, she lamented that Carlo beat her often and "that he copulated and had sexual commerce with his servant Paolina. With her he lived a while, and when she became pregnant, he dowered her with 50 ducats." This was a common solution to which noblemen resorted when their servants became pregnant. Dowering a single, pregnant woman and marrying her off restored her honor and reintegrated her into the community.

When Carlo asked Faustina for money, she took the opportunity to escape, telling him she wanted to take advice from her brother, sister, and brother-in-law. At first she stayed with her sister.[36] Later, while the proceedings developed, Faustina retreated to the convent of Sant'Anna, and Carlo was obliged to support her for the duration of the ecclesiastical investigation. This solution was for her own protection: husbands frequently became violent after their wives left them.

Faustina's servants came forward to corroborate her story. Lucretia, the widow of Bernardo Cadiani, had heard Carlo beat Faustina.[37] Sebastiana, the fifty-five-year-old widow of Dimitri Batron di Vassello, saw Faustina's body black and blue.[38] Sympathetic neighbors in the district of San Pietro di Castello, the area around the Arsenal, testified as well. Camillo de Venezia, an Arsenal worker, lived on the same street as Faustina. Word of Faustina's unhappy marriage had spread through the neighborhood.[39] Valeria, the twenty-eight-year-old wife of Aloisio Navetta, testified that Faustina had a black eye on occasion.[40] The neighbor upstairs, Isabetta, the wife of Gasparo Martini, a caulker at the Arsenal, recounted that Faustina used to confide in her about her marital problems and that she had seen her bruises. The neighbors were filled with compassion for Faustina. Fearing for her life, they urged her to take refuge with her sister.[41] Young and old, men and women from the popular orders came to this noblewoman's aid, and Patriarch Federico Cardinal Corner and his vicar Cristoforo Baldi granted Faustina the separation.[42]

There were no guarantees that noblewomen such as Faustina Gradenigo would be successful in their efforts to sever their marital ties. Given the importance of marriage alliances among the politically franchised, it was probably more difficult for a noblewoman than for a commoner to dissolve a marriage. A husband from the ruling class who was unwilling to dissolve the relationship publicly could potentially make use of his power and status to obstruct formal proceedings. Moreover, because the Patriarch was a member of the Venetian patriciate, he may have realized the broader significance of separating a patrician couple, for it would no doubt have an important impact on the wider network of relations and alliances tied to this union. The unhappy noblewoman Clara Gritti left the house of her husband, Paolo Priulo, three times over three years, claiming that Paolo beat her.[43] Once she had to have a tooth extracted because of one of his outbursts. Finally, she decided to separate definitively. Her brother took her to their mother's house, transporting furniture and valuables. Clara's mother came to her aid, sequestering 319 ducats, a fraction of her dowry of 8,300 ducats, for her support. In 1581, Clara filed for separation, producing eight female servants, her brother, a physician, a nephew, and a sister-in-law as witnesses who provided clear evidence that her husband had mistreated her. She lived with her mother while the proceedings went on. The couple selected *confidenti*, friends or relatives who would help them make decisions regarding the division of property, alimony, and child support. Each of them wrote their requests and responses to these arbitrators. Clara asked for a house, furniture, servants, a teacher for her daughter, food, and clothes. Paolo was obliged by the arbitrators to cover her expenses for food. He had to make an initial payment of 100 ducats while the ecclesiastical investigation was in process.

Despite the evidence that Clara produced to justify a separation, she lost the case.[44] Her husband claimed that her leaving the household had injured his honor. In addition, he alleged that she had attempted to poison him. One morning he found a Venetian coin in a pan of chopped herbs, "an act that could produce a thousand deaths," he exclaimed. Here again is the common accusation of poisoning, this time by the husband. Paolo objected to Clara's attempt to separate, to her having selected *confidenti*, and to her disposing of her patrimony without his permission. In essence, he objected to the independent decisions his wife was making; Paolo feared losing control of her. We cannot know why the judge ruled in Paolo's favor. It is plausible that he deferred to the power of the Priulo family.

In another instance of abuse in a patrician household, Cornelia Zane attempted to leave her husband, Giovanni Battista Salamon, on grounds of mistreatment. Her injuries were both verbal and physical.[45] In her deposition she stated that he rudely used foul and dishonest words. He hit and kicked her, even when she was pregnant, so that she had to be medicated by neighbors and others she knew, particularly in the town of Martinengo, where Salamon was rector. She claimed he did this because she gave him many children, and so he was especially cruel to her when the time of birth neared. Cornelia took refuge in her mother's house and initiated the case in court.

Giovanni Battista Salamon presented a different side to the marriage, denying he had inflicted any violence on his wife. He described his marriage of sixteen years in harmonious fashion and emphasized that he governed his house with dignity. The couple had ten children. His wife was mistress of the house and had everything she longed for. Giovanni Battista complained that she often screamed at him without cause, saying inappropriate and provocative things. He attempted to defame his wife's witnesses. Mandricardo the tailor, Iseppo Horlandi the weaver, Sister Marina, and Orsetta, the wife of Antonio the rower, he claimed, did not know what they were talking about. Still, Cornelia's uncle, a sister-in-law, and two cousins stood up for her. Unfortunately, the outcome of the case is unknown.

It is very clear in this series of cases regarding accusations of negligence and abuse that husbands did not favor separation. Perhaps some of these men were wrongly accused. The wife's initiation of an investigation in the Patriarchal Court constituted a serious offense to a man's public reputation and notions of honor. Faced with charges of abuse, husbands often tried to demonstrate that they were good providers. Alternatively, if they wished to be vindictive, they responded with a countersuit, accusing their wives of adultery. Either strategy enabled a successful husband to keep the dowry for himself. Perhaps more important, either strategy permitted him to keep his honor intact. Giovanni Paolo a Papis and Niccolò Montin, husbands whose wives filed for separation, are two cases in point.

Gratiosi Asolani, in the company of the ecclesiastical lawyer Pamphilo Corner, approached the Patriarchal Court on behalf of his daughter Franceschina in 1596.[46] Franceschina wanted to separate from the Venetian merchant Giovanni Paolo a Papis. She claimed her husband had abandoned her and her little boy and had consumed her dowry of 1,100 ducats, 800 of which was in capital. Giovanni Paolo had come to the marriage with inherited wealth valued at 3,000 or 4,000 ducats, but he had dissipated these assets. Giovanni Paolo, the wife declared, was a violent and vindictive husband who had struck her in the throat and wanted to kill her. He had even mistreated his own mother, dealing her blows. When Franceschina lived with him, she starved. He was incapable of supporting his family, so he abandoned them, closing up the house and auctioning off their possessions. When Giovanni Paolo was absent for fourteen months, Franceschina's father, moved by compassion, took his daughter and grandson in.

Giovanni Paolo had left Venice, and consequently did not appear before the Patriarchal Court to respond to his wife's allegations, but he did engage a procurator and he did depose. He argued that his parents in-law had consented to take in his wife and child while he was away, and they had agreed to feed them. He also pointed out that he had sent his brother-in-law 400 ducats for the support of his wife and child. He did not want a separation. He was gone only three months, and he was not without money. Franceschina, through the procurator who argued her position, continued to deny everything he said, but Giovanni Paolo won the case. Franceschina appealed, and he again was the victor; she was compelled to stay married to him.

When Niccolò Montin was thrown into prison in 1632 by the Venetian Council of Ten, his wife, Clara Vidali, approached the patriarchal vicar Cristoforo Baldi with her procurator Aloisio Zane and requested a separation.[47] She accused him of not supporting her, of wasting away her dowry by gambling, and of having a violent nature. Niccolò engaged Niccolò Noale as his procurator and quickly came to his own defense. He owned houses and land, he maintained, from which he had income and rents. He was not violent, but rather of a placid nature, and he minded his own business. He had never killed anyone, did not keep arms, and did not play cards except for recreation. When he lived with Clara, they never had any disagreements; they lived in tranquillity. Until he was imprisoned, he had always supported his wife financially. Niccolò tried to show that Clara did not really want the separation by declaring that she had cried and showed signs of great pain when the Council of Ten arrested him. In essence, Niccolò wanted to stay in the marriage and was trying to make a case that he was a good husband. Separation was dishonorable to men; women knew this would be a powerful offensive strategy in a court case.

Patriarch Federico Cardinal Corner and his vicar Cristoforo Baldi listed the questions they had about the Montin-Vidali case: Did Niccolò own his own house? Did he have rental income? If so, for how long and how much? Had he been a considerate husband, courteous and benevolent? What did the witnesses think was the cause of the disagreement between Niccolò and Clara, and which of the two did they think was right? Did they know why Clara did not want to return to her husband? What would this witness do or how would this witness resolve this problem if he or she were in Clara's position?

Niccolò's witnesses spoke well of him, but Clara sustained her allegations. When Clara's sister Angela deposed before the notary who visited her, she exclaimed that Niccolò had said "that he wanted terraces to sweat with blood from the great ills that could happen." When she asked him what he meant by this, he responded that if he had Clara in his hands, he wanted to kill her. Angela added that another day he visited her and once again told her that if he had his wife in hand, he wanted to vindicate himself. Angela concluded, "I knew him as a very angry man."

Clara's procurator then produced some of the letters her husband had written her from prison, in an effort to show his violent nature. One of them read as follows:

Listen, My Wife,
We are approaching the Carnival season and Fat Thursday. I know you like to have fun. You are that type. . . . Now I forbid you to go out of the house. Neither to your sister's or your friends', neither masked or without a mask. If you do, I'll give you plenty.
—Niccolò Montin, Your Husband

The vicar Cristoforo Baldi was convinced. He signed the verdict granting the separation on January 16, 1634.

What do these cases teach us about women who wished to dissolve marriages to violent or neglectful men? For one thing, they were not defenseless, nor were they without powers of decision. Moreover, the broader community approved of separation in instances of abuse or neglect, with the expectation that the wife would continue to lead an honorable life. Going off to live with someone else even because of a bad husband could not be condoned by civil or religious authorities, even though the members of the neighborhood communities presented no monolithic stance. The adultery suit of Antonia and Gregorio da Vegia is a case in point. In 1587 the Forty, a tribunal linked to the Avogaria di Comun, prosecuted Antonia, a gondolier's daughter, for adultery.[48] She admitted her errors in the course of the proceedings, which in many ways contained the same lines of questioning that would be carried out in an ecclesiastical investigation. Gregorio was not an ideal husband. The marriage had been arranged. He was much older. He stayed away from home for a week or two at a time. Antonia strayed. The state condemned her after witnesses described her comings and goings.

What is interesting here is the lines of argument of husband and wife, the testimony of neighbors in the vicinity of the *ospedale* at San Vido, and how their attitudes split along gender lines. Gregorio, the "injured" party, first wished to establish that he was a good husband and a good provider. To this, Paolo, the vegetable gardener, attested: "Gregorio treated his wife well. She did not lack food or drink. She had everything at her disposal except the savings box. She was well-dressed, with clothes and shoes."[49] Paolo also said there were rumors that Antonia had had sex with many men. Giovanni Maria Violi, a gondolier, and his wife, Zuana, sustained all this as well.[50] From where they lived, they could observe Gregorio's wife receiving other men. Gregorio also underlined that his injuries involved property. He claimed his wife had taken food and other possessions that belonged to him. The neighbor Lodovica sustained this. Giovanni Maria the gondolier also mentioned Antonia's taking food, wine, oil, and coal. Giovanni Maria's wife, Zuana, however, shifted focus. She testified that Antonia wanted to poison her husband.[51] It was a serious accusation, meant to show that Antonia was a bad wife. However, the Forty did not follow up. Perhaps they saw through this attempt to defame Antonia and did not find the attempted accusation of the desire to commit homicide credible. Many of Gregorio's witnesses had already testified about Antonia's goings-on with men, and that was the primary reason she was under investigation.

What defense did the wife provide?

> My husband says that I have made a mistake. That's not true. . . .
> My parents married me to Gregorio because he had money. The
> entire neighborhood was surprised. He was stingy, and he beat
> me when I was three or four months pregnant, so that I miscar-
> ried. He went outside [Venice] to his master's villa and stayed
> away eight, ten, fifteen days. And for the few mistakes I made, I
> made them out of great need . . . and if I had not gone to the
> chancellery and registered my possessions, he would not have
> come forward and said anything. [When asked why she married
> Gregorio, Antonia responded] Out of great fear of my father I
> said yes with my voice but not with my heart.[52]

Most of the witnesses for Antonia claimed they knew nothing about the allegations, and that what they did know was not from Antonia but from her mother. This undoubtedly hurt her defense. Still, some witnesses were forthcoming with their opinions.

Francesco Pasqualino said, "Antonia's parents should not have given her to that old man." Geronimo Pironi, a lawyer at one of the Venetian tribunals, remarked that Gregorio had gotten angry when Antonia had protected her dowry at the chancellery. In his opinion, what really interested Gregorio was the counterdowry he had given Antonia. Antonia had come to the marriage with a dowry of 100 ducats, which Gregorio had matched with another 100. When she left him and retreated to her mother's house, she took her clothes, pearls, head scarves, and other items with her. Gregorio went to court because she had injured his honor, but also to recover the property he believed was rightfully his and to protect his initial investment of 100 ducats. Antonia had been unhappy in the marriage. Feeling neglected and abused, she had turned elsewhere for help, and perhaps for affection as well. Although neighbors could sympathize over the age gap between husband and wife, and the husband's allegedly abusive behavior, infidelity was not an acceptable solution. But it was the solution that Antonia had chosen rather than suffer silently with a husband she detested. She would have time to think about it as she served the jail sentence she received from the Forty.

THESE TALES of violence, hunger, and betrayal offer us snapshots of wives availing themselves of the formal legal structures of Church and state to separate from their husbands. Like the annulment cases discussed in previous chapters, petitions to separate bed and board revolved around the legal reasons for which the Church would have sanctioned a separation. The narratives, thus, contain common themes of life and limb in grave peril.[53] Whether or not the dangers were exaggerated to win a positive verdict, what remains certain is that these women wished to change their marital status and that they had won the approval of their families and community.

Neighborhood communities remained an important part of family life, the part where women could perhaps more readily wield or manipulate the power of social control. Standards of behavior were not regulated only in the public spheres of Church and state. Marriage was not a private matter in Venetian neighborhoods: kinsmen and community had a decisive relationship with the married couple. The Venetian case demonstrates that they were, in effect, institutions of public life that protected women and disciplined men. Women in bad marriages had some powers of decision, and they were not alone.

"When a woman is free she does not possess clothing from her husband, and if he sold some things I had and with the money dressed me as a married woman, with clothing that was for his use, that's his business."

"A WOMAN WHO KNOWS HOW
TO TAKE CARE OF HERSELF WELL":
TALES FROM THE DOWRY WARS

CLARA VIDALI'S sorry marriage to Niccolò Montin disintegrated in 1633 after a mere four years.[1] All the while Niccolò had been steadily consuming her dowry of 1,600 ducats by playing cards. To pay for his gambling addiction, he had pawned and sold Clara's rings, gold necklaces, silver, and clothes. When Niccolò abandoned Clara to escape the prison sentence of the Venetian Council of Ten, her uncle Zuanne took her in. Niccolò had left her without the means to sustain herself. Claiming her reputation and honor had been offended, she returned to live with the aunt and uncle who had arranged the marriage in the first place, and filed for a separation.

Clara had come to her second marriage as a widow with considerable property. Niccolò's mother, eager to make the match, had guaranteed Clara's dotal goods with a lien on her own houses. Still, doubts about Niccolò's trustworthiness must have arisen early in the relationship because, just three months after the marriage contract, Clara drew up her testament. Four days later she voided it, making a new will with significant changes that reflected her worries over the match. In the first testament, dated November 13, 1629, she left Niccolò 300 ducats from her dowry of 1,600 ducats.[2] She appointed her son Francesco, her uncle Zuanne Vidali, Pietro Morcer, and her husband as executors. But Niccolò was named an executor only on condition that he not interfere with the testament. In the second testament, dated November 17, 1629, Clara reduced Niccolò's inheritance to 100 ducats and removed him from the list of executors.

When Niccolò began to falter in his financial responsibilities, Clara, with the support of her natal family, took action against him in the ec-

---

Facing page: Titian (c. 1488–1576). *Woman in a Fur Coat* (1536–1538). Vienna, Kunsthistorisches Museum. Photo: Alinari/Art Resource. Half garbed in sumptuous fur, the woman's assertive glance suggests she is aware of her powers over the beholder.

clesiastical court. Trying to save the union and no doubt interested in Clara's wealth, Niccolò built a defense in the ecclesiastical investigation to demonstrate how well he had supported his wife. The court investigated what he had bought for her, what she lacked, how she dressed, how well she ate, and, most important, Niccolò's sources of income. One witness remarked that Clara's husband treated her "with honor, both in the home and outside, with servants, with costly dresses, and with gold equal to the other citizens of Mestre."[3] Niccolò, however, did not present a convincing defense, and in the end the ecclesiastical court determined that Clara was better off living separately from her thriftless husband.

The Dowry Wars

Throughout the Renaissance, the dowry was widely regarded as an aid to husbands in sustaining the financial responsibilities of marriage and family.[4] In fact, it came to mean much more. If a Venetian husband governed dotal property responsibly, his wife could expect to find it intact for herself and her children, should he predecease her. Venetian law specifically obliged him to protect it with his own financial resources. Nonetheless, if a woman such as Clara Vidali married a wastrel, there might not be any dowry left, a situation resulting in significant loss for the wife. Because a widow could make no claim to her husband's patrimony unless he had specifically willed it to her, and was entitled to provision for food and lodgings from his estate for only a year after his death, a dowry could be a soft cushion for widowhood.[5] Dowry loss had broader implications as well, because it affected the financial future of male and female lineages alike.

Apart from estate planning, dowry mismanagement affected the stability of the wider community. Property that had not been clearly registered, for example, divided kin, rupturing family cohesion. Business relationships were jeopardized as well when creditors, seeking compensation, could not claim the assets placed under the umbrella of an *assicurazione di dote*, a kind of dowry insurance.[6] For example, in 1633 a baker named Francesco Trussardo quarreled with Antonio Zanchi before the Giudici del Procurator about taking possession of a boat as compensation for a debt. Trussardo complained that Zanchi had falsely registered the boat as a dowry resource so that it could not be confiscated.[7] In another case that year, Santo Martinazzi accused Marietta and Andrea di Giosio of collusion and gluttonous greed because they had neglected to repay their debt, even though Marietta owned a string of pearls worth thousands of ducats.[8] Examples of this sort abound, and they kept the courts busy.[9]

Ultimately, sound financial management of the dowry contributed to the stability and vitality of society as a whole. In contrast, its dissipation could render wives and children a burden to Church, state, and society. Law and custom placed the fate of this vital resource in the hands of husbands. Not all women were satisfied with this arrangement. Some were mindful of the wealth they had brought to the marriage and found resourceful ways to protect it.

Court activity in late Renaissance Venice clearly situates dowry litigation at center stage in the marriage wars, with women as eager as men to net that important resource. Examples of the terms of marriage contracts and the litigation over dotal goods during this period are telling: the registers of the Giudici del Procurator[10] were filled with contracts containing safety clauses protecting the dowry "in case of dissolution of the marriage." Here was a forthright statement admitting to the possibility of failed marriage and highlighting the reclamation of the dowry as a critical concern.[11] Even with these safety clauses and specific legal provisions protecting dotal property, however, there were no guarantees that women would recover this vital resource when couples were either having marital difficulties or in the process of separating. For example, in 1614 Angela Mastelaria, the wife of Jacobi Vidali called Orsetti, filed a protest with the Procurator against her husband of eighteen years. The two had been separated for many years because life circumstances, Angela recounted vaguely, had kept them apart. Friends had persuaded the couple to reunite. Angela, however, regretted the decision when her husband began liberally spending her life savings, largely in the form of loan investments. Jacobi persuaded Angela to donate her nest egg to his heirs. Meanwhile, he continued to spend the funds as he pleased. Angela denounced him before the magistrates of the Procurator in an effort to save her patrimony from eventual dissolution.[12]

Some women had to go to greater lengths than the Giudici del Procurator in order to prevent the dissipation of their dowries. Another secular magistracy, the State Prosecutors, were on hand in the event that a husband expropriated dotal goods. The magistracy might also delegate matters to yet another court, the Signori di Notte. Lucia

Grandajo resorted to the criminal branch of the Avogaria di Comun in 1596 to recover stolen property from her husband, Francesco. She complained that her standard of living had been very poor for ten or fifteen years. Francesco, she argued, had consumed her belongings; he had seriously beaten her and had threatened her life; and he was a public blasphemer banished from the city. When Francesco discovered that Lucia was planning to insure her dowry at the Procurator to protect herself against his insolvency, he stole her dotal goods. While Lucia took refuge at the house of a food vendor, officials from the Avogaria di Comun, under order from State Prosecutor Falier, retrieved the goods. In 1596 Lucia filed for a separation in the ecclesiastical court.[13]

Women had to strategize and to fight through the courts to ensure that legal prescriptions were honored and that the judicial process worked to their benefit. Men had to do the same with misbehaving wives, and judges and the community of common friends and acquaintances were called upon to decide which spouse was telling the truth. Venice's civil and criminal courts, under the aegis of the patriciate, thus served as secular theaters of domestic drama, but often the disputes over rightful ownership of dotal goods spilled over into the Patriarchal Court as well. Ecclesiastical and secular authorities in Venice achieved a measure of cooperation while formally maintaining a division of competencies.[14] In principle, secular magistracies oversaw the governance of contracts, dowries, spousal support, guardianship, inheritance, and legitimacy. They also resolved domestic discord which resulted in crime. The Church, on the other hand, judged the validity of the sacrament of marriage, acted as spiritual caretaker for the married couple, and ultimately determined whether or not to dissolve marriage ties. In practice, however, many of these assigned competencies overlapped. In particular, the investigation of deteriorating relationships often led the Patriarch or his vicar to examine conflicts over property in depth. At the same time, the Venetian state held a vested interest in keeping marriages together and seeing to it that wives were adequately supported.

The stories that follow offer us the opportunity to examine differing perspectives on dotal wealth. They illustrate as well important state concerns for the proper governing of dotal property; Church intervention in domestic financial conflicts; and the unique role of Venetian community members who were called upon to arbitrate the property disputes of married couples.

The Jew Who Would Be a Christian

In 1624 Catterina de Comitibus wrote her consort her thoughts about their disagreements over her dowry:

> There is no need to produce a multitude of documents, *Signore* Francesco my husband. You dream of confusing me. How many times have you said emphatically that I, having no one in the world, have your protection? Yet abusively you have done whatever you want, whatever was convenient for you, so that I would allow you to freely dispose of my patrimony. Admit it, this is not the way to live in peace, in love. May Justice protect me, or if I have no one else, then God will protect me. You should not complain about me but about yourself, as you have always failed to specify what little [of my dowry] remains. As I said, you are being false, with certain ends in mind. Now you are urging me to ask for a judgment from the Illustrious Patriarch, but that is contrary to the agreement we made with your lawyer. I am still willing to abide by that if you are, and we can live in peace. But as for your demands for a bigger dowry, your wanting to pursue further legal sentencing or to resort to other actions against me, according to your disturbing and unstable thoughts, I tell you, you must propose these things to our *confidenti*, as much as you like, and defend yourself reasonably, and I will abide by the judgment, and we will end all these demands. As you became a Christian out of love for me, pray to Jesus Christ that he remove all these thoughts and ideas from your heart about consuming all of my assets and bothering me, for I will denounce this. If you are just, I will always be your obsequious, humble servant and wife. May all that I have said be without offense.[15]

Fearing her entire estate was in jeopardy, Catterina requested a separation from Francesco Zacharia Conti alias Moisè Copie in 1624, just one year after the couple had concluded a marriage contract. A wealthy woman, Catterina claimed she had been deceived into marrying a man who was not of her faith. Francesco had courted her on several occasions when he visited her house on the pretense of purchasing silk. He presented himself as a rich merchant who would be fortunate to have her hand. Catterina hesitated because her suitor was not of her faith, but after he promised to convert from Judaism to Christianity, she agreed to the marriage. After the couple were joined in matrimony, Catterina discovered to her dismay that Francesco was still a practicing Jew. Moreover, he already had a wife and children. While her procurator, Giovanni Rossi, attempted to win an annulment on the grounds that Francesco was already married, Catterina also used religion as a pretext for requesting the dissolution of the union. She complained that Francesco ate meat on the prohibited days, and that he was baptized only on paper. Above all, he had no interest in the Christian religion but only in Catterina's wealth. Yet, clearly, there was more than religion and a previous marriage at stake in Catterina's complaint over Francesco alias Moisè's deceit: her property was in jeopardy. Catterina's dowry was very large, and she feared for its safety.[16]

When the couple married in May 1623, Francesco had registered the dowry at the Giudici del Procurator. Although Catterina had originally promised him 2,000 ducats in income per year and 4,000 ducats in gold, silver, and goods to be assessed by common friends,[17] her lawyer had negotiated the yearly income down to 1,334.5 ducats, 334.5 of which Catterina retained the right to dispose of at all times. The capital on which this annual yield was based was to be invested at 5 percent. Mutual friends had already concluded that Catterina's gold, silver, jewelry, and other possessions were worth 8,000 ducats. Francesco would be given half, and was obliged to insure it. He was forbidden to dissipate any part of the dowry. For his part of the agreement, he pledged a counterdowry of 400 ducats per year during Catterina's lifetime. In the event there were children and she predeceased them, Francesco was obliged to continue providing their heirs this annual sum.

The marriage contract also stated that Moisè Copie would become Francesco Conti and be baptized a Christian.[18] When Catterina discovered that her husband had deceived her, presumably to dispose of her lucrative dowry, she filed for a separation and moved to the convent of the Convertite, where on January 30, 1625, she deposed for the Patriarchal Court. The procurator Giovanni Rossi took down her main points.[19] The next day Francesco deposed, in his home, responding to Catterina's assertions as the notary read them to him. Francesco stated:

> I was at her house before I converted to Christianity. I went to buy some silks from her. . . . It is not true that I went to her house

to make her fall in love with me, but because she said she would like me to come. So I went, and I did send her some presents. . . . It is not at all true that I told her I knew of a merchant who would be a good match for her . . . she told me many times that if I converted to Christianity, she would marry me at once. . . . It is true that I did not make our vows public, because if my Jewish friends knew, they would poison me.[20]

Catterina's version of the betrothal, on the other hand, was that a Father Raffaele had made an agreement with her parish priest and had tried to convince her many times to marry Francesco, saying that she could save his soul. (One of the conditions upon which the Church would sanction marriage to a previously married non-Christian was to save the soul.) Francesco remained emphatic that he had not converted to Christianity for financial motives, but because his heart was in the new religion.

While Catterina insisted that the two priests had convinced her to marry Moisè in order to save his soul, her husband retorted that she had done all this for her own reputation. The couple had gathered information from various clerics about the possibility of their marrying. Catterina said they had sex after they agreed to the contract, but Francesco vehemently denied this. "That is not true at all, because she did not want to until I was baptized and gave her my hand in marriage. Not even when I was baptized. Not until I gave her my hand and the marriage rings."

Catterina lamented at length about Moisè. He had been previously married, to a Jewish woman named Regina, and he had two sons and a daughter. He tormented Catterina and her servants when they were praying before Jesus or the Blessed Virgin, saying that they were idolizing. He was indifferent to the prohibition against eating meat on forbidden days, and tried to prevent Catterina from abstaining. He was not interested in religion, but rather in her material goods. Francesco denied all of these accusations.

The ecclesiastical examiner noted that Francesco had been baptized on paper on July 17, 1623, and had left the ghetto and the Jews the evening of July 19. Two days later he married. Francesco affirmed that he and Catterina had married before the parish priest of Sant'Apostoli, in the presence of two witnesses, at two o'clock in the morning. The hour is indicative of a clandestine marriage.

In the end, Catterina and Francesco came to an agreement about dotal property. The discourse concerning Francesco's previous marriage and his religion was dropped. Catterina offered to withdraw her petition for separation from the ecclesiastical tribunal (together with all the other accusations) if Francesco would agree to her financial terms and then never ask for a divorce. Her procurator Francesco Pellizari, presented her case before the Venetian Signoria, in the Cancelleria Ducale, on November 28, 1624. Catterina proposed to select from their common possessions items valued up to 3,000 ducats. The items would be sold and put into loans or some other investment of her choice, which would serve as the basis of her dowry. She would divide the fruits of the investment with her husband. The rest of their goods would be assessed, but Francesco could not ask for more than what had already been promised. He would be allowed to keep the annual income of 1,000 ducats, guaranteeing the safety of these funds with his own property, as registered in the office of the Giudici del Procurator.[21] In the end this case seems to indicate that there were problems working out the dowry details. That is, that after an initial arrangement in principle, disagreements broke out over amounts or a payment schedule. This couple went to court, perhaps to force one another to accept the details of the dowry arrangements or to speed up payments. In fact, Catterina proved to be more concerned with a satisfying property agreement than with religious differences or Francesco's past relationship. She used the last two variables to her advantage in advancing the first goal, for if true, they were legitimate reasons to request a separation.[22] Motivated to remain with the wealthy widow he had married, Francesco professed Christianity, and the couple remained together.

A Refashioning of Self: An Honest Courtesan or a Courtesan Who Made Herself Honest?

It was Giovanni Battista Misserini who in 1612 initiated the proceedings in the ecclesiastical court for a formal separation, but his wife Foscarina Memo was in full agreement. The couple had never come to an understanding over rightful ownership of dotal goods. This disagreement had plagued them from the beginning of their marriage; meanwhile, their relationship had seriously deteriorated.

Foscarina Memo is an interesting woman to study because her social standing in Venetian society, an important determinant of experience, is not easy to classify. She was the illegitimate daughter of a prominent Venetian patrician, Giovanni Francesco Memo,[23] who had served as the castellan of Candia in the late sixteenth century. Foscarina felt closely tied to her Memo relatives, as evidenced in her will, but she was raised by her mother, Cornelia Livriera, who remained perhaps her closest companion throughout the courtship, marriage, and proceedings for separation. With her father deceased and her mother limited financially, Foscarina had little hope of enjoying a noble lifestyle, or even honorable status. Prior to her marriage, she lived with Cornelia in a rented apartment, costing 70 ducats annually, at the foot of the Ponte della Pana.[24] From there the women's standard of living descended. They moved to the parish of Santa Marina, where they shared a rented room in the house of *Madonna* Cecilia, which cost 30 ducats per year. Another woman rented there as well. It was in this house that Giovanni Battista first visited Foscarina. His court deposition sustained that at that time Foscarina earned her keep through prostitution. The assertion cannot be taken at face value, for it was quite common for husbands wishing to separate from their wives to slander their sexual reputations. Why would the rich son of a prosperous book publisher want to marry a dishonorable woman? Because he found in Foscarina attractive qualities that subordinated honor to passion? No male witnesses claiming to have had sex with Foscarina were called to the Patriarchal Court, and Giovanni Battista's accusations were never sustained. That does not necessarily mean the accusations were not true. Giovanni Battista was not the first, nor would he be the last, Venetian to fall in love with a courtesan.

Foscarina may have been one of the city's many prostitutes who worked independently, avoiding registration in order to skirt the Venetian sumptuary laws aimed, in theory, to prevent prostitutes from appearing as upper-class women. Her mother may have been her trainer and manager, as was frequently the case, beginning the process by procuring the Memo name for her daughter.[25] Foscarina clearly aspired to a higher standard of living. She could not boast a pure, noble bloodline, but neither was she confined in manners and associations to the lower ranks of Venetian society. Her financial resources a mystery, at least in the ecclesiastical record, it seems she used her charms to make a profitable match, one that would allow her to refashion her identity.

Clothes, jewels, furnishings, and other gifts would enable her to present herself as someone else, the Messer Giovanni Battista Misserini's wife—at least until the next opportunity came along.

For three years Giovanni Battista Misserini, the wealthy manager of a Venetian branch of his father's publishing firm on Venice's prestigious Merceria, had had a sexually intimate relationship with Foscarina. Not an unsuspecting foreigner, the Venetian Misserini knew of Foscarina's illegitimacy and lifestyle. In his court deposition he claimed he knew she was an experienced sexual partner before she became his lover. One of his corroborating witnesses described her as a kept woman.[26] Yet Giovanni Battista never explained why he ignored the questionable honor of this woman and took her in marriage on March 3, 1609. The couple joined according to the canons of Trent, with the knowledge of the bride's mother Cornelia Livriera but unbeknownst to Niccolò Misserini, Giovanni Battista's father. Giovanni Battista chose the mirror maker Vicenzo Bellana, the husband of Foscarina's sister, as his best man.

It was this kind of defiance of honor and public reputation, this crossing of class boundaries without regard for interests of lineage and property, that often landed young couples in "divorce" court. Authorities were attempting to protect the institution of marriage from the perils of mésalliance. After the Council of Trent, Venetians began issuing regulations to restrict clandestine marriage.[27] But both Church and lay magistrates discovered that clandestine marriages, because they did not follow the conventional norms of establishing a new union publicly before the community, often ended in dissolution.[28] This was a phenomenon that particularly affected families of economic substance and political weight. Presumably clandestine marriages did not include dowries if they took place against family wishes. Preventing them reflected the overall desire to ensure social stability by protecting the institution of marriage. It was important as well to support the practice of arranged marriage, a strategy which allowed parents some control over the social, financial, and, for the upper classes, political future of the lineage.[29] Arranged marriages normally affirmed traditional values, preserving the social order by encouraging socially sanctioned nuptial unions.

Giovanni Battista thus had good reason to fear his father's disapproval of his marriage to a "free woman," and for the first eight months of the marriage he put on a charade to protect himself and his inheritance. He ate and slept at his father's house in the parish of Sant'Apostoli, and paid daily visits to his new wife in Santa Marina. He brought Foscarina gifts and furnishings for their hidden nest. Eventually the prodigal son broke the news to Niccolò, whose reaction was, unsurprisingly, punitive. Niccolò dismissed Giovanni Battista from the family publishing house. The father had other sons managing branches of the firm in Rome and Naples, and it appears he ran a tight operation, controlling both his business and his sons' lives, as was the custom of the age. Niccolò also threw Giovanni Battista out of his house, but the son begged his friends to intervene and persuade the outraged father to accept his new arrangement.

Foscarina enjoyed her mother's wholehearted support for this prosperous match, whereas Giovanni Battista, in contrast, had to negotiate himself back into his father's graces. In the midst of these animated discussions, Cornelia and Foscarina made some compromises with Niccolò and Giovanni Battista, thereby sowing the seeds of the property dispute. The lengthy narratives that litigants and witnesses supplied to the Patriarchal Court further confuse matters but do not entirely obscure the wishes of an angry father, a love-struck and unruly son, and two women whose financially promising match had gone awry and who now had to negotiate through the administrative routes and financial procedures of the Venetian legal world. At the root of the men's and women's differences was that the exchange of vows had not been preceded by the required financial agreement that normally defined the dotal terms of the marriage pact. Foscarina did not bring a dowry to the marriage. Niccolò was set on remedying this by constraining her and her mother to sell off all their personal belongings in order to raise capital for the dowry. He wanted none of their possessions in his house, nor did he want Foscarina wearing costly fabrics that would weigh on family assets. In exchange, he would accept Foscarina's marriage to Giovanni Battista and take in the new daughter-in-law's mother and grandmother as well. The logic behind his request was explicitly stated: he was concerned that the eventual expense of this clandestine union would jeopardize his other sons' inheritances. Niccolò may not have had the resources to provide a marriage for Giovanni Battista. Moreover, Niccolò did not want to pledge his own wealth as collateral to insure Foscarina's dotal assets. The dowry would have to come from Foscarina, but Niccolò would have nothing to do with it —against conventional law and custom in Venice at the time.

Foscarina and Cornelia complied, although Cornelia had taken advice from a lawyer, who explained the disadvantages of the agreement. Perhaps the mother was willing to take the risk so that her daughter could leave the life of prostitution for a legitimate marriage. Moreover, both she and her own mother would enter the Misserini house, thereby resolving their difficulties with the expense of lodgings. Thus, Foscarina sold the furnishings of the rented apartment in Santa Marina and raised a dowry of cash and goods valued at 2,000 ducats.

However, there continued to be wrinkles in the financial part of the marriage agreement. Giovanni Battista and his father would not insure Foscarina's dowry against their own assets with the Giudici del Procurator, as was the custom and law. Cornelia exerted pressure on the men, creating more rifts in what were already precarious family ties. When personal relations between the couple broke down two and a half years after marriage, the unresolved issues over dotal goods came to the fore.

One of the twists in the disagreement was Giovanni Battista's claims that the goods Foscarina had sold to raise a dowry did not all belong to her, but that he had purchased them for her. In March 1610, a year into their marriage, the husband had demanded that his wife deposit 1,500 ducats for her dowry, and the following May another 500 ducats. Still, it was not clear whether the assets Foscarina sold to raise this capital were hers to begin with or the fruit of those months when she and Giovanni Battista had set up their clandestine nest. The details would eventually have to be straightened out in the Court of the Giudici del Procurator.

Further complicating the situation was the testament Foscarina had drawn up in the second year of her marriage, in order to protect what she thought were her dotal goods. She designated her parish priest as her executor, leaving him 300 ducats to say Masses for her. Another 300 ducats was designated for charity. Her half brother Marin Memo was to receive 100 ducats. She also left small tokens to her two uncles, Pietro and Giacomo Memo, to an uncle Alessandro who was a cloth merchant, and to a nephew. A third of her dowry would go to her husband, as stated in law; the rest would go to children if she had any. If she did not, her patrimony would go to her uncles, Giacomo and Piero, or to their children. Thus, we learn Foscarina maintained strong ties with her natal family, though they are conspicuously absent from the record of her marital litigation.[30]

The property issues were separated in the legal sphere from those contributing to the couple's deteriorating relationship. The division of property was relegated to the secular sphere and settled by a group of common friends, whom the spouses selected to arbitrate. Foscarina and Giovanni Battista each filed their claims: he on January 3 and she on January 30, 1612. The *confidenti* heard lawyers' arguments over the next several months and came to a decision in November of that year. *Confidenti* Francesco Loredan, Alvise di Dominici, Francesco Periglia, and Andrea Muschio came to the conclusion that all the goods, gold, and other items the couple were disputing should be sold, with the help of two common friends to be selected by each of them. Should they not agree on which friends to choose, the couple's possessions would be deposited in the Giudici del Procurator, which would invest the assets in landed property or loans, cautiously and securely, to insure the dowry. The arbitrators further judged that Foscarina was not obligated to pay the 1,500 ducats that Giovanni Battista had demanded on March 1, 1610, nor the 500 ducats he requested be paid in May 1610. The couple's notary, Andrea Spinelli, was paid 6 ducats for his services.

This segment of the dispute was clearly a victory for Foscarina, and the decision underlines once again the importance Venetian authorities placed on protecting a wife's dowry funds. The decisions of the arbitrators were emblematic of the social consciousness of the age: the separate bureaucracies of Church and state, as well as parish clergy and lay confraternities, worked consistently during the last half of the sixteenth century and the early decades of the seventeenth century to protect the financial and physical well-being of women, to promote social reform, and to uphold moral standards. Indigent women were thought particularly deserving of charity, in order to keep them from moral corruption.[31] Church, state, and lay benefactors all established institutions to address their needs. Several new asylums for women appeared in the city. First, through ecclesiastical sponsorship, the Convertite established a fixed site on the Giudecca in the 1540s where they built a community for reformed prostitutes and women who could afford neither lay nor spiritual dowries.[32] Two decades later the Zitelle Periclitanti, was founded for girls aged nine or older who were in danger of losing their virtue because of impoverishment and the negligent behavior of parents or guardians.[33] Around 1577 the Casa del Soccorso, believed to have been financed by the famous literary courtesan Veronica Franco, became a halfway house and refuge for women in

unstable marriages and adultresses.[34] The new institutions of poor re-
lief were intended to offer women both vocational skills and a Christian education, pillars of social stability, though how successfully the
needs of women were met is a separate issue.[35]

By the spring of 1612, Foscarina had filed her own petition for separation from Giovanni Battista in the Patriarchal Court. Although the
Patriarchal Court had delegated the division of property to *giudici
confidenti*, it nonetheless took a strong interest in how the patrimonial
dispute had begun and developed. Thus, the first phase of the investigation centered on the contested dowry funds. The Patriarch and his
vicar wanted to know more about the possessions that Giovanni Battista and his father Niccolò encouraged Foscarina and Cornelia to sell
to the two Jewish merchants who dealt in used merchandise. Did they
belong to Cornelia? To Foscarina? To Giovanni Battista? Did Giovanni
Battista purchase the allegedly fake pearls with his money, or Cornelia's, or Foscarina's? How did Foscarina know Giovanni Battista
spent 800 ducats of her dowry? Did he spend money or sell possessions? One would expect, according to Venetian norms, the secular
Avogaria di Comun to ask these questions, but they interested the ecclesiastical tribunal as well.

The court was also interested in the way Giovanni Battista had supported Foscarina. A bookseller, testifying for Giovanni Battista, took
great pains to describe Foscarina's lavish dress as a married woman:
raw and finished silks, a gold belt, a gold-handled fan, fine necklaces,
maninni [thin strands of gold chain], and pearls. He spoke of Niccolò's
situation with sympathy:

> With a clandestine marriage, against his will, as if at any time they
> [Foscarina and Cornelia] could pretend anything be counted as
> dowry, or that they could devise other conniving schemes with
> his son, and they should have been happy if [Niccolò] simply ac-
> cepted them naked. But *Madonna* Cornelia, who wanted nothing
> else but to deceive *Signor* Niccolò, had a brief document drawn
> up to her advantage where *Signor* Niccolò, against his word,
> would oblige his patrimony to insure the dotal goods. Their
> difficulties stem from this disagreement. *Madonna* Cornelia and
> *Madonna* Foscarina should remember when I reconciled every-
> one in the Church of the Peace in San Paolo, that Niccolò was
> ready to accept her and love her as a daughter.[36]

Attached to his statement for the Patriarchal Court was an inventory of everything Giovanni Battista had ever bought Foscarina during their marriage. After Foscarina was read the list, she replied:

> All the items you read to me were given to me, that is, those that were not part of the trousseau of dotal money, because when a woman is free, she does not possess clothing from her husband, and if he sold some things I had and with the money dressed me as a married woman, with clothing that was for his use, that's his business and I know nothing about it. On the contrary, for I do not recall whether he bought many items on the list for me or I already had them in the house.[37]

In all, the Patriarchal Court interrogated twenty-two witnesses in order to verify Foscarina's position, primarily people who had been involved in some way in the couple's financial affairs: bookseller friends of Giovanni Battista and Foscarina, the two used-furniture and clothing vendors, the pearl vendor, and the friend who accompanied Giovanni Battista to purchase the string of pearls. The vicar was particularly interested in how the two women had sold their belongings to amass a dowry. He questioned Jacobo, one of the two Jewish vendors:

> Tell me if *Signora* Cornelia was heated up and affected when she sold her furnishings, and whether her daughter Foscarina was present.
>
> I don't understand these words. I know the women sold their stuff, and *Madonna* Foscarina was present at the sale, and both of them indicated they wanted to make a good sale.
>
> Tell me if the two woman bargained, or tried to bargain with these Jews, exhibiting great eagerness to obtain an advantageous price.
>
> They negotiated the price with the Jewish merchants, and sought their own advantage the way every person does.[38]

The officials in the Venetian secular tribunals were also mandated by the Avogaria di Comun to testify in the ecclesiastical investigation. Among them were a guard and a lawyer from the Avogaria di Comun, an officer from the Giudici del Proprio, the notary at the Giudici del Procurator who had taken care of Foscarina's affairs, and a neighborhood shirt vendor who doubled as an amateur investment broker. The witnesses associated with the secular tribunals are of special interest, because they clearly reveal lines of cooperation between secular and ecclesiastical authorities. One official from the Giudici del Proprio testified:

> I know these women auctioned off their stuff. The man in charge was Ventura Gallina. The money they got from the auction was registered and deposited in the Avogaria [di Comun]. I know Niccolò, father of Giovanni Battista, did not want her to bring silk dresses, nor other pompous things. He wanted to dress her parsimoniously for his home. Those were the words I heard from Niccolò and Giovanni Battista, who made them [the women] sell their stuff because they did not want to insure it.[39]

Niccolò, it seems, wanted Foscarina to stop dressing like a courtesan.

Gaspar Fabrius, the notary who served Foscarina at the Giudici del Procurator, testified that Foscarina had told him that "her husband and father-in-law made her sell the little that she had, with great prejudice and damage to them [the women], and they collected several hundred ducats." He understood from her that the men had forced them to make bad financial deals.

Agostino Corner, a state prosecutor, sympathized with Foscarina, whom he had previously defended. He stated that Giovanni had tried to hoodwink his wife:

> I know that *Signor* Gasparo Fabrio, a notary at San Marco, told me that this Giovanni Battista and his father wanted to have in writing something that was to the disadvantage of this woman, and in his acts the [women] asked the notary's opinion. In good conscience he said he did not feel like giving his assent, as the document was of notable prejudice to her dowry.[40]

There is, thus, a protective note in these testimonies.

The shirt seller, Giovanni Battista Pizzinelli, had some knowledge of the women's attempts at investment. It seems they had not planned to relinquish the proceeds of their furniture sales to Giovanni Battista immediately, but rather to reap the fruits of investment first. Pizzinelli seems to have acted as a liasion between his customers and neighbors, and the local friars. He recounted:

> This woman invests. She told me three months after she had sold her stuff that, if I remember correctly, she had collected 800

ducats, which she wanted to invest with the friars of San Giorgio. And I told her they would offer 4 percent. She wanted me to ask them if they would give her 4.5 percent, and I told her that 4.5 percent was their returns, and that they did not want the investment if it was not for 4 percent. They [Foscarina and Cornelia] asked me if [the friars required] a certain type of currency. I responded that they wanted coinage at current city rates. They asked if the money had to be brought to the Mint or paid in the presence of the friars' notary. I told her the friars brought the money to their own residence, and that there was an order from the Pope stating that people who invest money with these friars cannot free it up whenever they want, but that the friars would return it at the pleasure of the creditors. And this woman and I had this discussion in my shop more than once.[41]

While Foscarina's witnesses tried to demonstrate that she had items to sell and then in turn capital to invest, the witnesses brought forth for Giovanni Battista emphasized that Foscarina's resources were extremely limited and that it was her husband who earned a lot of money and was capable of handling expenses and purchasing the property in question. The testimony of Pizzinelli suggests that Giovanni Battista underestimated the financial savvy of his wife and mother-in-law.

In the summer of 1612, Foscarina's lawyer submitted further accusations against Giovanni Battista to the Patriarchal Court, an effort to provide a more convincing argument that this was a bad marriage. Amid allegations of adultery and abuse were questions of property. Giovanni Battista's lawyer, Jacobo Pamphilum, made a detailed list of questions to help him characterize Cornelia and Foscarina. Among them, What were Cornelia's actual financial resources? Did she have income and property? What were her origins? As for Foscarina, was she a prostitute? Concerning *Madonna* Cornelia, whom did she associate with? Where did she live? Did she rent from someone, or did she rent to someone? Was it a room or an apartment? How much was her rent? Did she have that house when she was married? What does it mean for a woman to live comfortably? Does it mean she has income from property or that she is fed and maintained by men? Did *Madonna* Cornelia have property? Where? Was it inherited? Who left it to her? Did she have investments? How many? Who helped her with them? What dowries did she have? Was she a widow for a long time? Was

Foscarina legitimate or not? With which husband was she born? What did she inherit at her father's death? Giovanni Battista's lawyer did not find all the answers to his questions.

The court pursued financial matters a bit further before reaching a decision. How would Foscarina support herself, if separated from her husband? Foscarina had explained that her mother had covered her rent when she left Giovanni Battista, and if she left him permanently, she would support herself with the 20 *lire piccoli* a day he gave her, plus her dowry. When the vicar asked Foscarina whether her mother had property, or other means which would enable her to live honorably without working, she replied, "My mother does not have property, but my husband does not have to go crazy thinking about her welfare, because she is a woman who knows how to take care of herself well."

In the end the Patriarch was not convinced that Giovanni Battista and Foscarina should be granted a formal separation. He ordered Foscarina to return to her husband and to pay the expenses of the investigation,[42] a signal that he did not find her case convincing. The property dispute was settled by the *giudici confidenti* in the manner stated above. Thus, on May 22, 1613, Vicar-General Roberto Cusa drew up the list of expenses Foscarina had accumulated with the ecclesiastical court. Each part of the investigation was assigned a charge: her stated position, the justification that was outlined point by point, the examination of witnesses, and the verdict. It totaled 298 *lire* and 11 *soldi*. That was approximately 15 days' worth of subsistence for Foscarina, who had already claimed she could get by on 20 *lire* per day.

The case did not end there. Unwilling to accept the Patriarch's decision, Foscarina appealed to the papal nuncio in Rome. Once again she was ordered to return to Giovanni Battista. Foscarina and her mother ignored both ecclesiastical decisions, and instead they fled, taking some of the disputed belongings with them.[43] On December 18, 1613, Geronimo Rossi and Camillo Rincio posted a public notice on the steps of the Rialto on behalf of Giovanni Battista, stating the women had fled and stolen things of great value, and that Foscarina was an adulteress with someone whose name was not yet known.[44]

It took Giovanni Battista, with the help of his lawyer, eight months to discover Foscarina and Cornelia's whereabouts. Like his wife, he, too, filed once again for a separation with the Patriarchal Court on February 14, 1614, taking care to emphasize that he had tried to reconcile with his wife and that he was providing 1 *lira* every day for her support. He also filed a complaint with the Signori di Notte for the expropriation of his alleged belongings, but on March 11 this criminal tribunal of the secular sphere absolved Foscarina and Cornelia. It required Giovanni Battista to pay the expenses for the proceedings.[45] It was the husband's wish, at this point, for the wife to stay in a monastery rather than be known as a public prostitute. Their dispute was settled by August 1614. Their marriage was over, but the disputed dowry remained with the wife.

The Sum of Three Tales

The stories of Clara Vidali, Catterina de Comitibus, and Foscarina Memo reveal common priorities among Church, state, and community representatives arbitrating dowry litigation. The first was the cohesion of the family, in both its nuclear and extended forms. Property disputes between spouses, sometimes a symptom of deteriorating family relationships but often a cause, were a potential source of disruption. The second priority was the financial welfare of women. Though the Venetian ruling class had made legal provisions for the financial support of badly married women as early as 1374, charging the Procurators of Saint Mark with ensuring the victuals and lodgings of women who were legally separated from their husbands,[46] the issue of safeguarding married women's property persisted, emerging again during the mid-sixteenth century. There was a growing awareness of the financially poor, and attempts were made to address at least their minimum needs. However, poverty was not necessarily the only motivation behind making protective provisions for the dowry. It was widely known throughout the sixteenth century that dowries were rising to inflated levels in families with some financial security. Thus, they were a considerable investment of family resources, one that the natal family would want to supervise if not control.

In legal terms, a dowry ostensibly represented the wealth of a wife. Placed under husbandly control, however, ownership often became ambiguous, especially if the dowry was not registered. Yet the prescribed roles of husbands and wives emerge clearly from these stories, when one or both spouses stepped out of bounds. A husband was expected, by law, to register the dowry he received. Failure to do so could eventually lead to litigation over rightful ownership of capital and goods. A husband was also expected to behave responsibly with dotal wealth, which was in his safekeeping. A wastrel who consumed or expropriated dotal wealth was subject to the intervention and disciplinary action of Venetian authorities, for a wife was entitled, by law, to a dowry, which represented her share of the natal family's estate. However, she was expected to trust the laws in place that required her husband to insure the dowry while she stood by patiently. Clearly, women like Clara Vidali, Catterina de Comitibus, and Foscarina Memo understood that their dowries could be safety nets against eventual adverse financial circumstances. Thus they took an active part in protecting their wealth. They were not without support. Venetian law provided options for them, and civil and criminal authorities were prepared to come to their aid. So, too, were the ecclesiastical judges, who recognized the importance of dotal wealth.

Where women seem to have more radically crossed the boundaries of gender expectations was in attempting to separate from unwanted husbands, for whatever reason, and planning to use dowry resources to live independently. Foscarina Memo was a case in point. Like her mother, whose independence she admired, and the many other Venetian women who visited the courts to claim and protect their patrimony, she was a woman who knew how to take care of herself well.

CONCLUSION

OUR TALES OF THE marriage wars offer rich new insights into the hopes and desires of Venetian women and men who, after the Council of Trent, went to court seeking to change their marital status, to claim more satisfying intimate relationships for themselves, and to secure their financial resources. Their depositions offer us generous descriptions of both women's and men's expectations of domestic partnership. From them emerge wive's modes of agency, and the reactions of their husbands when they stepped out of prescribed roles. Wive's censorship of husbandly behavior also comes into view. Moreover, at another level the documents feature a broad spectrum of male authorities associated with the ecclesiastical and secular courts who were disposed to assisting husbands and wives with their difficulties.

One husband's tale of alleged fraud serves well to sum up the many themes running throughout the Venetian marriage wars, and it underlines once again the difficulties of reading court petitions as indices of social experience. Giacomo Savioni filed a grievance with State Prosecutor Paolo Donato on January 6, 1645, portraying his wife as both a thief and an imposter.[1] Laura Armana, he stated, was "the most perfidious and wicked person that nature has ever produced." He went on to explain:

> Knowing that I had a savings box containing gold and more than 2,000 ducats that my first wife left me for the dowries of our two noble daughters, [Laura] tried to say that one of my children had opened it and taken the money and valuables. She counseled me to put everything in a drawer in the room where I slept, or in the kneeling stool next to the bed, persuading me that even in plain sight the money and valuables would be more secure, and seeing that I would have placed the savings in the same drawer it had been in, in the first place. One day when I was not at home, she stole all my money and gold. She fled with the aid of Valentina [her maid], and she took shelter in the house of someone of authority, hiding there for many months, although I finally discovered where.

Giacomo lamented that his wife not only had been scheming to secure his daughters' inheritances but also that she had filed two claims at the Venetian mint for some money she said was part of her dowry.

Laura was not contrite about these allegations but instead expressed entitlement. She reponded by initiating three court cases against Giacomo. Two were before State Prosecutor Querini, for attempting to poison her, for mistreatment, and for filing a false claim to rob her of her property. The third, a petition for separation, was before the ecclesiastical court. In the secular disputes, State Prosecutor Querini found Giacomo innocent. Fed up, the unhappy husband also filed for a separation with the Patriarchal Court. In the course of preparing his case, Giacomo discovered further deceptions that raise questions about the accuracy of marriage records in post-Tridentine Venice:

> I was the one who saw a notation in the marriage registers of the Church of San Benedetto of this city that stated that she had been the wife of an Illustrious *Signore* Francesco Contarini, son of the Excellent Antonio. Seeming impossible to me that a woman of that quality had been the wife of that subject, I began to search more and to find that the notation was written anonymously, even though the signature read "I, the parish priest." At any rate, it was not in the hand of the priest of that time. What is more, the note stated that the banns had been announced, yet one cannot find any permission from the priest for that dispensation, and the priests always save those permissions. I would add that there was no record of where that marriage took place, nor were the witnesses noted, and all this is necessary for a marriage to be valid. This must be observed and not violated, according to the Council of Trent.

Digging deeper into the records, Giacomo discovered Laura had been married several times. He claimed she had made use of the courts to change her marital status as she pleased. Giacomo explained that Laura was not the widow of a nobleman, but rather of Giacomo di Zuanne Surian, who had died in 1607. That year she remarried one Antonio Zoppino, with whom she lived until 1612. Then she went to the ecclesiastical court and requested an annullment. In her court case, Giacomo alleged, she pretended that at the time of her marriage she was very young, fourteen, and that she had already been deflowered, on promise of marriage, by a *Signor* Vancastro. Zoppino, she claimed, never had sex with her, and she was forced to marry him because her mother and brother had threatened her. On these false pretenses, Giacomo continued, she had her wedding ties severed and she was free to marry again. This she did in February 1615; the groom was *Don* Gioseffe Guazzo, who, she claimed, mistreated her. She returned once again to the Patriarchal Court, asking for an annulment. She claimed that she had lived a dishonest life, one that she did not choose, one that her mother and her brother had forced her to lead; but principally she asserted that she was married by a priest who did not have the authority. Producing false testimonies about her residence, she claimed she lived in the parish of Santa Sofia but was married by a priest in San Geremia. Giacomo claimed she won her court case because she had not been married by her parish priest. The distraught husband concluded that Laura was "an expert at deceiving ecclesiastical justice, and of betraying and persecuting husbands."

Laura might see herself quite differently: as a woman who had grasped the correlation between financial independence, freedom, and power, and had learned how to manipulate her marriages, priests, and the courts in Venice to her advantage. Associations with men of high rank were an important variable in the success of common women who aspired to a better standard of living and who tried to make the judicial system work in their favor. Injured husbands often had no choice but to defer to the social superiors who philandered with their attractive wives and who held distinct advantages in the courts. At other times, however, they sought vindication from their wives, suing for adultery and theft. The wife and the household estate, minus the dotal goods, were the husband's legal possessions. Adultery made the dotal goods his as well.

Giacomo tells us that Laura made her way in life through fraud and theft, with the help of accomplices all along the way, among them her loyal maid and several parish priests willing to bend the rules of Trent. The husband complained that Laura had spun out a tale of forced union with a violent script to annul her first marriage, followed by a second annulment on technical grounds that the union had not been concluded properly. Laura also made Giacomo face charges in both criminal and ecclesiastical courts, using a common story: attempted homicide through poisoning and abuse.[2] Further, she accompanied the separation proceedings with a secular suit to net her dotal resources. Almost all of the themes found in Venetian marital litigation are present in this one accusatory tale. Giacomo's allegations cannot but raise the question of how many other women, like Laura, were reciting the tropes that would free them from unwanted husbands while protecting their dowries. The husband's story, like the others in this study, once again demonstrates the ambiguities and complexities of sorting through court tales to understand social realities. What emerges with more certainty is that women and men were unwilling to remain in unsatisfying relationships, and that after Trent, with the help of lawyers, they made use of the decrees defining valid marriage to break their vows.

Ordinary people had more flexibility in changing their marital status than did Venetian patricians tied to marriage and estate management systems that protected the lineages of a constitutional elite. Perhaps the individuals with the least freedom to alter their destinies were the daughters of the patriciate, who were firmly situated on the trajectory of marriage or monachization, and were well guarded.[3] Even some of them, however, like the women from below, were attempting to change their marital circumstances. Wives expected to be treated well, to be supported adequately, and even to have satisfying sex lives. Husbands expected loyalty and obedience. They frequently resisted wives' attempts to dissolve their marriages, in order to preserve male honor in the Venetian community as well as to keep dowry resources from escaping their grasp. Women, however, used (and perhaps misused) the courts to protect both themselves and their resources, thus manipulating a family system which normally favored the patriline.

In Venice, husbands whose wives aired their shortcomings in the courts more often than not tried to gloss over their problems, but it was difficult to keep secrets from the community. Gossip kept the intimacies of their marriages in the public domain, and both men and women who planned to go to court knew the value of disseminating knowledge throughout the community in this manner. The gossip flowed smoothly into the courts because there was a circle of learned male authorities ready to receive it. Officials at the patriarchal chancellery were adept at giving advice in canon law and in building legal arguments to settle marriage disputes. Here, learned authors and popular storytellers collaborated to form a repertoire of court stories that resembled each other. The language of complaint that reached the courts came in part from the parish priests who had counseled troubled spouses from the confessionals and had sometimes mediated the disputes on the sidelines. It came as well from the ecclesiastical lawyers who represented the disputing parties. Lawyers undoubtedly supplied the framework for the Venetian tropes, and their clients and supporting witnesses created improvised scripts. The familiar stories that reached the courts must have raised doubts among the Patriarch, his vicar, the state prosecutors, the community arbitrators, neighbors, and kin. In all probability the authorities of this closely knit society had more information to help them arrive at their decisions than has reached us through the written record. State prosecutors and other officials associated with the secular courts also assisted disputing husbands and wives, offering advice and enforcing the laws the Republic had established to stabilize the marital state.

Power was located both within the courts and outside these institutional venues—in the confessionals, in neighborhood chatter, in the secrets of midwives, and in the intimacies of marriage and sexuality that servants observed and reported. The cases also reveal the range of women's powers of decision and their manipulation of their connections with men of higher social rank to achieve their desired results. Their successes or failures in some measure were tied to their access to independent wealth, social status, and influential connections with the upper class.

Giacomo Savioni spun out a persuasive tale, telling us openly that a husband as well as a wife could be hurt by a misbehaving spouse. Sometimes that feeling is masked in the Venetian marriage wars, as we find husbands primarily protecting property and defending their honor rather than seeking justice for emotional injuries. The letter from this distraught husband, on the other hand, reveals his shock at betrayal, not only by his wife but also by the ecclesiastical authorities and influential patricians who, he felt, permitted the deceptions. He turned for redress and consolation to the most Serene Republic, which had established an institutional site for his supplication and those of other husbands in distress.

The emotional expectations of Venetian husbands and wives shed some light on the historical debate over whether affection was present in arranged marriages. Some historians have maintained that it was not, primarily when marriages were based on class and property arrangements.[4] It is difficult, however, to make universal pronouncements. Moreover, studies outside elite circles reach different conclusions. Steven Ozment's research on burgher society in Reformation

Europe, for example, points to intense emotional relationships between husbands and wives.[5] Protestant writers of the sixteenth and seventeenth centuries stressed the importance of companionate marriage and of mutual affection between spouses. The marriage cases in Venice confirm parts of both sides of the argument. Physical attraction and emotional love were not prerequisites for arranged unions, but couples desired them. Moreover, without the development of love and affection, marriages risked falling apart.

Giacomo's supplication to the state also reminds us that breaking marriage ties in late Renaissance Venice was never the sole domain of the Church. Although the Council of Trent undoubtedly changed the types of disputes that reached the Patriarchal Court after 1563, from enforcing promises of marriage to annulling invalid unions, marriage and "Catholic divorce" were too much a part of material life and secular culture for the state not to play an active role on a consistent basis in these spheres as well. Venetian patricians regularly served as Patriarch, arbitrated conjugal property disputes, regulated dowries, and judged accusations of adultery, theft, and breach of promise.

In the century following Giacomo Savioni's supplication, Venice's most powerful governing body, the Council of Ten, officially challenged the autonomy of the Patriarchal Court, claiming the right to screen petitions for separation before they reached what magistrates heatedly described as "all-too-liberal adjudicators" and "hungry lawyers" who manipulated proceedings. Too many tales had resulted in broken unions, claimed eighteenth-century patricians as they attempted to increase the powers of the secular state as well as to defend the social fabric of Venetian life. Whether eighteenth-century Venetian magistrates were successful censors of ecclesiastical decisions or had better success in keeping marriages together is a tale yet to be written. What these marriage wars reveal is that individual desires, even at the patrician level, overrode the broader principles of state that fueled the Venetian myth of peace and stability. As Renaissance twilight faded into starry Baroque nights, made merry with comic farce, carnival play, and opera, Venetians from every walk of life staged their own masked dramas in the courts, using language that artfully expressed resistance to conferred positions and status, and told tales to transform their life circumstances and make new identities.

NOTES

Abbreviations

ASPV Archivio Storico Patriarcale di Venezia

ASV Archivio di Stato di Venezia

BNMV Biblioteca Nazionale Marciana

CM *Causarum Matrimoniorum*

FC *Filciae causarum*

q. *quondam*

u.d. unfoliated document

Venetian Money

Monetary information from David Chambers and Brian Pullen, eds., *Venice: A Documentary History, 1450–1630* (Oxford: Blackwell, 1992). For *ducat* and *lira*, see p. 461; for *soldi*, see p. 463.

Introduction

1. Moderata Fonte, *Il merito delle donne*, intro. Adriana Chemello (Mirano and Venice: Editrice Eidos, 1988), 41.

2. Gaetano Cozzi, "Note e documenti sulla questione del 'divorzio' a Venezia (1782–1788)," *Annali dell'Istituto storico italo-germanico in Trento* 7(1981): 303.

3. Lynn Hunt, ed., *The New Cultural History* (Berkeley: University of California Press, 1989); Sara Maza, "Stories in History: Cultural Narratives in Recent Works in European History," *American Historical Review* 101 (1996): 1499–1503.

4. Mary Gergen, "The Social Construction of Personal Histories: Gendered Lives in Popular Autobiographies," in *Constructing the Social*, ed. Theodore R. Sarbin and John I. Kitsuse (London: Sage, 1994), 19–22.

5. Lucia Ferrante, "Il matrimonio disciplinato: Processi matrimoniali a Bologna nel cinquecento," in *Disciplina dell'anima, disciplina del corpo e disciplina della società tra medioevo ed età moderna*, ed. Paolo Prodi (Bologna: Il Mulino, 1994), 925–927.

6. Stanley Chojnacki finds that fifteenth-century Venetian patricians were sympathetic to the plight of women, more so than the patricians in fifteenth-century Florence studied by Cristiane Klapish-Zuber. Stanley Chojnacki, "The Power of Love: Wives and Husbands in Late Medieval Venice," in *Women and Power in the Middle Ages*, ed. Mary Erler and Maryanne Kowaleski (Athens: University of Georgia Press, 1988), 126–148; "'The Most Serious Duty': Motherhood, Gender, and Patrician Culture in Renaissance Venice," in *Refiguring Woman: Perspectives on Gender and the Italian Renaissance*, ed. Marilyn Migiel and Juliana Schiesari (Ithaca, N.Y.: Cornell University Press, 1991), 133–154, and "La posizione della donna a Venezia nel cinquecento," in *Tiziano e Venezia: Convegno internazionale di studi*, ed. Gaetano Cozzi (Vicenza: Neri Pozza, 1980), 65–70; Christiane Klapisch-Zuber, *Women, Family, and Ritual in Renaissance Italy*, trans. Lydia G. Cochrane (Chicago: University of Chicago Press, 1985). See the preface to this last book, in which David Herlihy expresses some reservations about Klapisch-Zuber's analyses of Florentine women's status in the family.

7. Peter Novick, *That Noble Dream: The "Objectivity Question" and the American Historical Profession* (Cambridge: Cambridge University Press, 1988), 600–601.

8. Natalie Zemon Davis, *Fiction in the Archives: Pardon Tales and Their Tellers in Sixteenth-Century France* (Stanford, Calif.: Stanford University Press, 1987).

9. Hayden White, "The Fictions of Factual Representation," in *Tropics of Discourse: Essays in Cultural Criticism*, ed. Hayden White (Baltimore: Johns Hopkins University Press, 1978), 124; the discussions in Novick, *That Noble Dream*, 600–601; and Davis, *Fiction in the Archives*, 3.

10. Joan Wallach Scott, *Gender and the Politics of History* (New York: Columbia University Press, 1988).

11. Joan Wallach Scott, "The Evidence of Experience," in *The Lesbian and Gay Studies Reader*, ed. Henry Abelove, Michèle Aina Barale, and David M. Halperin (New York and London: Routledge, 1993), 397–415, esp. 406–412.

12. Lawrence Stone, *The Family, Sex, and Marriage in England, 1500–1800*, abridged ed. (New York, Harper & Row, 1977); Sarah Hanley, "Family and State in Early Modern France: The Marriage Pact," in *Connecting Spheres: Women in the Western World, 1500 to the Present*, ed. Marilyn J. Boxer and Jean Quataert (New York and Oxford: Oxford University Press, 1987), 53–63; and "Social Sites of Political Practice in France: Lawsuits, Civil Rights, and the Separation of Powers in Domestic and State Government, 1500–1800," *American Historical Review* 102 (1997): 27–52.

13. Steven Ozment, *When Fathers Ruled: Family Life in Reformation Europe* (Cambridge, Mass.: Harvard University Press, 1983).

14. Jutta Sperling, *Convents and the Body Politic in Late Renaissance Venice* (Chicago: University of Chicago Press, 1999).

15. Gene Brucker, *Giovanni and Lusanna: Love and Marriage in Renaissance Florence* (Berkeley and Los Angeles: University of California Press, 1986).

16. Natalie Zemon Davis, *The Return of Martin Guerre* (Cambridge, Mass.: Harvard University Press, 1986).

17. See Sherrin Marshall, ed., *Women in Reformation and Counter-Reformation Europe: Public and Private Worlds* (Bloomington and Indianapolis: Indiana University Press, 1989), 2–3; Stanley Chojnacki, "Blurring Genders," *Renaissance Quarterly* 40 (1987): 743–751; and "'The Most Serious Duty'"; Natalie Zemon Davis, "Boundaries and the Sense of Self in Sixteenth-Century France," in *Reconstructing Individualism: Autonomy, Individuality, and the Self in Western Thought*, ed. Thomas C. Heller et al. (Stanford, Calif.: Stanford University Press, 1986), 53–63; Barbara Diefendorf, "Family Culture, Renaissance Culture," *Renaissance Quarterly* 40 (1987): 676–677, 679–680.

Chapter 1

1. Brian Pullan, *Rich and Poor in Renaissance Venice: The Social Institutions of a Catholic State, to 1620* (Cambridge, Mass.: Harvard University Press, 1971), 9.

2. Fernand Braudel, *The Mediterranean and the Mediterranean World in the Age of Philip II*, vol. 2 (London: Harper & Row, 1972), 1125.

3. Marin Sanudo, *Laus urbis Venetae* (1493), reprinted in *Venice: A Documentary History, 1450–1630*, ed. David Chambers and Brian Pullan (Oxford: Blackwell, 1992), 4–21.

4. Braudel, *The Mediterranean*, vol. 1, 390–391.

5. Cesare Vecellio, *Costumes anciens et modernes* (Paris: Tipographie de Firmin Didot Freres & Fils, 1860), vol. 1, 100–104, 111, 123.

6. "E di somma et notabile honestà l'uso et l'istituto d'allevar le donzelle nobili in Venetia; perchè sono così ben guardate et custodite nelle case paterne, che bene spesso ne anchi i più stretti parenti le veggono. Queste, nella fanciullezza loro, quando escono fuori di casa, il che accade di rado, portano in testa un velo di seta bianca, ch'esse chiamano fazzuolo, d'assai ampia larghezza, et con esso si coprono il viso e'l petto. Portano in questo tempo pochi ornamenti di perle, et qualche picciola collana d'oro di poca valuta. Le sopravesti di queste sono la maggior parte di color rovano o nere, di lana leggiera, overo ciambellotto o altra materia di poca valuta, benche sotto vadano vestite di colore, et vanno cinte d'uno di quei retini di seta ch'esse chiamano poste. Ma quando poi sono venute alla perfettione di grandezza, vanno vestite tutte di nero." Ibid., 101–102.

7. The precise figures are the following:

1581	134,000
1586	148,640
1593	139,459
1624	190,714
1632–33	98,244
1655	158,722

Karl Julius Beloch, "La popolazione di Venezia nei secoli xvi e xvii," *Nuovo archivio veneto* 2 (1902): 13–21. Beloch's figures, however, have been criticized. Compare Andrea Zannini, "Un censimento inedito del primo seicento e la crisi demografica ed economica di Venezia," *Studi veneziani* 26 (1993): 87–116. Only a few demographic studies of Venetian parishes exist. Among them are Analisa Bruni, "San Salvador: Storia demografica di una parrocchia di Venezia tra XVI e XVII secolo" (Undergraduate thesis, University of Venice, 1983– 1984); Laura Giannetti, "Venezia alla fine del XVI secolo: Le parocchie di Santa Maria Nova e San Canciano" Undergraduate thesis, University of Venice, 1977–1978).

8. Paolo Preto, "La società veneta e le grandi epidemie di peste," in *Storia della cultura veneta: Dalla controriforma alla fine della repubblica*, vol. 4, part 2 (Vicenza: Neri Pozza, 1984), 391–394.

9.
Year	Total Population	Approximate Number of Marriages
1581	134,871	1,539
1586	148,637	1,383
1624	141,125	1,461
1633	102,243	1,926
1642	120,307	1,238

Daniele Beltrami, *Storia della popolazione di Venezia dalla fine del secolo XVI alla caduta della repubblica* (Padua: 1954), 115; 180–183.

10. Bruni, "San Salvador," 22, 187–189, 201.

11. Michela Dal Borgo, "Venezia alla fine del '500. La zona di San Zaccaria" (undergraduate thesis, University of Venice, 1977–1978), unfoliated pages between 144 and 145.

12. Theologians at the Council of Trent also outlined a sermon program for priests. The subject of matrimony and the duties of husbands and wives was to be treated the second Sunday after Epiphany; the nature and quality of matrimony and the laws of the Church were scheduled for the nineteenth Sunday after Epiphany. Priests were instructed to teach people about the rites of marriage and to remind them that a priest needed to be present. Children, out of respect for their parents, should seek their consent before marrying. *Catechism of the Council of Trent for Parish Priests Issued by Order of Pope Pius V,* trans. John A. McHugh, O.P., and Charles J. Callan, O.P. (New York: Joseph F. Wagner, 1923), xli, 338–340, 351–354.

On clerical prescriptions for wives, see Agostino Valerio, *Istruttione delle donne maritate* (Venice: Bolognino Zaltieri, 1575). John Martin tells us Venetian women with abusive husbands sought counsel from their confessors. John Martin, "Out of the Shadow: Heretical and Catholic Women in Renaissance Venice" *Journal of Family History* 10 (1985): 25–26.

13. Antonio Niero, *I patriarchi di Venezia: Da Lorenzo Giustiniani ai nostri giorni* (Venice: Studium Cattolico Veneziano, 1961), 103.

14. Paul Grendler, *The Roman Inquisition and the Venetian Press, 1540–1605* (Princeton, N.J.: Princeton University Press, 1977), xx–xxii.

15. Paolo Prodi, "Chiesa e società," in *Storia di Venezia*, vol. 6, *Dal rinascimento al barocco*, ed. Gaetano Cozzi and Paolo Prodi (Rome: Istituto della Enciclopedia Italiana Fondata da Giovanni Treccani and Istituto Poligrafico e Zecca dello Stato, 1994), 320–323.

16. Husbands also brought adultery charges to the Avogaria di Comun. For a systematic study of adultery cases in Venice during the fourteenth and fifteenth centuries, see Guido Ruggiero, *The Boundaries of Eros: Sex Crime and Sexuality in Renaissance Venice* (New York and Oxford: Oxford University Press, 1985), 45–69; see also his valuable bibliographic essay, ibid., 199–201.

17. Trevor Dean, "Fathers and Daughters: Marriage Laws and Marriage Disputes in Bologna and Italy, 1200–1500," in *Marriage in Italy, 1300–1650*, ed. Trevor Dean and K. J. P. Lowe (Cambridge: Cambridge University Pres, 1998), 91–92. For the early modern Italian cities, see Lucia Ferrante, "Honor Regained: Women in the Casa del Soccorso in San Paolo in Sixteenth-Century Bologna," in *Sex and Gender in Historical Perspective: Selections from Quaderni Storici*, ed. Edward Muir and Guido Ruggiero (Baltimore: Johns Hopkins University Press, 1990), 46–72; Sandra Cavallo and Simona Cerutti, "Female Honor and the Social Control of Reproduction in Piedmont Between 1600 and 1800," in *Sex and Gender*, 73–109; Sherrill Cohen, *The Evolution of Women's Asylums Since 1500: From Refuge for Ex-Prostitutes to Shelters for Battered Women* (New York: Oxford University Press, 1992).

18. In Reformation Strasbourg and Nuremberg, marriage and divorce shifted to the jurisdiction of secular tribunals. Steven Ozment, *When Fathers Ruled: Family Life in Reformation Europe* (Cambridge, Mass.: Harvard University Press, 1983), 30. Civil authorities in early modern Freiburg also became increasingly involved in moral issues associated with marriage, and in Basel, ecclesiastical and secular jurisdictions were consolidated into a single court. Thomas Max Safley, *Let No Man Put Asunder: The Control of Marriage in the German Southwest* (Kirksville, Missouri: Sixteenth-Century Publishers, 1984), 184–185. What we see in Venice is the gradual encroachment of secular authority over the important institution of marriage, which was the backbone of this aristocratic polity. Studies elsewhere in Italy have reached similar conclusions. Compare Lucia Ferrante, "Il matrimonio disciplinato: Processi matrimoniali a Bologna nel cinquecento," in *Disciplina dell'anima, disciplina del corpo*

e disciplina della società tra medioevo ed età moderna, ed. Paolo Prodi (Bologna: Il Mulino, 1994), 901–927; Daniela Lombardi, "Il matrimonio: Norme, giurisdizioni, conflitti nello stato fiorentino del cinquecento," in *Istituzioni e società in Toscana nell' età moderna. Atti delle giornate di studio dedicate a Giuseppe Pansini, Firenze, 4–5 dicembre, 1992* (Rome: Ministero per i Beni Culturali e Ambientali, 1994), 787–805; and "Intervention by Church and State in Marriage Disputes in Sixteenth- and Seventeenth-Century Florence," in *Crime, Society, and the Law in Renaissance Italy*, ed. Trevor Dean and K. J. P. Lowe (Cambridge: Cambridge University Press, 1994), 142–156; Oscar Di Simplicio, *Peccato, penitenza, perdono: Siena 1575–1800: La formazione della coscienza nell'Italia moderna* (Milan: Franco Angeli, 1994); Cavallo and Cerutti, "Female Honor." For an overall synthesis, see Daniela Lombardi, "Fidanzamenti e matrimoni. Norme e consuetudini sociali del concilio di Trento alle riforme settecentesche," in *Storia del matrimonio*, ed. M. De Giorgio and Christiane Klapisch-Zuber (Rome and Bari: Laterza, 1996), 215–250.

19. Renzo Derosas, "Moralità e giustizia a Venezia nel '500–'600. Gli Esecutori contro la bestemmia," in *Stato, società e giustizia nella Repubblica Veneta (secolo XV–XVIII)*, vol. 1, ed. Gaetano Cozzi (Rome: Jouvence, 1980), 450; Gaetano Cozzi, "Note e documenti sulla questione del 'divorcio' a Venezia (1782–1788)," *Annali dell'Istituto storico italo-germanico in Trento* 7 (1981): 277. See also Gaetano Cozzi, *Religione, moralità e giustizia a Venezia: Vicende della magistratura degli Esecutori contro la bestemmia* (Padua: Cooperativa Libraria Editrice degli Studenti dell'Università di Padova, 1967–1968), 16. On fornication in Venice during the fourteenth and fifteenth centuries see Ruggiero, *Boundaries of Eros*, 16–44. Later the competencies of the Bestemmia extended to other perceived deviancies, such as gambling, public scandal, sex crimes, prostitution, and licentious publications. It had enormous powers over popular customs, with procedures similar to those of the Council of Ten, based on anonymity and secret procedures. See Prodi, "Chiesa e società," 323.

20. Ozment, *When Fathers Ruled*, 37.

21. *Statutorum legum, ac iurium DD. Venetorum*, fols. 194r–195v, November 4, 1553.

22. Ibid., fol. 199r, August 6, 1559. The *giudici confidenti* were supposed to help make decisions concerning the division of property, according to a law established in 1539. Cozzi notes, however, that the eighteenth-century canon lawyers discovered that this practice had lapsed because it was more lucrative for them to carry out these battles before the various tribunals. Cozzi, "Note e documenti," 310.

23. For a full treatment of protocol in matrimonial trials, see P. Chas. Augustine, *A Commentary on the New Code of Canon Law*, bk. III, vol. 5 (London and St. Louis: Herder, 1935).

24. The ecclesiastical lawyers and notaries remain to be studied. A useful

model for research is Andrea del Col, *L'Inquisizione nel patriarcato e diocesi di Aquileia, 1557–59* (Valcellina: Edizione Università di Trieste, 1998).

25. Arturo Carlo Jemolo, *Il matrimonio nel diritto canonico dal concilio di Trento al codice del 1917* (repr. Bologna: Il Mulino, 1993), 457–462.

26. Prodi, "Chiesa e società," 324–335; and "The Structure and Organization of the Church in Renaissance Venice: Suggestions for Research," in *Renaissance Venice*, ed. John Rigby Hale (London: Faber and Faber, 1973), 416. On the history of the patriarchate, see Niero, *Patriarchi*, 93–127. On the *vicario generale*, see Giuseppe Cappelletti, *Storia della chiesa di Venezia dalla sua fondazione sino ai nostri giorni*, vol. 1 (Venice: Tipografia Armena di San Lazzaro, 1849).

27. After the papal visit in 1581, Trevisan asserted to Rome that the Venetian clergy did not need synods or annual visits to check on whether the decrees at Trent were being implemented. Silvio Tramontin, "Venezia tra riforma cattolica e riforma protestante," in *Patriarcato di Venezia*, ed. Silvio Tramontin (Padua: Giunta Regionale del Veneto and Gregoriana Libreria Editrice, 1991), 119.

28. Joanne M. Ferraro, *Family and Public Life in Brescia, 1580–1650: The Foundations of Power in the Venetian State* (Cambridge: Cambridge University Press, 1993).

29. Matteo Zane (1600–1605), a senator and the Procurator of St. Mark, had also had a diplomatic career in Italian and European courts. Paul Grendler, "The Leaders of the Venetian State, 1540–1609: A Prosopographical Analysis," *Studi veneziani* 19 (1990): 76, 84. On Zane, see ibid, 80. Cardinal Francesco Vendramin (1605–1619), the son of Marco and Maria Contarini, had been a Venetian ambassador in Madrid, Paris, and Rome in the last two decades of the sixteenth century. The pope made him a cardinal in 1615. The tradition of lay patriarchs broke in 1619 with Giovanni Tiepolo (1619–1631). A Bragadin by birth, he had first had a government career and then became a cleric and scholar. His successor, Cardinal Federico Corner (1631–1644), had a more traditional clerical career. The son of a Doge, Corner was one of the few patriarchs who had a degree from the University of Padua in canon law. He had been the bishop of Padua, another town in the regional state. In 1632 the pro-Church Corner party held sway in Venice, sealing its power with his election to the patriarchate. The patriarchate subsequently remained with a cleric, Gianfrancesco Morosini (1644–1678), who, like all the others, was a scion of the Venetian nobility. Niero, *Patriarchi*, 93–127.

30. Tramontin, "Venezia tra riforma," 124.

31. Antonio Niero, "Dal '600 alla caduta della Repubblica," in *Patriarcato di Venezia*, ed. Silvio Tramontin (Padua: Giunta Regionale del Veneto and Gregoriana Libreria Editrice, 1991), 141–143.

32. ASPV, *Curia II*, Liber *actorum mandatorum*, 1580–1581, 1581–1587, 1587–1590, 1591–1594, 1595–1598, 1599–1600, 1601–1605, 1602–1607, 1608–

1611, 1611–1614, 1614–1617, 1620–1621, 1621–1623, 1623–1624, 1624–1625, ASPV, *Curia II*, Liber *sententiarum 1600–1607.*

33. Ferrante has reached similar conclusions for Bologna. See her "Il matrimonio disciplinato," 908.

34. The requests for annulment and separation for these years may be found in ASPV, *Curia II*, Liber *actorum mandatorum*, according to date. Between January and October 1621, for example, there were twenty-six requests for separation. For 1620–1621, fols. 126r–126v, 134v–135r, 152r–152v; for 1621–1623, fols. 13r, 24v, 46r, 50v–51v, 52r–52v, 54v–55r, 73r–73v, 77r, 80r, 89v–90r, 102v–103r, 112v, 113v, 117r–117v, 129r, 131r–132r, 135r, 140r, 144r–144v, 147r–147v. The verdicts are in ASPV, *Curia II*, Liber *sententiarum 1600–1607*, fols. 5r–374r, June 4, 1601–May 4, 1607; Liber *sententiarum civilium* (1620–1631), fols. 57r–152r, August 8, 1621–June 8, 1626.

35. Cozzi's study of the conflict between Church and state in eighteenth-century Venice for jurisdiction over divorce offers supportive evidence for this point of view. The Venetian patriciate intervened between 1782 and 1788, lamenting that the Church had been granting divorces too liberally. Ecclesiastical lawyers were also blamed for the defects in the system, for supposedly encouraging discontented wives to take their grievances to court. Cozzi, "Note e documenti," 275, 321.

36. Jeffrey R. Watt, "Divorce in Early Modern Neuchâtel, 1547–1806," *Journal of Family History* 14 (1989): 135, 139–140. Access to the courts in Neuchâtel was not restricted to the elite.

37. Safley, "Marital Litigation," 72.

38. Watt, "Divorce in Early Modern Neuchâtel," 142.

39. Ozment, *When Fathers Ruled*, 55–56.

Chapter 2

1. ASPV, *Curia II, CM, busta* 85, Camilla *q.* Mattheo Belloto and Angelo de Bollis *q.* Pauli, July 12 and 30, 1617, fols. 1r–1v; 8v–10v.

2. Ibid., fols. 23v–25v.

3. Ibid., testimony of Paolo *q.* Giovanni Aloyisi Zanfardo, September 27, 1617, fols. 7v–11v; testimony of Cornelia *q.* Natalini Bozeti, wife of Paolo, September 27, 1617, fols. 11v–16r.

4. ASPV, *Curia II, FC, filza* 35, unfoliated *fascicolo* labeled "Bellota, Nullitatis," dated April 8, 1620.

5. It is important to note that people were casual about reporting their age. Some did not know precisely how old they were.

6. Adultery has usually been characterized, at least in Venetian historiography, as a crime identified from a patriarchal perspective, one in which the

husband is considered the primary victim. Guido Ruggiero, *Eros*, 45. Camilla's and her mother's testimony present adultery from another perspective, one linked to a female angle of vision, in which mother and daughter are the primary victims.

7. ASPV, *Curia II, FC, filza* 35, petition of Camilla Belloto presented by her procurator, Pietro Abettino, April 8, 1620, u.d.

8. Ibid., testimony of Veronica Belloto, April 9, 1620, u.d.

9. Ibid., testimony of Marietta, April 9, 1620, u.d.

10. For the Esecutori contro la Bestemmia, see Renzo Derosas, "Moralità e giustizia a Venezia nel '500–'600," in *Stato, società e giustizia nella Repubblica Veneta*, ed. Gaetano Cozzi (Rome: Jouvence, 1980), 431–528; see also Ruggiero, *Boundaries of Eros*, 188, n. 50.

11. ASPV, *Curia II, FC, filza* 35, testimony of Jacobo *q. Clarissimi* Marini Justiniani, April 9, 1620, u.d.

12. Ibid., testimony of Marietta *q.* Mattheo Bellotto, wife of Andrea Taleapetra, April 9, 1620, u.d.; testimony of Veronica *q.* Bernardini Lutieri and widow of Matthei Belloti, April 9, 1620, u.d.

13. ASPV, *Curia II, Liber sententiarum civilium 1620–1631, fascicolo* 2, May 13, 1620, fols. 15v–16r.

14. Jean-Louis Flandrin, *Families in Former Times: Kinship, Household, and Sexuality in Early Modern France*, trans. Richard W. Southern (Cambridge and New York: Cambridge University Press, 1979), 131. On the confusion and conflict this created in Venice, see Ruggiero, *Boundaries of Eros,* 28–29. Compare Ruggiero, *Binding Passions: Tales of Magic, Marriage, and Power at the End of the Renaissance* (Oxford and New York: Oxford University Press, 1993), 59. The Tridentine rules published in Venice are in BNMV, Misc. 2689.7, *Parte sostantiale delli decreti del sacro et general concilio di Trento*, fols. 1r–4r.

15. Late medieval courts in Troyes, Châlon-sur-Marne, and Strasbourg were filled with cases of contested betrothal, as were those of sixteenth-century Zurich and Nuremberg. Steven Ozment, *When Fathers Ruled: Family Life in Reformation Europe* (Cambridge, Mass.: Harvard University Press, 1983), 25–26, 34. In Constance, Thomas Safley tells us, there was much confusion over the exact moment at which a marriage agreement became binding. One third of the procedures of the marriage court revolved around determining whether to enforce an alleged agreement to marry. Most of the plaintiffs were single, and women sought redress from the court twice as often as men. Thomas Max Safley, "Marital Litigation in the Diocese of Constance, 1551–1620," *Sixteenth Century Journal* 12 (1981): 65, 73, 77. We have as yet no systematic study of marriage disputes in Venice prior to the Council of Trent.

16. Flandrin, *Families*, 131–135; Sarah Hanley, "Family and State in Early Modern France: The Marriage Pact," in *Connecting Spheres: Women in the Western World, 1500 to the Present*, ed. Marilyn J. Boxer and Jean Quataert (New York

and Oxford: Oxford University Press, 1987), 53–63, and "Social Sites of Political Practice in France: Lawsuits, Civil Rights, and the Separation of Powers in Domestic and State Government, 1500–1800," *American Historical Review* 102 (1997): 30–32.

17. *Enciclopedia cattolica*, vol. 8 (Florence: G. C. Sansoni, 1952), 407–475. See also Gabriela Zarri, "Il matrimonio tridentino," in *Il concilio di Trento e il moderno*, ed. Paolo Prodi and Wolfgang Reinhard (Bologna: Il Mulino, 1996), 437–484.

18. Gaetano Cozzi, "Padri, figli, e matrimoni clandestini (metà secolo XVI–metà secolo XVIII)," *La cultura* 14 (1976): 171–173, 184–189.

19. Margaret R. Sommerville, *Sex and Subjection: Attitudes to Women in Early Modern Society* (London: Arnold, 1995), 182–183. Sommerville refers to Filippo Pascale, *Tractatus amplissimus de viribus patriae potestatis* (Venice: Bertanorum, 1655).

20. Marco Ferro, "Matrimonio," in *Dizionario del diritto comune e veneto*, 2nd ed. (Venice: Modesto Fenzo, 1845–1847) vol. 7, 152–153.

21. On how the message on marriage from Trent spread in the Venetian community, see Joanne Ferraro, "The Power to Decide: Battered Wives in Early Modern Venice," *Renaissance Quarterly* 48 (1995): 496.

22. For a valuable analysis of the performative aspect of narrative and a superb review of the literature, see Sarah Maza, "Stories in History: Cultural Narratives in Recent Works in European History," *American Historical Review* 101 (1996): 1499–1503.

23. On female and male honor in Venice, see Ruggiero, *Binding Passions*, 59.

24. Camilla stated that her father would have killed her—"che l'havrebbe fatta morir sotto un legno"—and that he gazed at her with threatening eyes when the priest asked her to say yes or no at the marriage ceremony. ASPV, *Curia II, FC, filza* 35, petition of Camilla Belloto presented by her procurator, Pietro Abettino, April 8, 1620, u.d.

25. Sommerville, *Sex and Subjection*, 184, 204, n. 36: grave fear is incompatible with free choice. Sommerville cites the following theorists: Johannes Lancelottus, *Institutionum iuris canonici libri quatuor* (Venice, 1564), fol. 45r; Marco Antonio Cucchi. *Istitutiones iuris canonici* (Pavia, 1565), fol. 97r; Alberico Gentili, *Disputationum de nuptiis libri septem* (Hanau, 1614), 242; Filippo Pascale, *Tractatus amplissimus de viribus patriae potestatis* (Naples, 1618), 318–319.

26. ASPV, *Curia II, FC, filza* 42, testimony of Vittoria Cesana, May 4, 1629, u.d. All subsequent quotes for Vittoria are from this source.

27. *The Canons and Decrees of the Council of Trent*, trans. Rev. H. J. Schroeder, O.P. (Rockford, Ill.: Tan Books, 1978), 184.

28. ASPV, *Curia II, CM, busta* 90, testimonies of Marieta, *figlia di* Aloysio Brazzera and wife of Joannis Marmota, a domestic servant, November 13, 1628, fols. 3r–10r; *Nobile Dominus* Theodorus Minio *q.* Domini Pauli, No-

vember 11, 1628, fols. 10r–24r; Antonio Baldù, *Nobile Veneziano, figlio q. Nobile Veneziano* Nicolai, December 16, 1628, fols. 24r–35r. Copies of the testimonies are found in ASPV, *Curia II, FC, filza* 42, unfoliated *fascicolo* labeled "Cesana," dated October 16, 1628.

29. ASPV, *Curia II, CM, busta* 90, fols. 10r–24r.

30. ASPV, *Curia II, Liber sententiarum civilium 1620–1631, fascicolo* 2, May 11, 1629, fols. 202r–202v.

31. ASPV, *Curia II, CM, busta* 86, Magdalena Filosi *q.* Bartolomeo and Anzolo Faniente *q.* Jacobo, March 1, 1621, u.d.

32. ASPV, *Curia II, CM, busta* 90, Paolina *q.* Giovanni Pirron, tailor, and Lorenzo, son of Lorenzo Comelli, a cloth merchant, May 16, 1629, fols. 10v–12v.

33. ASPV, *Curia II, FC, filza* 43, testimony of Paolina Pirron, August 20 and 22, 1629, u.d. All subsequent quotes for Paolina are from this source.

34. *Curia II, CM, busta* 90, no date, fols. 1v–2r.

35. Ibid., fols. 3r–11v.

36. ASPV, *Curia II, FC, filza* 43, testimony of Pasqueta, daughter of Giovanni de Presbiterus and widow of Giovanni the tailor, no date, u.d.

37. Ibid., testimony of Thomasina, widow of Lorenzo Comelli, May 25, 1629, u.d.

38. Ibid., testimony of Lorenzo Comelli, August 27, 1629, u.d.

39. ASPV, *Liber sententiarum civilium 1620–1631, fascicolo* 2, August 27, 1629, fols. 213v–214v.

40. ASPV, *Curia II, CM, busta* 86, Arcangela Ceraione, *filia Domini* Horatij Ceraione, Florentini, and Bernardino Gisbè, Bergomensis, July 9, 1620.

41. Ibid., March 6, 1621, fols. 5r–6r.

42. "Et essendo quella sera fatta andare a dormire per forza col detto Bernardino, tutta la notte gridò, et contrastò con lui, non volendo lasciarsi conoscere carnalmente, et tanto fu il rumore che quelli di casa furono neccessitati a correrli, et agiutarla, dove restò vergine come hor si ritrova, ne mai è stato possibile indurla ad acconsentire, è perciò è stata sempre separata da lui." Ibid., fols. 7r–7v.

43. ASPV, *Curia II, Liber sententiarum civilium 1620–1631*, March 24, 1621, fols. 43v–44r.

44. ASPV, *Curia II, CM, busta* 90, Isabetta Damiani *q.* Francesco and Josepho Sansoni *q.* Gasparo, February 21, 1629, fol. 31r; ASPV, *Curia II, FC, filza* 36, February 8 and November 17, 1621, u.d.; ibid., *filza* 42, January 9, 1629, u.d. Isabetta engaged Francesco Lazaroni on November 17, 1628. ASV, *Notarile. Testamenti, busta* 502, *atti* of Bartholomeo Bresciani *q.* Francesco, fol. 143r.

45. ASPV, *Curia II, FC, filza* 42, *fascicolo* produced by Francesco Lazaroni, procurator (*procurator fiscalis* for the Patriarchal Court), August 18, 1628, u.d.

46. ASPV, *Curia II, CM, busta* 90, August 25, 1620, fols. 36v–37r.

47. ASV, *Notarile. Testamenti, busta* 72, no. 90, March 28, 1631, u.d., *atti* Paolo T. Balbi.

48. ASPV, *Curia II, CM, busta* 83, Cornelia *q.* Jacobi Calzago and Paula Archaina versus Joanne Francesco Fisaro, August 8, 1597, fols. 11r–13v.

49. ASPV, *Curia II, Liber sententiarum 1600–1607*, January 24, 1597, fols. 309r–309v; a note about the appeal is in ASPV, *Curia II, CM, busta* 83, April 1, 1597, fols. 310r–310v.

50. ASPV, *Curia II, CM, busta* 90, *Dona* Joannetta, *figlia q.* Valentini Hortolani and Domino Francesco, son of Baptista Zanatta, a carpenter, May 4, 1628, u.d.; ASPV, *Curia II, FC, filza* 42, *fascicolo* dated July 21, 1628, testimony of *Dona* Joannetta, *figlia q.* Valentini Hortolani, u.d.

51. ASPV, *Curia II, CM, busta* 90, *Dona* Joannetta, *figlia q.* Valentini Hortolani, and Domino Francesco, son of Baptista Zanatta, a carpenter, May 4, 1628, u.d.

52. Ibid.

53. ASPV, *Curia II, FC, filza* 42, unfoliated *fascicolo* dated July 21, 1628, *Dona* Clementia, widow *q. Dona* Baptista Picioli, August 7, 1628; Lucieta, widow of Michaelis *q.* Joannis, August 9, 1628; Lucretia, *figlia q.* Rugieris de Cabrieli, widow of Domiti Colgira, August 10, 1628. All quotes are from this source.

54. ASPV, *Curia II, Liber sententiarum civilium 1620–1631, fascicolo* 2, September 11, 1628, fols. 191r–191v.

55. Sommerville, *Sex and Subjection*, 183.

56. ASPV, *Curia II, CM, busta* 82, *Clarissima Dona* Helena Cornelia and *Clarissimo Domino* Zuanne Badoer *q.* Sig. Candiano. 1596.

57. ASPV, *Curia II, CM, busta* 82, testimony of *Dona* Alba, *figlia q.* Domini Bartholomei Boseleti of Padua, wife of Domini Aloisij Bonhomo Zergostini, a spicier in Padua, May 8, 1596, u.d. (a family friend); testimony of Julia Boldù, May 13, 1596, u.d. (Helena's aunt); testimony of Petrus Antonio Battalea *q.* Domini Joannis Ludovici, May 14, 1596, u.d. (Helena's uncle); testimony of *Dona* Helisabet, wife of *Clarissimo Domino* Antonij Boldù, May 18, 1596, u.d. (Helena's aunt); testimony of *Dona* Donata Donato, May 25, 1596, u.d. (Helena's aunt); testimony of *Dona* Hiermina, *figlia q.* Domini Gasparus Boldù, May 30, 1596, u.d. (Helena's cousin).

58. ASPV, *Curia II, Liber sententiarum 1600–1607*, January 27, 1597, fols. 321r–322r.

59. ASPV, *Curia II, CM, busta* 88, Magdalena de Francisus *q.* Giovanni Battista Toscani and Aloysio Bonamico, September 20, 1625, fols. 1r–9v.

60. Ibid., testimony of Franceschina, widow of Joannes Baptista de Francescius, May 19, 1626, fols. 4r–6r.

61. ASPV, *Curia II, Liber sententiarum civilium 1620–1631, fascicolo* 2, July 23, 1627, fols. 172r–172v.

62. Sommerville, *Sex and Subjection*, 182.

63. ASPV, *Curia II, CM, busta* 84, Paolina Businelli *q.* Sebastiano and Giro-lamo Cernotta, December 19, 1607, u.d.

64. ASPV, *Curia II, CM, busta* 82, Arsilia Pegorini *q.* Iseppo and *Magistro* Bernardino Struppiolo, April 20, 1593, u.d.; ASPV, *Curia II, FC, filza* 21, testi-monies dated April 30, 1593, u.d.

65. ASPV, *Curia II, FC, filza* 21 (1593–1594), u.d.

66. No record of the decision could be retrieved, but the material in *busta* 82 contains discussion of appealing the unfavorable verdict Arsilia obtained.

67. Jutta Gisela Sperling, *Convents and the Body Politic in Late Renaissance Venice* (Chicago: University of Chicago Press, 1999), 37–38.

68. Ibid., 38–39.

69. *The Simon and Schuster Book of the Opera* (New York: Simon and Schus-ter, 1977), 1597–1598.

70. Joseph Spencer Kennard, *Masks and Marionettes* (Port Washington, N.Y.: Kennikat Press, 1935), 38–39, 69–70; Giacomo Oreglia, *The Commedia dell'Arte*, trans. Lovett F. Edwards (London: Methuen, 1968), 79–80; Katherine Marguerite Lea, *Italian Popular Comedy: A Study in the Commedia dell'Arte, 1560–1620* (New York: Russell and Russell, 1962), 183–184, 195; Richard An-dres, *Scripts and Scenarios: The Performance of Comedy in Renaissance Italy* (Cam-bridge: Cambridge University Press, 1993), 121–122, 161–165.

71. On all three writers, see Patricia Labalme, "Venetian Women on Women: Three Early Modern Feminists," *Archivio veneto* 5th ser., 117 (1981): 81–109; Satya Datta, "La presenza di una coscienza femminista nella Venezia dei primi secoli dell'età moderna," *Studi veneziani* 32 (1996): 105–137; Paul F. Grendler, *Schooling in Renaissance Italy: Literacy and Learning, 1300–1600* (Balti-more and London: Johns Hopkins University Press, 1989), 94–95.

72. The tyrannical father was a polemic aimed not just at forced unions but also at forcing young girls to live their lives in the monastery. On this im-portant subject, see Francesca Medioli, *L'"Inferno monacale" di Arcangela Tarabotti* (Turin: Rosenberg & Sellier, 1990). See also Labalme, "Venetian Women," 100–105.

73. Sperling, *Convents and the Body Politic*, 18–71.

74. Merry E. Wiesner, *Women and Gender in Early Modern Europe* (Cam-bridge: Cambridge University Press, 1993), 57.

75. ASPV, *Curia II, CM, busta* 80, Angela *q.* Petri de Fais and Bartholomeo de Albertis, February 3, 1586, u.d.

76. Ibid., fol. 23r.

77. ASPV, *Curia II, FC, filza* 35, petition of Camilla Belloto presented by her lawyer, Pietro Abettino, April 8, 1620, u.d.; ASPV, *Curia II, FC, filza* 35, tes-timonies of Jacobus *q. Clarissimi* Marini Justiniani, April 11, 1620, u.d., and *Domino* Paulus *q. Domino* Giovanni Aloysij Cafardi, April 13, 1620, u.d.

78. Andres, *Scripts and Scenarios*, 145–153.

79. *Simon and Schuster Book of the Opera*, 1597–1598.

80. Quoted from Kennard, *Masks and Marionettes*, 52.

81. Isabella Andreini, *Lettere della Signora Isabella Andreini, Padovana. Comica gelosa ed Academica intenta* (Venice: Presso Giovanni Battista Combi, 1617), fols. 119–122.

82. Moderato Fonte, *Il merito delle donne*, intro. Adriana Chemello (Mirano and Venice: Editrice Eidos, 1988), 41–43. Virginia to Cornelia: "Volete voi dunque che s'amino i vecchi? Non ammettendo gli adolescenti e meno gli maturi?" Cornelia to Verginia: "Io non dico cotesto perche ben sapete, che un uccello in man d'un putto e una giovene in man d'un vecchio non stette mai bene. I vecchi partecipano dell'astuzia delli maturi, anzi gli eccedono in ciò e nel resto poi son manchevoli di molte buone parti, poiche hanno passato gli anni dell'allegrezza ed insieme e consumata ogni lor venusta e leggiadria, hanno mangiato il fior della lor farina e non e avanzato altro in loro che crusca o semola, che si dice. Oltra di ciò sono gelosissimi e sospettosi per natura, pegri e inabili a i pericoli, alle fatiche e lunghe osservazioni de gli amanti; sono fastidiosi ed avari."

Virginia asks Cornelia whom she defines as old. Cornelia responds:

"In fin quaranta cinque anni ed ancor fino li cinquanta puo amarsi un uomo di buona e leal qualità ma andatelo a trovar voi. Che ne fanciullo, ne giovene, ne vecchio si trova alcun che ami di vero cuore."

83. ASPV, *Curia II, CM, busta* 81, Isabella Floriani and Ambrosio Mazzoni, August 5, 1588.

84. ASPV, *Curia II, Liber sententiarum 1600–1607*, March 26, 1596, fols. 323r–323v.

85. ASPV, *Curia II, CM, busta* 90. Vittoria, *figlia Eccellente Domino* Antonij Cesana and *Nobile* Giovanni Battista Barbaro, July 1, 1628; ASPV, *Curia II, FC, filza* 42, testimony of Vittoria Cesana, May 4, 1629, u.d.

86. ASPV, *Curia II, FC, filza* 42, testimony of *Nobile* Theodorus Minio, November 15, 1628, u.d.

87. Women's hostility over unwanted arrangements was rooted not just in forced unions but also in compelling young girls to live out their lives in monasteries. On this important subject, see Medioli, *L'"Inferno monacale."*

88. See Ruggiero, *Binding Passions*, 60–61, 143–147; Ferraro, "The Power to Decide," 505, 505 notes 38–39.

Chapter 3

1. See James A. Brundage, "The Problem of Impotence," in *Sexual Practices and the Medieval Church*, ed. James Brundage and Vern L. Bullough (Buffalo,

N.Y.: Prometheus Books, 1982), 135–140; James A. Brundage and Vern L. Bullough, eds., *Law, Sex, and Christian Society in Medieval Europe* (Chicago: University of Chicago Press, 1987), 143–145, 163–164, 200–203, 224–225, 290–292, 376–378.

2. On crossing boundaries of marriage and sexual behavior, see Guido Ruggiero, *The Boundaries of Eros* (New York and Oxford: Oxford University Press, 1985), and *Binding Passions* (New York and Oxford: Oxford University Press, 1993).

3. ASPV, *Curia II, CM, busta* 82, November 28, 1590, Camilla, *filia q. Magnifico Domino* Giorgio Benzoni, *civic venetiarum*, and *Domino* Gasparo Centani, son of *Magnifico Domino* Lorenzo.

4. See Margaret R. Sommerville, *Sex and Subjection* (London: Arnold, 1995), 126–132.

5. See Jeffrey R. Watt, "Divorce in Early Modern Neuchâtel, 1547–1806," *Journal of Family History* 14 (1989), 143; Thomas Max Safley, *Let No Man Put Asunder: The Control of Marriage in the German Southwest* (Kirksville, Mich.: Sixteenth-Century Publishers, 1984), 19–20, 36. Protestants, in contrast to Catholics, allowed divorce in the case of impotence that developed after marrying.

6. Citizens, though not patricians, held illustrious status in Venetian society. Some were admitted to the ducal chancellery and exercised important government responsibilities. Citizens had to be the legitimate offspring of members of this class for three generations, and neither they nor their ancestors could be associated with the mechanical arts. Marco Ferro, *Dizionario del diritto comune e veneto* (Venice: Modesto Fenzo, 1780), vol. 1, 396. The term *cittadino* was used in other contexts as well. For example, in the 1607 census, civil professionals such as lawyers, physicians, notaries, and priests who were not from noble families were classified as *cittadini*. See the discussion of this term in Andrea Zannini, "Un censimento inedito del primo seicento e la crisi demografica ed economica di Venezia," *Studi veneziani* 26 (1993): 92–95.

7. Testimony of Camilla, ASPV, *Curia II, CM, busta* 82, December 18, 1590, fols. 13r–23v. All quotes for Camilla are from this source.

8. The evidence here supports Ruggiero's conclusion that women were not necessarily passive in their sexuality. Ruggiero, *Boundaries of Eros*, 164.

9. Sommerville, *Sex and Subjection*, 28.

10. Richard Palmer, "Pharmacy in the Republic of Venice in the Sixteenth Century," in *The Medical Renaissance of the Sixteenth Century*, ed. A. Wear, R. K. French, and I. M. Lonie (Cambridge: Cambridge University Press, 1985), 102–103, 105.

11. Angus Mclaren, *A History of Contraception: From Antiquity to the Present Day* (Oxford, UK and Cambridge, Mass.: B. Blackwell, 1990), 154.

12. Ruggiero, *Binding Passions*, 168–170.

13. Alberto Bolognetti, "Report to the Papal Nuncio in Venice, 1578–81," in *Venice: A Documentary History, 1450–1630,* ed. David Chambers and Brian Pullan (Oxford: Blackwell, 1992), 237.

14. For a full discussion, see Angus Mclaren, *Reproductive Rituals: The Perception of Fertility in England from the Sixteenth Century to the Nineteenth Century* (London and New York: Methuen, 1984), 40–41. See also Emmanuel Le Roy Ladurie, "The Aiguillette: Castration by Magic," in *The Mind, the Method, and the Historian,* ed. Emmanuel LeRoy Ladurie (Chicago: University of Chicago Press, 1981), 84–96.

15. McLaren, *Reproductive Rituals,* 40.

16. Jane Sharp, *The Midwives' Book,* ed. Randolph Trumbach (New York and London: Garland Press, 1985), 18, 101.

17. Rudolph Bell, *How to Do It: Guides to Good Living for Renaissance Italians* (Chicago: University of Chicago Press, 1999), 41–57. Among the advice manuals Bell cites are Charles Estienne, *L'agricoltura et casa di villa Carlo Stefano gentil'huomo francese, nuovamente tradotta dal Cavaliere Hercole Cato* (Venice: Aldo Manuzio, 1581); Leonardo Fioravanti, *La chirugia* (Venice: Gli Eredi di Melchiorre Sess, 1570); *I secreti della signora Isabella Cortese* (Venice: Giacomo Cornetti, 1584); Girolamo Mercurio, *La commare* (Venice, 1596), reprinted in Luisa Altieri Biagi et al., *Medicine per la donna nel '500* (Turin: Einaudi, 1992).

18. ASPV, *Curia II, CM, busta* 82, testimony of *Magnificus Dominus* Gasparo Centani *filius Magnifici Domini* Laurentij, December 19, 1590, fols. 23v–58r, 71r–74r. All quotes from the dialogue between Gasparo and the vicar are from this source.

19. Dante Olivieri, *Dizionario etimologico italiano* (Milan: Casa Editrice Ceschina, 1961), 597.

20. Using the most formal form of "you," the second-person plural, was not just particular to Camilla and Gasparo, but rather a general cultural construct that implied some form of psychological distance and inequality in the marital relationship, with the husband in the position of power.

21. Giovanni Marinello, *Medicine per le donne nel cinquecento: Testi di Giovanni Marinello e di Girolamo Mercurio,* ed. Maria Luisa Altieri Biagi, Clemente Mazzotta, Angela Chiatera, and Paola Altieri (Turin: UTET and Tipografia Torinese, 1992), bk. 2, 48–50. See also McLaren, *Reproductive Rituals,* 43–44.

22. Sharp, *Midwives' Book,* 21.

23. ASPV, *Curia II, CM, busta* 82, *Dona* Bona, *filia q. Domini* Petri di Pestoribus, *veneta, et uxor Domini* Pompei Phillippi, *drapperij,* fols. 50r–51r.

24. Ibid., *Dona* Catherina, *filia q. Domini* Joannis di Frescis, *brixien, et uxor Domini* Sancti de Galenis a Coreis, *aureis,* fols. 51r–52r.

25. Ibid., *Dona* Oliva, *uxor* Franchi, *obstetrici,* August 16, 1591, fols. 107v–109r; *Dona* Lucieta, widow of Jacobi, *obstetrix,* August 16, 1591, fols. 109r–110r;

Dona Maria, *obstetricibus*, August 16, 1591, fols. 110v–111v; *Dona* Lucretia, *uxor* Bastiani di Capite, *agens matrona*, August 16, 1591, fols. 112r–113r.

26. ASPV, *Curia II, Liber sententiarum 1500–1663*, fols. 165r–165v, 168r.

27. Ruggiero, *Boundaries of Eros,* 109–145.

28. ASPV, *Curia II, CM, busta* 78, testimony of *Dona* Lucretia, *filia q.* Baptista *q.* Antonij Balatini, March 5 and 20, 1584, fols. 7r–10r, 35v–38r. All quotes for Lucretia are from this source.

29. ASPV, *Curia II, FC, filza* 16, u.d. (the *filza* is dated July 6, 1584); testimony of Matteo *q.* Franci de Castro, *comitatus* de Mel Bellune, July 24, 1584; testimony of *Dona* Aquilina *q.* Jacobi Moschini, July 24, 1584.

30. Merry Wiesner, *Women and Gender* in *Early Modern Europe* (Cambridge: Cambridge University Press, 1993), 63.

31. ASPV, *Curia II, CM, busta* 78, testimony of Francesco, April 18, 1584, fols. 10v–12r. All subsequent quotes for Francesco are from this source.

32. Wiesner, *Women and Gender,* 46–47.

33. See John T. Noonan, Jr., *Contraception: A History of Its Treatment by Catholic Theologians and Canonists* (Cambridge, Mass., and London: Belnap Press of Harvard University Press, 1986), 337. Galenic anatomy has been described in recent scholarship as the "one-sex model," in which the woman's organs were considered an interior version of the man's genitals. Women's organs were on the inside, according to Galen, because a lack of heat had failed to turn them outside. Thomas Laqueur, *Making Sex: Body and Gender from the Greeks to Freud* (Cambridge, Mass.: Harvard University Press, 1990). See also Ian Maclean, *The Renaissance Notion of Woman: A Study in the Fortunes of Scholasticism and Medical Science in European Intellectual Life* (Cambridge: Cambridge University Press, 1980), 33; and Winfried Schleiner, "Early Modern Controversies About the One-Sex Model," *Renaissance Quarterly* 53 (2000): 180–191.

34. Marinello, *Medicine per le donne,* 51.

35. ASPV, *Curia II, CM, busta* 78, Lucretia Balatini and Francesco Revedin. Francesco's position is stated on fols. 51v–52v.

36. Ibid., *Dominus* Franciscus Battalea *q.* Laurentij, June 2, 1584, fols. 29r–29v.

37. Ibid., *Dominus* Hermolaus de Hermolais *q.* Dominus Hieronymi, June 2, 1584, fols. 29v–30r.

38. ASPV, *Curia II, FC, filza* 16, testimony of Mattheo de Castro, July 24, 1584, u.d.

39. Ibid., testimony of Aquilina figlia di Jacobo Moschini, July 24, 1584, u.d.

40. Ibid., testimony of Marieta Viviani, July 24, 1584, u.d.

41. ASPV, *Curia II, CM, busta* 78, *Magnificus* Joannis *q.* Joannes Francisci and Lucieta *q.* Baptista Paduani, November 24, 1583, fols. 1v–2r.

42. Ibid., *Dona* Marietta Filacaipo, April 27, 1584, fols. 13r–13v; June 12, 1584, fol. 28v.

43. Marinello, *Medicine per le donne,* 51.

44. ASPV, *Curia II, CM, busta* 78, *Dona* Catherina, April 27, 1584, fols. 14r–14v.

45. Ibid., *Dona* Magdalena Scuda, May 29, 1584, fols. 25v–26v.

46. ASPV, *Curia II, FC, filza* 16, February 27, 1586, u.d.

47. Ibid., testimony of Belisario Gadaldono, January 15, 1584, fols. 63v–64r.

48. ASPV, *Curia II, FC, filza* 16, testimony of Lucia Paduana *q.* Baptista, June 14, 1584, u.d.

49. Ibid., testimony of *Dona* Helena, *brixien, q.* Petri Marini and wife of Hieronimo Corfiati, November 14, 1584, u.d. (*fascicolo* labeled "Attestationis Lutieta," dated July 11, 1584).

50. Ibid., *Dona* Laura *q.* Angeli, wife of Petri Cebibi, November 27, 1585, u.d.

51. Nadia Maria Filippini, "The Church, the State and Childbirth: The Midwife in Italy During the Eighteenth Century," in *The Art of Midwifery: Early Modern Midwives in Europe and North America,* ed. Hilary Marland (London and New York: Routledge, 1993), 155–161. For a general discussion of the competencies of midwives in early modern Europe, see Wiesner, *Women and Gender,* 66–69.

52. Filippini, "The Church, the State and Childbirth," 159.

53. Nadia Maria Filippini, "Levatrici e ostetricanti a Venezia tra sette e ottocento," *Quaderni storici* 58 (1985): 152.

54. ASPV, *Curia II, FC, filza* 16, testimony of Giovanni Domenico 9, Antonio, Nov. 29, 1585, u.d.

55. Ibid., testimony of *Dona* Helena *q.* Nicolai, *remarij in arsenatu venetu, Dalmatini, et relicta q.* Jacobi Calafati *in arsenatu venetu,* January 30, 1586, u.d.

56. Ibid.

57. Ibid., testimony of *Domino* Aloysius *q. Don* Ludovici, *draperius,* January 23, 1586, u.d.

58. Ibid., *Dona* Angela *q.* Francesco, *brixien,* widow of Joannis Petri Boara Calderarij, January 30, 1586, u.d.

59. Ibid., *Dona* Julia *q.* Sebastiani, *forojiulien, laboratorius campo,* January 30, 1586, u.d.

60. ASPV, *Curia II, CM, busta 78,* unbound u.d., dated May 16, 1586.

61. ASPV, *Curia II, CM, busta* 86, April 5, 1619, fols. 24v–27r.

62. Ibid.

63. ASPV, *Curia II, FC, filza* 34, *fascicolo* dated August 9, 1619; testimony of Cornelia, wife of Julius de Venetijs, a shoemaker, August 30, 1619, u.d.; testimony of Julius *q.* Rugerij Paduani, September 3, 1619, u.d.; testimony of Alessandro Marinonus *q.* Joannis, August 31, 1619, u.d. All quotes are from this source.

64. ASPV, *Curia II, FC, filza* 34, *fascicolo* dated August 9, 1619. The *articolos additionales* are dated January 29, 1620.

65. Ibid., *articolo* 4.

66. ASPV, *Curia II, FC, filza* 34, testimony of *Dona* Lucieta *q.* Joannis Francesci and wife of Anastasij Bigarelli, February 20, 1620, fols. 1r–3r.

67. Ibid., testimony of *Dona* Faustina, February 20, 1620, fols. 4r–4v.

68. Ibid., testimony of Felicità, *filia* Anastasij *q.* Nicolaide, June 5, 1620, in unfoliated *fascicolo* dated April 17, 1620. All quotes for Felicità are from this source, unless noted otherwise.

69. Ibid., July 17, 1620.

70. ASPV, *Curia II, Liber sententiarum civilium 1620–1631, fascicolo* 2, July 8, 1620, fols. 21r–21v.

71. Bell, *How to Do It*, 192–197, 239–240, 257. See also Stephen Haliczer, *Sexuality in the Confessional: Sacrament Profaned* (New York: Oxford University Press, 1996); Jean-Louis Flandrin, *Sex in the Western World: The Development of Attitudes and Behavior*, trans. Sue Collins (Chur, Switzerland, and Philadelphia: Harwood Academic Publishers, 1991); Thomas Tentler, *Sin and Confession on the Eve of the Reformation* (Princeton, N.J.: Princeton University Press, 1977).

Chapter 4

1. On restricted marriage, see James C. Davis, *The Decline of the Venetian Nobility as a Ruling class* (Baltimore: Johns Hopkins University Press, 1962); compare Ferraro, *Family and Public Life in Brescia, 1580–1650: The Foundations of Power in the Venetian State* (Cambridge: Cambridge University Press, 1993), 106–109; Marzio Barbagli, *Sotto lo stesso tetto: Mutamenti della famiglia in Italia dal XV al XX secolo* (Bologna: Il Mulino, 1984), 199.

2. See also Alexander Cowan, "Patricians and Partners in Early Modern Venice," in *Medieval and Renaissance Venice*, ed. Ellen E. Kittell and Thomas F. Madden (Urbana and Chicago: University of Illinois Press, 1999), 276–293.

3. ASPV, *Curia II, CM, busta* 82, Laura Belfante and Andrea Goleno, May 26, 1595.

4. ASPV, *Curia II, Liber sententiarum civilium 1600–1607*, February 26, 1597, fols. 335r–335v.

5. ASPV, *Curia II, CM, busta* 84, Isabella Cigala and Adriano Fostinello, December 17, 1617. All quotes for Isabella are from this source.

6. ASPV, *Curia II, Liber sententiarum 1620–1631, fascicolo* 2, February 7, 1620, fols. 3r–3v.

7. ASPV, *Curia II, CM, busta* 60, Vicenza Dandolo *q.* Marci (*q.* Antonio is supplied, too) and Iseppo, *figlio* Antonij Samitarij, a weaver, June 29 and July 27, 1560.

8. ASPV, *Giudici di Petizion, Inventari, busta* 337/2, nos. 30–47, January 16, 1580–July 19, 1581.

9. Jutta Sperling, *Convents and the Body Politic in Late Renaissance Venice* (Chicago: University of Chicago Press, 1999), passim. See also Sherrill Cohen, *The Evolution of Women's Asylums Since 1500: From Refuge for Ex-Prostitutes to Shelters for Battered Women* (New York: Oxford University Press, 1992); Lucia Ferrante, "Honor Regained," in *Sex and Gender in Historical Perspective*, ed. Edward Muir and Guido Ruggiero (Baltimore: Johns Hopkins University Press, 1990), 46–72; David I. Kertzer, *Sacrificed for Honor: Italian Infant Abandonment and the Politics of Reproductive Control* (Boston: Beacon, 1993).

10. ASPV, *Curia II, CM, busta* 74, Zuane Bonifacio Facini and Zuana q. Zuane Bagolin, cobbler. (A copy of the proceedings of the Avogaria di Comun and the Signori di Notte al Criminal are included in this ecclesiastical investigation); ASPV, *Curia II, Liber actorum mandatorum*, reg. 74, April 24, 1582, fol. 38r; all quotes for this case are from ASPV, *Curia II, FC, filza* 15, *fascicolo* "Facini and Bagolin," 1582–1583.

11. Margaret F. Rosenthal, *The Honest Courtesan* (Chicago: University of Chicago Press, 1992), 66.

12. Ibid., 67.

Chapter 5

An earlier version of this chapter was published in *Renaissance Quarterly* 48 (1995): 492–512.

1. ASPV, *Curia II, CM, busta* 78, Pasquetta Peregrinus and Romano Cavatia, April 26–October 12, 1584, fols. 1r–46v; *FC, filza* 16, Peregrinus and Cavatia, u.d.; *Liber actoum mandatorum*, reg. 74 (1581–1587), April 26, 1584, fol. 134r; May 5, 1584, fol. 136v; May 14, 1584, fol. 139.

2. *Malmaritate*, asylums for unhappy wives, had sprung up in many northern Italian cities, including Venice. They were a Catholic alternative to divorce. See Sherrill Cohen, "Asylums for Women in Counter-Reformation Italy," in *Women in Reformation and Counter-Reformation Europe: Public and Private Worlds*, ed. Sherrin Marshall (Bloomington and Indianapolis: Indiana University Press, 1989), 166, 169, 182–183; Brian Pullan, *Rich and Poor in Renaissance Venice: The Social Institutions of a Catholic State, to 1620* (Cambridge, Mass.: Harvard University Press, 1971), 388–394; and Lucia Ferrante, "Honor Regained: Women in the Casa del Soccorso in San Paolo in Sixteenth-Century Bologna," in *Sex and Gender in Historical Perspective: Selections from Quaderni Storici*, ed. Edward Muir and Guido Ruggiero (Baltimore: Johns Hopkins University Press, 1990), 46–72.

3. ASPV, *Curia II, CM, busta* 78, June 12, 1584, fols. 20r–23v.

4. It would be fruitful to study the attractiveness of this option for

some women. Convents in sixteenth-century Italy were refuges for unhappy wives. Those which accommodated women in Venice still require systematic study.

5. Gaetano Cozzi, "Note e documenti sulla questione del'divorzio'a Venezia (1782–1788)," *Annali dell'Istituto storico italo-germanico in Trento* 7(1981): 303.

6. Property is an important issue in these cases of separation. Women did not have the liberty to dispose of clothing purchased with the husband's resources. This remained the husband's property.

7. ASPV, *Curia II, FC, filza* 16, "Pasqueta. Attestationes," testimony of Isabella, daughter of *q.* Niccolò di Pirano, October 25, 1584, fols. 1r, 8v.

8. Ibid., fol. 9r.

9. ASPV, *Curia II, FC, filza* 16, Giovanni *q.* Luca Meneghetti, February 5, 1585, fols. 26r–26v.

10. ASPV, *Curia II, FC, filza* 16, Jacobo *q.* Martini de Vassalino, *brixien, baiulus,* January 30, 1585, fols. 11v–16r.

11. Ibid., testimony of Benvenuto Doni, son of Lorenzo, January 31, 1585, fols. 16–24v.

12. Ibid., testimony of Lucretia *q.* Antonio Lorenzo Patavini, wife of Jacobo Terrazzina; testimony of Claudia *q.* Domenico Pelizzario, wife of Francesco, February 12, 1585, fols. 34r–40v.

13. Klapisch-Zuber has characterized the husband's giving of gifts at marriage in fifteenth-century Florence as primarily ritual and notes their temporary nature. Christiane Klapisch-Zuber, "The Griselda Complex: Dowry and Marriage Gifts in the Quattrocento," in *Women, Family, and Ritual in Renaissance Italy*, ed. Christiane Klapisch-Zuber, trans. Lydia G. Cochrane (Chicago: University of Chicago Press, 1985), 224–231. In contrast, the nuptial gifts of the husband to the wife take on a very different complexion in sixteenth-century Venice if we view them from a gendered perspective. Gifts might be viewed as temporary by husbands, as evidenced by the fact that they gambled them away. Wives, however, took a very different stance: when their husbands tried to take gifts back, they protested and fought through the courts to protect their trousseaus.

14. Ibid., 224–225.

15. ASPV, *Curia II, FC, filza* 16, testimony of Isabella, October 25, 1584, fol. 7r.

16. ASPV, *Curia II, FC, filza* 16, testimony of *Dominus* Benvenuto Doni, son of Lorenzo, fol. 20r. On the competencies of the Uffizio del Petizione, see Marco Ferro, *Dizionario del diritto comune e veneto* (Venezia: Modesto Fenzo, 1780), vol. 4, 202–204.

17. ASPV, *Curia II, CM, busta* 78, testimony of D. Romanus Cavatri, son of Franco, fols. 23v–27r.

18. On the functions of the procurator see Ferro, *Dizionario*, Vol. 5, 46.

19. Dennis Romano has identified the urban spaces in fifteenth-century

Venice commonly associated with women: houses, parish neighborhoods, and convents. The neighborhood community was the central place where a woman's honor and reputation were defended. Dennis Romano, "Gender and the Urban Geography of Renaissance Venice," *Journal of Social History* 23 (1989), 342–344.

20. Ruggiero argues that gossip, particularly that of women, was a form of power that could shape honor and reputation. Guido Ruggiero, "'Più che la vita caro': Onore, matrimonio, e reputazione femminile nel tardo Rinascimento," *Quaderni storici* 66 (1987), 756. On the social functions of gossip, see Mary Beth Norton, "Gender and Defamation in Seventeenth-Century Maryland," *William and Mary Quarterly* 44 (1987): 3–39, esp. 4–7. (I thank Eve Kornfeld for this reference.) Norton argues that for seventeenth-century Marylanders, gossip was the community's method of defining standards of behavior, of identifying misbehavior, of targeting misbehavers, and of establishing social order. Women could not draft laws, but they could use gossip to advance and protect their interests and to define rules of behavior.

21. Cavallo and Cerutti demonstrate that wives made their husbands' misbehavior part of the public domain by confiding in female neighbors. They argue that female solidarity should be read as "attempts to rebalance the power relationships between the sexes." Sandra Cavallo and Simona Cerutti, "Female Honor and the Social Control of Reproduction in Piedmont Between 1600 and 1800," in *Sex and Gender in Historical Perspective: Selections from Quaderni Storici*, ed. Edward Muir and Guido Ruggiero (Baltimore: Johns Hopkins University Press, 1990), 88–89, 90–94. In the Venetian marriage cases it is evident that wives were confiding in both men and women of their communities.

22. ASPV, *Curia II, CM, busta* 75, Cecilia Bartholomeo Bressan Garzoti and Horatio *q.* Baptista Cerdonis, January 8, 1580.

23. Ibid., testimony of Cornelia *q.* Petri Baffo Venosa, widow of Domenico Cimatoro, March 17, 1580, u.d.

24. Ibid., testimony of Battista *q.* Geronimo da Venezia, *spicularius*, April 13, 1580, u.d.

25. Ibid., testimony of Marco Cerdo Gardolino, *figlio q.* Jacobi, October 24, 1580, u.d.

26. ASPV, *Curia II, CM, busta* 84, Paola da Venezia *q.* Andrea and Jacobo Furlano, unnumbered *fascicoli*, May 1610–April 1611.

27. Joanne M. Ferraro, "Building Context for Marital Litigation: The Dispute of Orsetta Targhetta and Annibale Bassi (1634)," in *I coniugi nemici: Separazione in Italia dal XV al XVII secolo*, ed. Silvana Seidel Menchi and Diego Quaglioni (Bologna: Il Mulino, 2000), 141–190.

28. ASPV, *Curia II, CM, busta* 84, testimony of Giovanni *q.* Pietro de Federico, unnumbered *fascicolo*, July 19, 1610, fols. 14r–19r.

29. Ibid., testimony of Andriana, *figlia di* Andrea *q.* Giovanni Antonio da Venezia, July 29, 1610, fols. 19r–22v.

30. Ibid., testimony of Maddalena *q.* Jacobi Apolonio da Venezia, July 19, 1610, fols. 10v–14r.

31. Ibid., testimony of Jacoba *q.* Bartholomeo Disdini, July 19, 1610, fols. 7v-10r.

32. Ibid., testimony of Geronimo *q.* Niccolò de Arboribus, July 19, 1610, fols. 3v–7v.

33. On Venetian women's networks in the fourteenth and fifteenth centuries, see Dennis Romano, *Patricians and Popolani: The Social Foundations of the Venetian Renaissance State* (Baltimore and London: Johns Hopkins University Press, 1987), 133–138; and on their relations with servants, ibid., 134–138.

34. ASPV, *Curia II, CM, busta* 87, Isabetta Bembo *q. Clarissimo Dominici* and *Clarissimo* Francesco Priuli *q. Domini*, May 19, 1623; *FC, filza* 38, "Bemba separationis," June 16, 1623.

35. ASPV, *Curia II, CM, busta* 92, Faustina Gradenici *q. Clarissimo* Marco and Carlo de Cappis, *fascicolo* 1, January 5, 1637, fol. 1v; January 14, 1637, fol. 3r.

36. Ibid., evidence presented by Niccolò Noale, *procuratore*, on January 26, 1637, *more veneto*; testimony of Francesca, wife of Domenico Garemberti, March 5, 1637, u.d.

37. Ibid., testimony of Lucretia, widow of Bernardo Cadiani, March 5, 1637, u.d.

38. Ibid., testimony of Sebastiana, widow of Dimitri Batron di Vassello, June 8, 1637, u.d.

39. Ibid., testimony of Camillus *q.* Geronimo da Venezia, March 6, 1637, u.d.

40. Ibid., testimony of Valeria, wife of Aloisio *q.* Bilasio Navetta, June 6, 1637, u.d.

41. Ibid., testimony of Isabetta, wife of Gasparo Martini, June 17, 1637, u.d.

42. ASPV, *Curia II, CM, busta* 92, unbound document, *fascicolo* 1, August 14, 1637, u.d.

43. ASPV, *Curia II, CM, busta* 75, Clara Gritti and Paolo Priulo *q.* Hieronimo, August 21, 1581, fols. 26v–34v; *FC, filza* 14, unnumbered *fascicolo*, "*parte* P. Priulo e Gritta *positiones*," August 21, 1581, u.d.

44. ASPV, *Curia II, CM, busta* 75, Gritti and Priulo, unbound document, December 18, 1581, u.d.

45. ASPV, *Curia II, CM, busta* 92, Cornelia Zane *q.* Camillo and Giovanni Battista Salamone *q.* Alvise, January 29, 1641. Their marriage on July 19, 1625, is noted in ASV, *Avogaria di Comun, Matrimoni-Libri d'oro*, Reg. IV, p. 250.

46. ASPV, *Curia II, CM, busta* 83, Giovanni Paolo *q.* Camillo a Papa and Franceschina, *f.* Gratiosi Asolani. Sentence is dated May 7, 1604, fols. 89r–89v;

appeal, June 14, 1604, fols. 96v–99r. Final decision is registered in ASPV, *Curia II, Liber sententiarum 1600–1607*, June 4, 1604, fols. 164r–165r.

47. ASPV, *Curia II, CM, busta* 90, Clara Vidali and Niccolò Montin, 1633, u.d.

48. ASV, *Avogaria di Comun, Miscellanea penale, busta* 366, Antonia di Bernardo and Gregorio *q.* Zuane da Vegia, *fascicolo* 5, fols. 1r–55r.

49. Ibid., fol. 14r.

50. Ibid., fol. 2v.

51. Ibid., Ludovica, fols. 4v–5r; Zuana, fols. 4r–4v, 18r–18v; Giovanni Maria, fols. 2r–2v, 15v–16r; Paolo, fols. 2v–3r, 14r.

52. Ibid., fols. 8r, 25r–26r.

53. Cozzi, "Note e documenti," 303.

Chapter 6

1. ASPV, *Curia II, CM, busta* 90, Clara Vidali and Niccolò Montin, 1633, u.d.

2. ASV, *Notarile. Testamenti, busta* 177, no. 244, u.d.

3. ASPV, *Curia II, CM, busta* 90, Melchior *q.* Joannis Tomasseti of Mestre, April 14, 1633.

4. On the legal status of the dowry in Italy, see Francesco Ercole, "L'istituto dotale nella pratica e nella legislazione statutaria dell'Italia superiore," *Rivista/Italiana per le scienze giuridiche* 45 (1909):191–302; 46 (1910): 167–257, both of which are bound in the volume dated 1908. On husbands' rights and limitations, see 46 (1910):167–182, 222–223, 246. See also Stanley Chojnacki, "Dowries and Kinsmen in Early Renaissance Venice," *Journal of Interdisciplinary History* 5 (1975): 41–70, esp. 47, and "Patrician Women in Early Renaissance Venice," *Studies in the Renaissance* 21 (1974): 176–203. James C. Davis, *A Venetian Family 1500–1900* (Philadelphia: American Philosophical Society, 1975), 107; Joanne Ferraro, *Family and Public Life in Brescia, The Foundations of Power in the Venetian State* (Cambridge: Cambridge University Press, 1993), 112–113, 122 (and on women's property, 111–130); Julius Kirshner, "Pursuing Honor While Avoiding Sin: The Monte delle Doti of Florence," *Quaderni di "Studi Senesi"* 41 (1978): 1–82; Julius Kirshner and Anthony Molho, "The Dowry Fund and the Marriage Market in Early Quattrocento Florence," *Journal of Modern History* 50 (1978), 403–416.

5. *Statuta veneta cum correctionibus et additionibus novissimis* (Venice: Ex Typographia Ducali Pinelliana, 1691), fols. 28r, 94r.

6. See Julius Kirshner, "Wives' Claims Against Insolvent Husbands in Late Medieval Italy," in *Women of the Medieval World: Essays in Honor of John H. Mundy*, ed. Julius Kirshner and S. F. Wemple (Oxford: Basil Blackwell, 1985), 256–303, esp. 298, 302; for an overview of early modern Europe in general, see

Merry Wiesner, *Women and Gender in Early Modern Europe* (Cambridge: Cambridge University Press, 1993), 59–60.

7. ASV, *Giudici del Procurator. Scritte, domande e risposte, busta* 6, January 18 and 26, 1633, fols. 453r, 464r, 472r.

8. Ibid., November 12 and January 24, 1633, fols. 403r, 443r.

9. The evidence is substantial, as I will demonstrate in a future article featuring colluding spouses.

10. In 1553 the Venetian state established legal recourse for women whose husbands were dissipating dotal goods. A wife could protect her dowry by means of the *interdetto*, a petition requesting the intervention of the three magistrates (Venetian patricians) of the Giudici del Procurator. *Statuta veneta*, August 6, 1559, fol. 195v. Argelati explained the procedure:

> Wives whose husbands are on the verge of poverty insure their dowries in the following way: they warn all the husband's creditors by engaging a town crier. The day this is executed, they file a *Terminazione* to insure the dowry, where they must warn [creditors] and explain what they intend to do. They must claim the same goods that were part of their dowry. Should anyone wish to impede the insurance of the dowry, he must intervene at that point.

Francesco Argelati, *Practica del foro veneto* (Venice: Agostino Savioli a San Salvadore, 1737), 29: "Si fanno l'assicurazione di dote da quelle Mogli, li di cui Mariti tendano a povertà: nella seguente forma: si citano per stridor dei vivi tutti li creditori del Marito, ed il giorno, che cade la citazione, si fa un'atto a Lire . . . , vale a dire una Terminazione d' assicurazione di dote, dovendosi avvertire, che nelle citazioni e di necessità spiegare quello si vuol fare, e di più che pratticandisi a suo tempo il pagamento di dote, devono apprendersi gli stessi beni, che si sono appresi in assicurazione, e chi volesse impugnar tali assicurazioni deve qui interdirle con l'ordine solito degli'Interdetti." Appeals went from the Procurator to the Auditor Vecchio.

The Procuratori would seek to recoup the wife's losses by pursuing her husband's creditors. This same tribunal had the authority to discipline husbands who failed to provide adequate support for their wives. *Statuta veneta*, November 4, 1553, fol. 195v. See also Angelo Rigo, "Giudici del Procurator e donne 'malmaritate' a Venezia in epoca tridentina," *Atti dell'Istituto veneto di scienze, lettere ed arti, Classe di scienze morali, lettere, ed arti* 151 (1993): 241–266, esp. 247.

11. In 1639 Barbera Mazzeti brought the silk weaver Marco Michel a dowry valued at 556.5 ducats, 330 of which were in movable goods. In return the groom promised to safeguard the dotal goods and to return them in the event the marriage dissolved. Marco also gave Barbera a counterdowry of 143.5 ducats, essentially a supplement, making her total resources in monies

and goods 700 ducats. He promised to return the counterdowry as well in the event the couple separated. ASV, *Giudice del Procurator. Interdetti e Terminazioni di Assicurazione di dote*, Reg. 93, May 26, 1640, fols. 46v–47r. Likewise, in 1631 a couple of noble rank in the Trivigiano agreed to similar terms over a sizable dowry and counterdowry. Betta Trevisan brought Anzolo dall'Oglio 4,000 ducats in cash and goods, and Anzolo offered a counterdowry of 2,000 ducats. Betta's family would not approve the marriage contract unless Anzolo promised to return the entire sum (not minus the "third" of the dowry, which was customary in Venetian law) in the event the couple separated. ASV, *Giudice del Procurator. Interdetti e terminazioni di assicurazioni di dote*, reg. 86, marriage contract dated November 15, 1631, fols. 53r–53v.

12. ASV, *Giudice al Procurator. Scritte domande, e risposte, busta* 2, *fascicolo* 27, dated September 6, 1614, u.d.; *fascicolo* 37, dated October 9, 1614, u.d.

13. ASPV, *Curia II, CM, busta* 83, Lucia and Francesco *q.* Silvestri Grandajo, June 17, 1596, u.d.

14. ASV, *Compilazione Legge, busta* 277, *fascicolo* 1, "Matrimoni. Nullità Matrimoni," fols. 304r, 310r–310v, 311v, 314r.

15. ASPV, *Curia II, CM, busta* 88, Catterina de Comitibus and Francesco Zacharia Conti alias Moisè Copie, May 13, 1624, fols. 65r–74v. Catterina's letter is labeled *foglio* 53, August 3, 1624, fols. 45v–48r.

16. Ibid., marriage contract dated May 20, 1623, fols. 75r–80r.

17. Venetian legislators in the Major Council sought the aid of the community at large by further establishing in 1559 that spouses granted separations would chose *confidenti* (also called *giudici arbitri*), mutual friends who would arbitrate a fair property settlement. This might include determining to whom property had belonged prior to the marriage, negotiating the terms of a dowry that had not been officially registered or recorded, and settling on a monthly sum that would cover the needs of the wife. This was particularly critical for the financial protection of wives who would thenceforward be living apart from their husbands. *Statuta veneta*, August 6, 1559, fol. 199r: "Una de le cose, che con displicenza è udita, non solamente dal Serenissimo Prencipe, et Signoria Nostra, quando vanno a visitazione delli Officij de Palazzo, ma insieme da tutta la Città per l'intender che fra il marito, et moglier vertisca differentie tale, che dalli Giudici di esso Palazzo si ricerchi il modo, che le parti possino viver divise dal matrimonio, facendosi publicamente tali et così importanti opposizioni, con perpetua nota, et vergogna, infamia delle famiglie, che li parenti et amici di quelli disperano poter componer in alcun tempo, et ridur insieme quelli, che col solenne Sacramento del matrimonio si sono per tutto il tempo della vita loro congiunti, et ligati, cosa che non seguirà quando tale differentie fussero delli proprij lor parenti senza strepito terminate, per la qual cosa dovendosi proveder ad uno così inonesto et dannoso disordine.

"L'andera parte, che così come è stato provisto di dar giudici compromissarij fra padre, madre, figlioli, figliole, fratelli, barbani, con figlioli de fratelli, &

c. & specialmente per la parte presa in questo Conseglio sotto di 26 Marzo 1555. Così nell'avvenire in tutte le differentie che vertiranno fra marito, & moglie siano dati Giudici confidenti, i quali possano giudicar, si circa alimenti, come ogn'altra cosa, si come horo possono li giudici de procurator nella materia soprascritta iusta in omnibus, & per omnia la forma della parte soprascritta."

See also Pompeo Molmenti, *La storia di Venezia*, vol. 2 (Trieste: Lint, 1981), 322–323.

The deliberations of the Major Council read as follows:

One of the unpleasant things the Serene Prince and Signoria hear when subjects visit the Palace Courts, but also the entire city [hears], is that husbands and wives have such great differences that the judges of the Palace search for a way that the two parties can live separately in marriage, making this [separation] and opposition public, to the eternal bother and infamous shame of the families, so that friends and kin despair of being able to reconcile those who took the solemn sacrament of matrimony and joined together for all their lives. This would not happen if those differences were solved by their own kin without an uproar. ASV, *Maggior Consiglio*, Reg. Rocca, n. 35, August 21, 1559, fol. 89r, republished in Molmenti, *Storia della Repubblica*, vol. 2, 323.

18. ASPV, *Curia II, CM, busta* 88, fols. 75r–79v.

19. Ibid., fols. 80r–81r.

20. Ibid., January 31, 1625, fols. 81r–86r.

21. Ibid., fols. 49r–51r.

22. This was not the only time Moisè found himself answering to authorities. Jutta Sperling found that "in 1625 Moisè Coppio, 'jew, but now Christian of appearance,' was denounced for having 'noisy,' 'licentious,' and 'scandalous' conversations with several nuns of Santa Maria Maddalena, to whom he sent letters and gifts." Jutta Sperling, *Convents and the Body Politic* (Chicago: University of Chicago Press, 1999), 158.

23. ASPV, *Curia II, CM, busta* 85, February 8, 1612, *Dona* Foscarina filia *q. Clarissimo Domino* Giovanni Francesco Memo, *et uxoris Domino* Giovanni Battista Misserini. From Barbaro we learn that Giovanni Francesco was born in 1559 and married *Dona* Marina Querini *q.* Francesco *q.* Sebastiano *q.* Zaccaria Barbaro *q.* Piero Alessandro. M. Barbaro, *Arbori dei patritii veneti*, in ASV, Miscellanea codici, s. I, *Storia veneta*, vol. 21, 48.

24. ASPV, *Curia II, CM, busta* 85, renter's contract, unbound folio dated August 10, 1600.

25. See Ruggiero's discussion of courtesans in *Binding Passions*, 38–48.

26. ASCPV, *Curia II, CM, busta* 85, *Memo/Misserini*, testimony of Pietro *q.* D. Antonij Bertani.

27. ASV, *Capi Consiglio dei Dieci, Consulti e memorie sui divorzi, busta* 1, un-

numbered *fascicolo* entitled "Memoria Privata" contains a list of laws on clandestine marriage; *Consiglio dei Dieci, Decreti*, March 9, September 28, and November 13, 1571; August 27, 1577; January 15, 1578; ASV, *Compilazione legge, busta 277, fascicolo* 1, "Matrimoni. Nullità di Matrimoni," u.d. See also G. Cozzi, *Religione, moralità e giustizia a Venezia: Vicende della magistratura degli Esecutori contro la bestemmia* (Padua: Cooperativa Libraria Editrice degli Studenti dell'Università di Padova, 1967–1968), 16–18, and *Il dibattito sui matrimoni clandestini. Vicende giuridiche, sociali, religiose dell'istituzione matrimoniale tra medioevo ed età moderna* (Venice: University of Venice History Department, 1985–1986); Paolo Prodi, "Chiesa e società," in *Storia di Venezia*, vol. 6, *Dal rinascimento al barocco*, ed. Gaetano Cozzi and Paolo Prodi (Rome: Istituto della Enciclopedia Italiana Fondata da Giovanni Treccani, 1994), 320.

28. See Gabriele Martini, "La donna veneziana del '600 tra sessualità legittima ed illegittima: Alcune riflessioni sul concubinato," *Atti dell'Istituto Veneto di Scienze, Lettere ed Arti* 145 (1986–1987): 301–339.

29. ASV, *Compilazione Legge, busta 277, fascicolo* 1, "Matrimoni. Nullità Matrimoni," fol. 313r. One concern, for example, was the long-term relationships between nobles and women of lower social stations. On this problem see Andrea Zannini, "Burocrazia e burocrati a Venezia in età moderna: I cittadini originari (sec. XVI–XVIII)," *Istituto veneto di scienze, lettere ed arti. Memorie Classe di scienze morali, lettere, ed arti* 47 (1993): 339–363.

30. ASV, *Notarile. Testamenti, notaio* Gaspar Favio, *busta* 423, testament of Foscarina Memo q. *Clarissimo* Giovanni Francesco, January 24, 1611.

31. See Prodi, "Chiesa e società," 308. For early modern Italy, see Sherrill Cohen, "Asylums for Women in Counter-Reformation Italy," in *Women in Reformation and Counter-Reformation Europe: Public and Private Worlds*, ed. Sherrin Marshall (Bloomington and Indianapolis: Indiana University Press, 1989), 166–188. For an overview of the status of unmarried women in early modern Europe, see Wiesner, *Women and Gender*, 62.

32. Brian Pullan, *Rich and Poor in Renaissance Venice: The Social Institutions of a Catholic State, to 1620* (Cambridge, Mass.: Harvard University Press, 1971), 377–378.

33. Ibid., 388–391.

34. Ibid., 391–393.

35. Sperling, *Convents and the Body Politic*, passim. See also Sherrill Cohen, *The Evolution of Women's Asylums Since 1500: From Refuge for Ex-Prostitutes to Shelters for Battered Women* (New York: Oxford University Press, 1992); Lucia Ferrante, "Honor Regained: Women in the Casa del Soccorso in San Paolo in Sixteenth-Century Bologna," in *Sex and Gender in Historical Perspective: Selections from Quaderni Storici*, ed. Edward Muir and Guido Ruggiero (Baltimore: Johns Hopkins University Press, 1990), 46–72; David Kertzer, *Sacrificed for Honor: Italian Infant Abandonment and the Politics of Reproductive Control* (Boston: Beacon, 1993).

36. ASPV, *Curia II, CM, busta* 85. Testimony of *D.* Baretius *filius D.* Giovanni Maria Barechi de Cremona, *librarius,* June 22, 1612, u.d.

37. Ibid., testimony of Foscarina Memo, May 1, 1612, u.d.

38. Ibid., testimony of Jacobo di Muggia, April, 1612, u.d.

39. Ibid., testimony of Angeles Filius *q.* Blasij Fanonij, minister in the Uffizio del Proprio, April 3, 1612, u.d.

40. Ibid., testimony of Agostino Corner, no date, u.d.

41. Ibid., testimony of Giovanni Battista Pizzinelli, April 13, 1612, u.d.

42. ASPV, *Liber actum mandatorum,* reg. 82, May 30, 1613, fols. 247r–247v.

43. ASPV, *Curia II, CM, busta* 85, May 10, 1614, u.d. According to Misserini's statement, produced by *D.* Jacobo Pamphilus, April 21, 1614, unbound folio.

44. Ibid. Unbound folio labeled "Proclama," produced by Pietro Abetinus on February 14, 1614.

45. Ibid. Signed by Camillus Pincio, *coaduatore,* August 30, 1614.

46. *Statuta veneta,* fol. 145r.

Conclusion

1. ASV, *Avogaria di Comun. Misto, busta* 3015/7, *fascicolo* 11, u.d. All quotes are from this source.

2. Joanne M. Ferraro, "Coniugi nemici: Orsetta, Annibale ed il compito dello storico (Venezia 1634)," in *I coniugi nemici: La separazione in Italia dal XII al XVIII secolo,* ed. Silvana Seidel Menchi and Diego Quaglioni (Bologna: Mulino, 2000), 141–190.

3. Jutta Sperling has argued that patriarchal honor, coupled with high dowries, severely limited the opportunities of Venetian daughters of the patriciate for self-actualization. Jutta Sperling, *Convents and the Body Politic in Late Renaissance Venice* (Chicago: University of Chicago Press, 1999), 24.

4. Philip Ariés, *Centuries of Childhood: A Social History of Family Life,* trans. Robert Baldick (New York: Vintage, 1962); Jean-Louis Flandrin, *Families in Former Times: Kinship, Household, and Sexuality in Early Modern France,* trans. Richard W. Southern (Cambridge and New York: Cambridge University Press, 1979); David Hunt, *Parents and Children in History: The Psychology of Family Life in Early Modern France* (New York: Basic Books, 1970); Lawrence Stone, *The Family, Sex, and Marriage in England, 1500–1800* Abridged ed. (Harmondsworth, UK: Penguin Books, 1977).

5. Ozment, *When Fathers Ruled* and *Magdalena and Balthasar* (New York: Simon and Schuster, 1986).

BIBLIOGRAPHY

Archival Sources

Archivio Storico Patriarcale di Venezia. Curia II

    Causarum matrimoniorum
    Filciae causarum
    Liber actorum mandatorum
    Liber sententiarum 1500–1663
    Liber sententiarum 1600–1607
    Liber sententiarum civilium 1620–1631

Archivio di Stato di Venezia

    Avogaria di Comun. Miscellanea penale
    Avogaria di Comun. Misti
    Avogaria di Comun. Raspe
    Giudici del Procurator. Interdetti e terminazioni di dote
    Giudici del Procurator. Scritte, domande, e risposte
    Giudici del Proprio. Vadimoni
    Giudici del Petizione
    Notarile. Testamenti

Contemporary Works (in print)

Andreini, Isabella. *Lettere della Signora Isabella Andreini, Padovana, Comica gelosa, ed Academica intenta.* Venice: Presso Giovanni Battista Combi, 1617.

Argelati, Francesco. *Pratica del Foro veneto.* Venice: Agostino Savioli a San Salvator, 1737.

Barbaro, M. *Arbori dei patritii veneti.* In ASV, *Miscellanea codici,* s.I.: *Storia veneta.*

Ferro, Marco. *Dizionario del diritto comune e veneto.* Venice: Modesto Fenzo, 1780.

Marinella, Lucrezia. *La nobiltà e eccellenza della donna.* Venice: G. B. Ciotti, 1601.

Parte sostantiale delli decreti del sacro et generale concilio di Trento che furono publicati nella sinodo diocesana di Venezia il dì xvii di settembre 1564. Venice: Francesco Rampazetto, 1564.

Valerio, Agostino. *Istruttione delle donne maritate.* Venice: Bolognino Zaltieri, 1575.

Contemporary Works (reprinted)

Aretino, Pietro. *The Ragionamenti: The Lives of Nuns, The Lives of Married Women, The Lives of Courtesans.* Intro. Peter Stafford. London: Odyssey Press, 1970.

Bandello, Matteo. *Le quattro patri de le Novelle del Bandello.* Ed. Gustavo Balsamo-Crivelli. Turin: Unione Tipographico and Editrice Torinese, 1924.

Boccaccio, Giovanni. *The Decameron.* Harmondsworth, UK: Penguin, 1982.

Bolognetti, Alberto. "Report to the Papal Nuncio in Venice, 1578–81." In *Venice: A Documentary History, 1450–1630.* Ed. David Chambers and Brian Pullan, 236–237. Oxford: Blackwell, 1992.

Catechism of the Council of Trent for Parish Priests Issued by Order of Pope Pius V. Trans. John A. McHugh, O.P., and Charles J. Callan, O.P. New York: Joseph F. Wagner, 1923.

Fonte, Moderata. *Il merito delle donne.* Intro. Adriana Chemello. Mirano and Venice: Editrice Eidos, 1988.

Marinello, Giovanni. *Medicine per le donne nel cinquecento. Testi di Giovanni Marinello e di Girolamo Mercurio.* Ed. Maria Luisa Altieri Biagi, Clement Mazzetta, Angela Chiatera, and Paolo Altieri. Turin: UTET and Tipografia Torinese, 1992.

Ruzzante (Angelo Beolco). *Teatro.* Ed. and trans. Ludovico Zorzi. Turin: Einaudi, 1967.

Sanudo, Marino. *Laus urbis Venetae.* 1493. Reprinted in *Venice: A Documentary History, 1450–1630.* Ed. David Chambers and Brian Pullan, 4–21. Oxford: Blackwell, 1992.

Sharp, Jane. *The Midwives' Book.* Ed. Randolph Trumbach. New York and London: Garland, 1985.

Tassini, Giuseppe. *Veronica Franco: Celebre poetessa e cortigiana del secolo XVI.* 1874. Reprinted Venice: Alfieri, 1969.

The Canons and Decrees of the Council of Trent. Trans. Rev. H. J. Schroeder, O.P. Rockford, Ill.: Tan Books, 1978.

Vecellio, Cesare. *Costumes anciens et modernes.* 2 vols. Paris: Tipographie de Firmin Didot Freres & Fils, 1860.

Modern Works

Abelove, Henry, Michèle Aina Barale, and David M. Halperin, eds. *The Lesbian and Gay Studies Reader*. New York and London: Routledge, 1993.

Accati, Luisa. "The Spirit of Fornication: Virtue of the Soul and Virtue of the Body in Friuli, 1600–1800." In *Sex and Gender in Historical Perspective: Selections from Quaderni Storici*. Ed. Edward Muir and Guido Ruggiero, 110–140. Trans. Margaret A. Gallucci, Mary M. Gallucci, and Carole C. Gallucci. Baltimore: Johns Hopkins University Press, 1990.

Agnew, John, and James S. Duncan, eds. *The Power of Place: Bringing Together Geographical and Sociological Imaginations*. Boston: Unwin Hyman, 1989.

Andres, Richard. *Scripts and Scenarios: The Performance of Comedy in Renaissance Italy*. Cambridge: Cambridge University Press, 1993.

Ariés, Philip. *Centuries of Childhood: A Social History of Family Life*. Trans. Robert Baldick. New York: Vintage, 1962.

Augustine, P. Chas. *A Commentary on the New Code of Canon Law*, bk. 3, vol. 5. London and St. Louis: Herder, 1935.

Bakhtin, Mikhail. *Rabelais and His World*. Trans. Helene Iswolsky. Bloomington: Indiana University Press, 1984.

Barbagli, Marzio. *Sotto lo stesso tetto: Mutamenti della famiglia in Italia dal XV al XX secolo*. Bologna: Il Mulino, 1984.

Barzaghi, Antonio. *Donne o cortigiane? La prostituzione a Venezia: Documenti di costume dal XVI al XVIII secolo*. Verona: Bertani, 1980.

Bell, Rudolph. *How to Do It. Guides to Good Living for Renaissance Italians*. Chicago: University of Chicago Press, 1999.

Bellomo, Manlio. *La condizione giuridica della donna in Italia*. Turin: Eri, 1970.

———. *Ricerche sui rapporti patrimoniali tra conjugi*. Milan: Giuffre, 1961.

Bistort, Giulio. *Il magistrato alle pompe nella repubblica di Venezia*. Venice: Emiliana, 1912. Reprinted Bologna: Forni Editore, 1969.

Boerio, Giuseppe. *Dizionario del dialetto veneziano*. Venice: Tipografia di Giovanni Cecchini, 1856.

Bortolan, Gino. *Il patriarcato di Venezia*. Venice: Tipo-Litografia Armena-Isola di S. Lazzaro, 1974.

Bossy, John. *Christianity in the West 1400–1700*. New York and Oxford: Oxford University Press, 1985.

———. "The Counter-Reformation and the People of Catholic Europe." *Past and Present* 47 (1970): 51–70.

———, ed. *Disputes and Settlements: Law and Human Relations in the West*. Cambridge and New York: Cambridge University Press, 1983.

Boxer, Marilyn J., and Jean Quataert, eds. *Connecting Spheres: Women in a Globalizing World, 1500 to the Present*. New York and Oxford: Oxford University Press, 1999.

Braudel, Fernand. *The Mediterranean and the Mediterranean World in the Age of Philip II.* 2 vols. London: Harper & Row, 1972.

Bridenthal, Renate, and Claudia Koonz, eds. *Becoming Visible: Women in European History.* Boston: Houghton Mifflin, 1977.

Brucker, Gene. *Giovanni and Lusanna: Love and Marriage in Renaissance Florence.* Berkeley and Los Angeles: University of California Press, 1986.

Brundage, James A. "The Problem of Impotence." In *Sexual Practices and the Medieval Church.* Ed. Vern L. Bullough and James A. Brundage, 135–140. Buffalo, N.Y.: Prometheus Books, 1982.

———. "Prostitution in the Medieval Canon Law." *Signs* 1 (1976): 825–845.

Brundage, James A., and Vern L. Bullough, eds. *Law, Sex, and Christian Society in Medieval Europe.* Chicago: University of Chicago Press, 1987.

Bullough, Vern L., and Bonnie Bullough. *The History of Prostitution.* New Hyde Park, N.Y.: University Books, 1964.

Bullough, Vern L. and James A. Brundage, eds. *Sexual Practices and the Medieval Church.* Buffalo, N.Y.: Promethus Books, 1982.

Buonanno, Milly, ed. *Le funzioni sociali del matrimonio: Modelli e regole della scelta del coniuge dal XIV al XX secolo.* Milan: Edizioni di Comunità, 1980.

Burghartz, Susanna. "Tales of Seduction, Tales of Violence: Argumentative Strategies Before the Basel Marriage Court." *German History* 17 (1999): 41–56.

Burke, Peter. *Popular Culture in Early Modern Europe.* London: Temple Smith, 1978.

Calvino, Italo. *Italian Folktales Selected and Retold by Italy Calvino.* Trans. George Martin. New York: Harcourt Brace Jovanovich, 1980.

Canosa, Romano, and Isabella Colonnello. *Storia della prostituzione in Italia dal quattrocento alla fine del settecento.* Rome: Sapere 2000, 1989.

Cappelletti, Giuseppe. *Storia della chiesa di Venezia dalla sua fondazione sino ai nostri giorni.* 8 vols. Venice: Tipografia Armena di San Lazzaro, 1849–1860.

Carroll, Linda. "Who's on Top? Gender as Societal Power Configuration in Italian Renaissance Painting and Drama." *Sixteenth Century Journal* 20 (1989): 531–558.

Cavallo, Sandra. "Assistenza femminile e tutela dell'onore nella Torino del XVIII secolo." *Annali della Fondazione Luigi Einaudi* 14 (1980): 127–155.

Cavallo, Sandra, and Simona Cerutti. "Female Honor and the Social Control of Reproduction in Piedmont Between 1600 and 1800." In *Sex and Gender in Historical Perspective: Selections from Quaderni Storici.* Ed. Edward Muir and Guido Ruggiero, 73–109. Baltimore: Johns Hopkins University Press, 1990.

Chambers, David, and Brian Pullan, eds. *Venice: A Documentary History, 1450–1630.* Oxford: Blackwell, 1992.

Chojnacki, Stanley. "Blurring Genders." *Renaissance Quarterly* 40 (1987): 743–751.

———. "Dowries and Kinsmen in Early Renaissance Venice." *Journal of Interdisciplinary History* 5 (1975): 571–600.

————. "'The Most Serious Duty': Motherhood, Gender, and Patrician Culture in Renaissance Venice." In *Refiguring Woman: Perspectives on Gender and the Italian Renaissance*. Ed. Marilyn Migiel and Juliana Schiesari, 133–154. Ithaca, N.Y.: Cornell University Press, 1991.

————. "Nobility, Women and the State: Marriage Regulation in Venice, 1420–1535." In *Marriage in Italy, 1300–1650*. Ed. Trevor Dean and K. J. P. Lowe, 128–154. Cambridge: Cambridge University Press, 1998.

————. "Patrician Women in Early Renaissance Venice." *Studies in the Renaissance* 21 (1974): 176–203.

————. "La posizione della donna a Venezia nel cinquecento." In *Tiziano e Venezia: Convegno internazionale di studi*. Ed. Gaetano Cozzi, 65–70. Vicenza: Neri Pozza, 1980.

————. "The Power of Love: Wives and Husbands in Late Medieval Venice." In *Women and Power in the Middle Ages*. Ed. Mary Erler and Maryanne Kowaleski, 126–148. Athens: University of Georgia Press, 1988.

Ciammitti, Luisa. "Quanto costa essere normali: La dote nel Conservatorio femminile di Santa Maria del Baraccano (1630–1680)." *Quaderni storici* 53 (1983): 469–497.

Cohen, Elizabeth S. "'Courtesans' and 'Whores': Words and Behavior in Roman Streets." *Women's Studies* 19 (1991): 201–208.

Cohen, Sherrill. "Asylums for Women in Counter-Reformation Italy." In *Women in Reformation and Counter-Reformation Europe: Public and Private Worlds*. Ed. Sherrin Marshall, 166–188. Bloomington and Indianapolis: Indiana University Press, 1989.

————. "Convertite e malmaritate: Donne 'irregolari' ed ordini religiosi nella Firenze rinascimentale." *Memoria: Rivista di storia della donne* 5 (1982): 23–65.

————. *The Evolution of Women's Asylums Since 1500: From Refuge for Ex-Prostitutes to Shelters for Battered Women*. New York: Oxford University Press, 1992.

Conti Odorisio, Ginevra. *Donne e società nel seicento: Lucrezia Marinelli e Arcangelo Tarabotti*. Rome: Bulzoni Editore, 1979.

Cowan, Alexander. "Patricians and Partners in Early Modern Venice." In *Medieval and Renaissance Venice*. Ed. Ellen E. Kittell and Thomas F. Madden, 276–293. Urbana and Chicago: University of Illinois Press, 1999.

Cozzi, Gaetano. *Il dibattito sui matrimoni clandestini: Vicende giuridiche, sociali, religiose dell'istituzione matrimoniale tra medioevo ed età moderna*. Venice: University of Venice History Department, 1985–1986.

————. "Note e documenti sulla questione del 'divorzio' a Venezia (1782–1788)." *Annali dell'Istituto storico italo-germanico in Trento* 7 (1981): 275–360.

————. "Padri, figli e matrimoni clandestini (meta sec. XVI–meta sec. XVIII." *La cultura* 14 (1976): 169–212.

————. *Religione, moralità e giustizia a Venezia: Vicende della magistratura degli*

Esecutori contro la bestemmia. Padua: Cooperativa Libraria Editrice degli Studenti dell'Università di Padova, 1967–1968.

―――, ed. *Stato, società e giustizia nella Repubblica Veneta (sec. xv–xviii).* Rome: Jouvence, 1980.

Darton, Robert. *The Great Cat Massacre and Other Episodes in French Cultural History.* New York: Vintage Books, 1985.

―――. "The Symbolic Element in History." *Journal of Modern History* 58 (1986): 218–234.

Datta, Satya. "La presenza di una coscienza femminista nella Venezia dei primi secoli dell'età moderna." *Studi veneziani* 32 (1996): 105–137.

Davidoff, Leonore, and Catherine Hall. *Family Fortunes: Men and Women of the English Middle Class, 1780–1850.* Chicago: University of Chicago Press, 1987.

Davis, James C. *The Decline of the Venetian Nobility as a Ruling Class.* Baltimore: Johns Hopkins University Press, 1962.

―――. *A Venetian Family 1500–1900.* Philadelphia: American Philosophical Society, 1975.

Davis, Natalie Zemon. "Boundaries and the Sense of Self in Sixteenth-Century France." In *Reconstructing Individualism: Autonomy, Individuality, and the Self in Western Thought.* Ed. Thomas C. Heller et al., 53–63. Stanford, Calif.: Stanford University Press, 1986.

―――. "City Women and Religious Change." In *Society and Culture in Early Modern France.* Ed. Natalie Zemon Davis, 65–95. Stanford, Calif.: Stanford University Press, 1975.

―――. *Fiction in the Archives: Pardon Tales and Their Tellers in Sixteenth-Century France.* Stanford, Calif.: Stanford University Press, 1987.

―――. "Ghosts, Kin, and Progeny: Some Features of Family Life in Early Modern France." *Daedalus* 106 (1977): 87–114.

―――. *The Return of Martin Guerre.* Cambridge, Mass.: Harvard University Press, 1986.

―――. "The Sacred and the Body Social in Sixteenth-Century Lyon." *Past and Present* 90 (1980): 40–70.

―――, ed. *Society and Culture in Early Modern France.* Stanford, Calif.: Stanford University Press, 1975.

Dean, Trevor, and K. J. P. Lowe, eds. *Marriage in Italy, 1300–1650* (Cambridge: Cambridge University Press, 1998.

Del Col, Andrea. *L'Inquisizione nel patriarcato e diocesi di Aquileia, 1557–59.* Montereale Valcellina: Edizioni Università di Trieste, 1998.

Derosas, Renzo. "Moralità e giustizia a Venezia nel '500–'600: Gli Esecutori contro la bestemmia." In *Stato, società e giustizia nella Repubblica Veneta (Secolo xv–xviii),* vol. 1. Ed. Gaetano Cozzi, 431–528. Rome: Jouvence, 1980.

Diefendorf, Barbara. "Family Culture, Renaissance Culture." *Renaissance Quarterly* 40 (1987): 661–681.

Di Simplicio, Oscar. *Peccato, penitenza, perdono: Siena 1575–1800: La formazione della coscienza nell'Italia moderna.* Milan: Franco Angeli, 1994.

Ercole, Francesco. "L'istituto dotale nella pratica e nella legislazione statutaria dell'Italia superiore." *Rivista italiana per le scienze giurdiche* 45 (1909): 191–302; 46 (1910): 167–257.

Farr, James R. "Crimine nel vicinato: Ingiurie, matrimonio e onore nella Digione del XVI e XVII secolo." *Quaderni storici* 66 (1987): 839–854.

Ferguson, Margaret W., Maureen Quilligan, and Nancy J. Vickers, eds. *Rewriting the Renaissance: The Discourses of Sexual Difference in Early Modern Europe.* Chicago: University of Chicago Press, 1986.

Ferrante, Lucia. "Honor Regained: Women in the Casa del Soccorso in San Paolo in Sixteenth-Century Bologna." In *Sex and Gender in Historical Perspective: Selections from Quaderni Storici.* Ed. Edward Muir and Guido Ruggiero, 46–72. Baltimore: Johns Hopkins University Press, 1990.

———. "'Malmaritate': Tra assistenza e punizione (Bologna sec. XVI–XVII)." In *Forme e soggetti dell'intervento assistenziale in una città di antico,* 65–109. Ed. Mario Fanti. Bologna: Istituto per la Storia di Bologna, 1986.

———. "Il matrimonio disciplinato: Processi matrimoniali a Bologna nel cinquecento." In *Disciplina dell'anima, disciplina del corpo e disciplina della società tra medioevo ed età moderna.* Ed. Paolo Prodi, 901–927. Bologna: Il Mulino, 1994.

———. "Pro mercede carnali: Il giusto prezzo rivendicato in tribunale." *Memoria* 17 (1986): 42–58.

Ferraro, Joanne. "Coniugi nemici: Orsetta, Annibale ed il compito dello storico (Venezia, 1634)." In *I coniugi nemici: La separazione in Italia dal XII al XVIII secolo.* Ed. Silvana Seidel Menchi and Diego Quaglioni, 141–190. Bologna: Il Mulino, 2000.

———. *Family and Public Life in Brescia, 1580–1650: The Foundations of Power in the Venetian State.* Cambridge: Cambridge University Press, 1993.

———. "Honor and the Marriage Wars of Late Renaissance Venice," Contributions from the International Meeting, Honour: Identity and Ambiguity of an Informal Code (The Mediterranean, 12th–20th Centuries), in *Acta Histriae* 9 (2000): 41–48.

———. "The Power to Decide: Battered Wives in Early Modern Venice." *Renaissance Quarterly* 48 (1995): 492–512.

Filippini, Nadia Maria. "The Church, the State and Childbirth: The Midwife in Italy During the Eighteenth Century." In *The Art of Midwifery: Early Modern Midwives in Europe and North America.* Ed. Hilary Marland, 152–175. London: Routledge, 1993.

———. "Levatrici e ostetricanti a Venezia tra sette e ottocento." *Quaderni storici* 58 (1985): 150–180.

Fiume, Giovanna, ed. *Onore e storia nelle società mediterranea.* Palermo: La Luna, 1989.

Flandrin, Jean-Louis. *Families in Former Times: Kinship, Household, and Sexuality in Early Modern France*. Trans. Richard W. Southern. Cambridge and New York: Cambridge University Press, 1979.

———. *Sex in the Western World: The development of attitudes and behavior*. Trans. Sue Collins. Chur, Switzerland, and Philadelphia: Harwood Academic Publishers, 1991.

Foucault, Michel. *The History of Sexuality*. Vol. 1, *An Introduction*. Harmondsworth, U.K.: Penguin, 1981.

Gaudemet, Jean. "Il legame matrimoniale nel XVII secolo: Legislazione canonica e tendenze laiche." In *Le funzioni sociali del matrimonio: Modelli e regole della scelta del coniuge dal XIV al XX secolo*. Ed. Milly Buonanno, 64–79. Milan: Edizioni di Comunità, 1980.

Gélis, Jacques. *History of Childbirth: Fertility, Pregnancy and Birth in Early Modern Europe*. Boston: Northeastern University Press, 1991.

Gelles, Richard J. "No Place to Go: The Social Dynamics of Marital Violence." In *Battered Women: A Psychosociological Study of Domestic Violence*. Ed. Maria Roy, 46–63. New York: Van Nostrand Reinhold, 1977.

Gergen, Mary. "The Social Construction of Personal Histories: Gendered Lives in Popular Autobiographies." In *Constructing the Social*. Ed. Theodore R. Sarbin and John I. Kitsuse, 19–44. London: Sage, 1994.

Giannetti, Laura. "Venezia alla fine del XVI secolo: Le parocchie di Santa Maria Nova e San Canciano." Undergraduate thesis, Università degli Studi di Venezia, Facoltà di Lettere e Filosofia. 1977–1978.

Goffen, Rona. "Renaissance Dreams." *Renaissance Quarterly* 40 (1987): 682–706.

———. *Titian's Women*. New Haven, Conn., and London: Yale University Press, 1997.

Gottlieb, Beatrice. "The Meaning of Clandestine Marriage." In *Family and Sexuality in French History*. Ed. Robert Wheaton and Tamara K. Hareven, 49–83. Philadelphia: University of Pennsylvania Press, 1980.

Grazzini, Anton Francesco. *Le rime burlesche edite e inedite*. Ed. Carlo Veronese. Florence: Sansone, 1882.

Green, Monica. "Women's Medical Care in Medieval Europe." *Signs: Journal of Women in Culture and Society* 14 (1989): 434–473.

Greenblatt, Stephen Jay. *Renaissance Self-Fashioning from More to Shakespeare*. Chicago: University of Chicago Press, 1980.

Grendler, Paul. *Critics of the Italian World, 1530–1560: Antonio Francesco Doni, Nicolò Franco, and Ortensio Lando*. Madison: University of Wisconsin Press, 1969.

———. "The Leaders of the Venetian State, 1540–1609: A Prosopographical Analysis." *Studi veneziani* 19 (1990): 35–86.

———. *The Roman Inquisition and the Venetian Press, 1540–1605*. Princeton, N.J.: Princeton University Press, 1977.

————. *Schooling in Renaissance Italy: Literacy and Learning, 1300–1600*. Baltimore and London: Johns Hopkins University Press, 1989.

Grieco, Sara F. Mathews. "Pedagogical Prints: Moralizing Broadsheets and Wayward Women in Counter-Reformation Italy. In *Picturing Women in Renaissance and Baroque Italy*. Ed. Geraldine A. Johnson and Sara F. Mathews Grieco, 61–87. Cambridge: Cambridge University Press, 1997.

Guerci, Luciano. *La sposa obbediente: Donna e matrimonio nella discussione dell' Italia del settecento*. Turin: Editrice Tirrenia Stampatori, 1988.

Hale, John Rigby, ed. *Renaissance Venice*. London: Faber and Faber, 1973.

Haliczer, Stephen. *Sexuality in the Confessional: Sacrament Profaned*. New York: Oxford University Press, 1996.

Hanley, Sarah. "Family and State in Early Modern France: The Marriage Pact." In *Connecting Spheres: Women in the Western World, 1500 to the Present*. Ed. Marilyn J. Boxer and Jean Quataert, 53–63. New York and Oxford: Oxford University Press, 1987.

————. "Social Sites of Political Practice in France: Lawsuits, Civil Rights, and the Separation of Powers in Domestic and State Government, 1500–1800." *American Historical Review* 102 (1997): 27–52.

Horowitz, Maryanne C. "Aristotle and Women." *Journal of the History of Biology* 9 (1979): 183–213.

Hughes, Diane Owen. "Sumptuary Laws and Social Relations in Renaissance Italy." In *Disputes and Settlements: Law and Human Relations in the West*. Ed. John Bossy, 69–99. Cambridge and New York: Cambridge University Press, 1983.

Hunt, David. *Parents and Children in History: The Psychology of Family Life in Early Modern France*. New York: Basic Books, 1970.

Hunt, Lynn, ed. *The New Cultural History*. Berkeley: University of California Press, 1989.

Johnson, Geraldine A., and Sara F. Mathews Grieco, eds. *Picturing Women in Renaissance and Baroque Italy*. Cambridge: Cambridge University Press, 1997.

Jones, Ann. "City Women and Their Audiences: Louise Labé and Veronica Franco." In *Rewriting the Renaissance: The Discourses of Sexual Difference in Early Modern Europe*. Ed. Margaret W. Ferguson, Maureen Quilligan, and Nancy J. Vickers, 299–316. Chicago: University of Chicago Press, 1986.

Kennard, Joseph. *Masks and Marionettes*. Port Washington, N.Y.: Kennikat Press, 1935.

Kertzer, David. *Sacrificed for Honor: Italian Infant Abandonment and the Politics of Reproductive Control*. Boston: Beacon, 1993.

King, Margaret. *Women of the Renaissance*. Chicago: Chicago University Press, 1991.

King, Margaret L., and Albert Rabil, Jr., eds. *Her Immaculate Hand: Selected Works by and About the Women Humanists of Quattrocento Italy*. Binghamton, N.Y.: Center for Medieval and Early Renaissance Studies, 1983.

Kirshner, Julius. "Pursuing Honor While Avoiding Sin: The Monte delle Doti of Florence." *Quaderni di "Studi senesi"* 41 (1978): 1–82.

——. "Wives' Claims Against Insolvent Husbands in Late Medieval Italy." In *Women of the Medieval World: Essays in Honor of John H. Mundy*. Ed. Julius Kirshner and S. F. Wemple, 256–303. Oxford: Basil Blackwell, 1985.

Kirshner, Julius, and Anthony Molho. "The Dowry Fund and the Marriage Market in Early Quattrocento Florence." *Journal of Modern History* 50 (1978): 403–438.

Kirshner, Julius, and S. F. Wemple, eds. *Women of the Medieval World: Essays in Honor of John H. Mundy*. Oxford: Basil Blackwell, 1985.

Kittell, Ellen E., and Thomas F. Madden, eds. *Medieval and Renaissance Venice*. Urbana and Chicago: University of Illinois Press, 1999.

Klapisch-Zuber, Christiane. "The Griselda Complex: Dowry and Marriage Gifts in the Quattrocento." In *Women, Family, and Ritual in Renaissance Italy*. Ed. Christiane Klapisch-Zuber, 224–231. Trans. Lydia G. Cochrane. Chicago: University of Chicago Press, 1985.

——, ed. *Women, Family, and Ritual in Renaissance Italy*. Trans. Lydia G. Cochrane. Chicago: University of Chicago Press, 1985.

Labalme, Patricia C. *Beyond Their Sex: Learned Women of the European Past*. New York: New York University Press, 1980.

——. "Sodomy and Venetian Justice in the Renaissance." *Legal History Review* 52 (1984): 217–254.

——. "Venetian Women on Women: Three Early Modern Feminists." *Archivio veneto* 5th ser., 117 (1981): 81–109.

Ladurie, Emmanuel Le Roy. "The Aiguilette: Castration by Magic." In *The Mind, the Method, and the Historian*. Ed. Emmanuel Le Roy Ladurie, 84–96. Chicago: University of Chicago Press, 1981.

——, ed. *The Mind, the Method, and the Historian*. Chicago: University of Chicago Press, 1981.

La Fond, Jean, and Augustin Redondo, eds. *L'image du monde renversé et ses représentations littéraires et para-littéraires de la fin du XVI siècle au milieu du XVIIe*. Paris: Librairie Philosophique J. Vrin, 1979.

Laqueur, Thomas. *Making Sex: Body and Gender from the Greeks to Freud*. Cambridge, Mass.: Harvard University Press, 1990.

Lazzaretti, Lorella. "La donna attraverso i processi per causa matrimoniale nella diocesi di Feltre del '500." *Studi veneziani* 32 (1996): 49–82.

Lea, Kathleen Marguerite. *Italian Popular Comedy: A Study in the Commedia dell' Arte, 1560–1620*. New York: Russell and Russell, Inc., 1962.

Lombardi, Daniela. "Fidanzamenti e matrimoni. Norme e consuetudini sociali del concilio di Trento alle riforme settecentesche." In *Storia del matrimonio*. Ed. M. De Giorgio and Christiane Klapisch-Zuber, 215–250. Rome and Bari: Laterza, 1996.

————. "Intervention by Church and State in Marriage Disputes in Sixteenth- and Seventeenth-Century Florence," In *Crime, Society, and the Law in Renaissance Italy*. Ed. Trevor Dean and K. J. P. Lowe, 142–156. Cambridge: Cambridge University Press, 1994.

————. "Il matrimonio: Norme, giurisdizioni, conflitti nello stato fiorentino del cinquecento." In *Istituzioni e società in Toscana nell' età moderna. Atti delle giornate di studio dedicate a Giuseppe Pannsini, Firenze, 4–5 dicembre, 1992*, 787–805. Rome: Ministero per i Beni Culturali e Ambientali, 1994.

Lottin, Alain. "Vie et mort du couple: Difficultés conjugales et divorces dans le nord de la France aux XVIIe et XVIIIe siècles." *XVIIe siècle* 102–103 (1974): 68–71.

Maclean, Ian. *The Renaissance Notion of Woman: A Study in the Fortunes of Scholasticism and Medical Science in European Intellectual Life*. Cambridge: Cambridge University Press, 1980.

Maldini, Daniela. "Donne sole, 'figlie raminghe,' 'convertite' e 'forzate.' Aspetti assistenziali nella Torino di fine settecento." *Il Risorgimento* 33 (1980): 115–138.

Marcolini, Giuliana, and Giulio Marcon. "Prostituzione e assistenza a Venezia nel secolo XVIII: Il pio loco delle povere peccatrici penitenti di San IOB." *Studi veneziani* 10 (1985): 99–136.

Marland, Hilary, ed. *The Art of Midwifery: Early Modern Midwives in Europe and North America*. London: Routledge, 1993.

Marshall, Sherrin, ed. *Women in Reformation and Counter-Reformation Europe: Public and Private Worlds*. Bloomington and Indianapolis: Indiana University Press, 1989.

Martin, John, "Out of the Shadow: Heretical and Catholic Women in Renaissance Venice." *Journal of Family History* 10 (1985): 21–33.

Martin, Ruth. *Witchcraft and the Inquisition in Venice, 1550–1650*. Oxford: Basil Blackwell, 1989.

Martini, Gabriele. "La donna veneziana del '600 tra sessualità legittima ed illegittima: Alcune riflessioni sul concubinato." *Atti dell'Istituto veneto di scienze, lettere, ed arti* 145 (1986–1987): 301–339.

Maza, Sarah. "Stories in History: Cultural Narratives in Recent Works in European History." *American Historical Review* 101 (1996): 1499–1503.

Mclaren, Angus. *A History of Contraception: From Antiquity to the Present Day*. Oxford, U.K. and Cambridge, Mass.: B. Blackwell, 1990.

————. *Reproductive Rituals: The Perception of Fertility in England from the Sixteenth Century to the Nineteenth Century*. London and New York: Methuen, 1984.

Medioli, Francesca. *L' "Inferno monacale" di Arcangela Tarabotti*. Turin: Rosenberg & Sellier, 1990.

Messbarger, Rebecca. "Woman Disputed: Representations of Women in 18th Century Italian Public Discourse." Ph.D. diss., University of Chicago, 1994.

Migiel, Marilyn, and Juliana Schiesari, eds. *Refiguring Woman: Perspectives on Gender and the Italian Renaissance.* Ithaca and London: Cornell University Press, 1991.

Molmenti, Pompeo. *La storia di Venezia nella vita privata: Dalle origini alla cadutta della republicca.* Vol. 2, *Lo splendore.* Trieste: Lint, 1981.

Monter, William. "Women and the Italian Inquisitions." In *Women in the Middle Ages and the Italian Renaissance and Historical Perspectives.* Ed. Mary Beth Rose, 73–87. Syracuse, N.Y.: Syracuse University Press, 1985.

Moscucci, Ornella. *The Science of Woman: Gynaecology and Gender in England, 1800–1929.* Cambridge and New York: Cambridge University Press, 1990.

Muir, Edward. *Civic Ritual in Renaissance Venice.* Princeton, N.J.: Princeton University Press, 1981.

———. "Images of Power: Art and Pageantry in Renaissance Venice." *American Historical Review* 84 (1979): 16–52.

———. "The Virgin on the Street Corner: The Place of the Sacred in Italian Cities." In *Religion and Culture in the Renaissance and Reformation.* Ed. Steven Ozment, 25–40. Kirksville, Missouri: Sixteenth-Century Publishers, 1989.

Muir, Edward, and Guido Ruggiero, eds. *Microhistory and the Lost Peoples of Europe: Selections from Quaderni Storici.* Trans. Eren Branch. Baltimore: Johns Hopkins University Press, 1991.

———. *Sex and Gender in Historical Perspective: Selections from Quaderni Storici.* Trans. Margaret A. Gallucci, Mary M. Gallucci, and Carole C. Gallucci. Baltimore: Johns Hopkins University Press, 1991.

Muir, Edward, and Ronald F. E. Weissman. "Social and Symbolic Places in Renaissance Venice and Florence." In *The Power of Place: Bringing Together Geographical and Sociological Imaginations.* Ed. John Agnew and James S. Duncan, 81–103. Boston: Unwin Hyman, 1989.

Niero, Antonio. *I patriarchi di Venezia: Da Lorenzo Giustiniani ai nostri giorni.* Venice: Studium Cattolico Veneziano, 1961.

Noonan, John T., Jr. *Contraception: A History of Its Treatment by Catholic Theologians and Canonists.* Cambridge, Mass., and London: Belnap Press of Harvard University Press, 1986.

Norton, Mary Beth. "Gender and Defamation in Seventeenth-Century Maryland." *William and Mary Quarterly* 44 (1987): 3–39.

Novick, Peter. *That Noble Dream: The "Objectivity Question" and the American Historical Profession.* Cambridge: Cambridge University Press, 1988.

Odorisio, Ginevra Conti. *Donna e società nel seicento.* Rome: Bulzoni, 1979.

Olivieri, Dante. *Dizionario etimologico italiano.* Milan: Casa Editrice Ceschina, 1961.

Oreglia, Giacomo. *The Commedia dell'Arte.* Trans. Lovett F. Edwards. London: Methuen, 1968.

Ozment, Steven. *Magdalena and Balthasar.* New York: Simon and Schuster, 1986.

————. *When Fathers Ruled: Family Life in Reformation Europe*. Cambridge, Mass.: Harvard University Press, 1983.

————, ed. *Religion and Culture in the Renaissance and Reformation*. Kirksville, Mich.: Sixteenth-Century Publishers, 1989.

Padoan, Giorgio. "Il mondo delle cortigiane nella letteratura rinascimentale." In *Il gioco dell'amore: Le cortigiane di Venezia dal trecento al settecento*, 63–71. Milan: Berenice, 1990.

Palmer, Richard. "Pharmacy in the Republic of Venice in the Sixteenth Century." In *The Medical Renaissance of the Sixteenth Century*. Ed. A. Wear, R. K. French, and I. M. Lonie, 100–117. Cambridge: Cambridge University Press, 1985.

Park, Katharine. *Doctors and Medicine in Early Renaissance Florence*. Princeton, N.J.: Princeton University Press, 1985.

Park, Katharine, and Robert A. Nye. "Destiny Is Anatomy." *The New Republic* 3970 (1991): 53–57.

Perry, Mary Elizabeth. "Deviant Insiders: Legalized Prostitutes and a Consciousness of Women in Early Modern Seville." *Comparative Studies in Society and History* 27 (1985): 138–158.

————. *Gender and Disorder in Early Modern Seville*. Princeton, N.J.: Princeton University Press, 1990.

————. "'Lost Women' in Early Modern Seville: The Politics of Prostitution." *Feminist Studies* 4 (1978): 195–214.

Phillips, Roderick. *Putting Asunder: A History of Divorce in Western Society*. Cambridge: Cambridge University Press, 1988.

Pollick, Linda. *Forgotten Children: Parent-Child Relations from 1500–1900*. Cambridge and New York: Cambridge University Press, 1983.

Prodi, Paolo. "Chiesa e società." In *Storia di Venezia*. Vol. 6, *Dal rinascimento al barocco*. Ed. Gaetano Cozzi and Paolo Prodi, 305–339. Rome: Istituto della Enciclopedia Italiana Fondata da Giovanni Treccani and Istituto Poligrafico e Zecca del Stato, 1994.

————. "The Structure and Organization of the Church in Renaissance Venice: Suggestions for Research." In *Renaissance Venice*. Ed. John Rigby Hale, 409–430. London: Faber and Faber, 1973.

Pullan, Brian. *Rich and Poor in Renaissance Venice: The Social Institutions of a Catholic State, to 1620*. Cambridge, Mass.: Harvard University Press, 1971.

Ravagnan, Angela. "'Servata forma sacri concilii Tridentini': L'applicazione delle disposizioni tridentine sul matrimonio nel patriarcato di Venezia e nella diocesi di Chioggia (1564–1610)." Undergraduate thesis, University of Venice, 1988–1989.

Rigo, Angelo. "Giudici del Procurator e donne 'malmaritate' a Venezia in epoca tridentina." *Atti dell Istituto veneto di scienze, lettere, ed arti*, Classe di scienze morali, lettere, ed arti 151 (1993): 214–266.

———. "Secondo comanda Dio et la Sancta Madre Giesia. Vicende matrimoniali a Venezia all'epoca del concilio di Trento (1545–1563)." Venice: University of Venice, 1988–1989.

Rocke, Michael J. *Forbidden Friendships: Homosexuality and Male Culture in Renaissance Florence.* New York and Oxford: Oxford University Press, 1996.

Romano, Dennis. "Gender and the Urban Geography of Renaissance Venice." *Journal of Social History* 23 (1989): 339–354.

———. *Housecraft and Statecraft: Domestic Service in Renaissance Venice 1400–1600.* Baltimore: Johns Hopkins University Press, 1996.

———. *Patricians and Popolani: The Social Foundations of the Venetian Renaissance State.* Baltimore and London: Johns Hopkins University Press, 1987.

Rose, Mary Beth, ed. *Women in the Middle Ages and the Italian Renaissance and Historical Perspectives.* Syracuse, N.Y.: Syracuse University Press, 1985.

Rosenthal, Margaret F. *The Honest Courtesan: Veronica Franco, Citizen and Writer in Sixteenth-Century Venice.* Chicago: University of Chicago Press, 1992.

———. "Venetian Women Writers and Their Discontents." In *Sexuality and Gender in Early Modern Europe: Institutions, Texts, Images.* Ed. James Grantham Turner, 107–132. Cambridge: Cambridge University Press, 1993.

———. "Veronica Franco's Terze Rime: The Venetian Courtesan's Defense." *Renaissance Quarterly* 42 (1989): 227–258.

Roy, Maria, ed. *Battered Women: A Psychosociological Study of Domestic Violence.* New York: Van Nostrand Reinhold, 1977.

Ruggiero, Guido. *Binding Passions: Tales of Magic, Marriage, and Power at the End of the Renaissance.* Oxford and New York: Oxford University Press, 1993.

———. *The Boundaries of Eros: Sex Crime and Sexuality in Renaissance Venice.* New York and Oxford: Oxford University Press, 1985.

———. " 'Più che la vita caro': Onore, matrimonio, e reputazione femminile nel tardo Rinascimento." *Quaderni storici* 66 (1987): 753–775.

———. "Re-Reading the Renaissance: Civic Morality and the World of Marriage, Love and Sex." In *Sexuality and Gender in Early Modern Europe: Institutions, Texts, Images.* Ed. James Grantham Turner, 10–30. Cambridge: Cambridge University Press, 1993.

Sadie, Stanley, ed. *The Grove Dictionary of Opera.* Vol. 4. London: Macmillan, 1992.

Safley, Thomas Max. *Let No Man Put Asunder: The Control of Marriage in the German Southwest.* Kirksville, Mich.: Sixteenth-Century Publishers, 1984.

———. "Marital Litigation in the Diocese of Constance, 1551–1620." *Sixteenth Century Journal* 12 (1981): 61–78.

Sarbin, Theodore, ed. *Narrative Psychology: The Storied Nature of Human Conduct.* New York: Praeger, 1986.

Scarabello, Giovanni. "Devianza sessuale ed interventi di giustizia a Venezia nella prima metà del XVI secolo." In *Tiziano e Venezia, Convegno internazionale di studi,* 75–84. Venice: Neri Pozza Editore, 1976.

_____. "Le 'signore' della repubblica." In *Il gioco dell'amore: Le cortigiani di Venezia dal trecento al settecento*, 11–35. Milan: Berenice, 1990.

Schleiner, Winfried. "Early Modern Controversies About the One Sex Model." *Renaissance Quarterly* 53 (2000): 180–191.

Schneider, Jane. "Of Vigilance and Virgins: Honor and Shame and Access to Resources in Mediterranean Societies." *Ethnology* 10 (1971): 1–23.

Schutte, Anne Jacobson. "The Image of a Creative Woman in Late Renaissance Italy." *Renaissance Quarterly* 44 (1991): 42–61.

Scott, Joan Wallach. "The Evidence of Experience." In *The Lesbian and Gay Studies Reader*. Ed. Henry Abelove, Michèle Aina Barale, and David M. Halperin, 397–415. New York and London: Routledge, 1993.

————. *Gender and the Politics of History*. New York: Columbia University Press, 1988.

The Simon and Schuster Book of the Opera. New York: Simon and Schuster, 1977.

Seidel Menchi, Silvana and Diego Quaglioni, eds. *Coniugi nemici. La separazione in Italia dal XII al XVIII secolo*. Bologna: Il Mulino, 2000.

Smart, Carol, and Barry Smart, eds. *Women, Sexuality and Social Control*. London: Routledge and Kegan Paul, 1978.

Sommerville, Margaret R. *Sex and Subjection: Attitudes to Women in Early Modern Society*. London: Arnold, 1995.

Sperling, Jutta Gisela. *Convents and the Body Politic in Late Renaissance Venice*. Chicago, University of Chicago Press, 1999.

Stone, Lawrence. *The Family, Sex, and Marriage in England, 1500–1800*. Abridged ed. New York: Harper & Row, 1977.

————. "Wife Beating as a Social Problem: The Process of Definition." *International Journal of Women's Studies* 7 (1984): 412–422.

Tamassia, Nino. *La famiglia italiana nei secoli decimoquinto e decimosesto*. Rome: Multigrafica, 1971.

Tassini, Giuseppe. *Curiosità veneziane*. 8th ed. Venice: Filippi Editore, 1970.

Tentler, Thomas. *Sin and Confession on the Eve of the Reformation*. Princeton, N.J.: Princeton University Press, 1977.

Turner, James Grantham, ed. *Sexuality and Gender in Early Modern Europe: Institutions, Texts, Images*. Cambridge: Cambridge University Press, 1993.

Vitali, Achille. *La moda a Venezia attraverso i secoli: Lessico ragionato*. Venice: Filippi Editore, 1992.

Watt, Jeffrey R. "Divorce in Early Modern Neuchâtel, 1547–1806." *Journal of Family History* 14 (1989): 137–155.

Wear, A. R. K. French, and I. M. Lonie, eds. *The Medical Renaissance of the Sixteenth Century*. Cambridge: Cambridge University Press, 1985.

Wheaten, Robert, and Tamara K. Hareven, eds. *Family and Sexuality in French History*. Philadelphia: University of Pennsylvania Press, 1980.

White, Hayden. "The Fictions of Factual Representation." In *Tropics of Dis-*

course: Essays in Cultural Criticism. Ed. Hayden White, 121–134. Baltimore: Johns Hopkins University Press, 1978.

———, ed. *Tropics of Discourse: Essays in Cultural Criticism.* Baltimore: Johns Hopkins University Press, 1978.

Wiesner, Merry. *Women and Gender in Early Modern Europe.* Cambridge: Cambridge University Press, 1993.

Zannini, Andrea. "Burocrazia e burocrati a Venezia in età moderna: I cittadini originari (sec. XVI–XVIII)." In *Istituto veneto di scienze, lettere, ed arti. Memorie Classe di scienze morali, lettere, ed arti* 47 (1993): 339–363.

———. "Un censimento inedito del primo seicento e la crisi demografica ed economica di Venezia." *Studi veneziani* 26 (1993): 87–116.

Zarri, Gabriela. "Il matrimonio tridentino." In *Il Concilio di Trento e il moderno.* Ed. Paolo Prodi and Wolfgang Reinhard, 437–484. Bologna: Il Mulino, 1996.

Zoppelli, Luca. "Venice." In *The Grove Dictionary of Opera.* Ed. Stanley Sadie. Vol. 4, 913–915. London: Macmillan, 1992.

INDEX

Bruni, Analisa—researcher, 19
Buonamico, Alvise—husband of
    Magdalena de Francisus, 56
Busellino, Alessandro—step-brother
    of Camilla Benzoni, 72, 82

Calafati, Helena—witness for Lucieta
    Paduani, 96
Calafaro, Zuanne—fiancé of Joannetta
    Hortolani, 52, 54–55
Calmo, Andrea—playwright, 63
Cancelleria Ducale, 142
Candia, 143
Canon law, 8
    and impotence, 70
    theory, 40
canonists, 40, 52, 66
Capello, Piero—guardian of Vicenza
    Dandolo, 108
Carnival, 50, 60, 94, 110, 131
Casa del Soccorso, 57, 147
Causarum Matrimoniorum, 31
Cavatia, Antonio—husband of Isabella
    Cavatia, 121
Cavatia, Romano—husband of Pas-
    quetta Peregrini, 120, 122–123
Centani, Gasparo—husband of
    Camilla Benzoni, 71–74, 77, 79,
    83-85
Ceraione, Antonia—mother of Ar-
    cangela Ceraione, 49
Cernotta, Girolamo—husband of
    Paolina Businelli, 57
certitude, 24
Cesana, Antonio—father of Vittoria
    Cesana, 41, 43-44
child bearing, 71
childlessness, 87
children, 4, 5
Chojnacki, Stanley—historian, 162 n. 6
Christian morality, 36
Christians and Christianity, 139
church authority, over married
    women, 102
citizens (*cittadini*), 18, 39, 64, 71,
    175 n. 7
Ciurano, Iseppo—guardian of Mag-
    dalena Filosi, 45

clandestine marriage, 10, 39
clerics, 70
clothing
    of Clara Vidali, 135
    maidens, 18, 47
    and male citizens, 18
    and marriage disputes, 18
    and noblemen, 18
    and noblewomen, 18
    purchased by husbands for wives,
        181 n. 6
    and social hierarchy, 18
    and social identity, 144
    of wives, 121
coaching, by lawyers, 37
codes of conduct, 7
Codevigo—district of the Padovano,
    99
coercion, 45, 99
    of Arsilia Pegorin, 58
    of Camilla Belloto, 41
    of children by parents, 40, 47
    of Cornelia Calzago, 51
    and ecclesiastical judges, 41
    of Felicità Fada, 99
    and invalidity of the marriage con-
        tract, 40, 57
    and legal theorists, 41
    of Paolina Pirron, 45
    stories about, 41
    of Vittoria Cesana, 41, 44
cohabitation, 106
Collegio degli Speziali, 76
Comelli, Lorenzo—husband of
    Paolina Pirron, 45
community
    anxiety, 122
    assistance to wives, 124
    attitudes toward bad husbands, 121,
        126
    attitudes toward dissolving mar-
        riage, 41, 121, 131
    as censors of family behavior, 34
    and domestic discord, 5, 122
    and dowries, 138
    expectations of husbands, 34, 122
    and mediation of property disputes,
        5

gifts, 122, 144–145, 181 n. 13
Gisbè, Bernardino—husband of
    Arcangela Ceraione, 49, 50
Giudecca, 107–108, 147
giudici arbitri. See arbitrators and
    confidenti
Giudici del Procurator, 17, 22, 123,
    136–137, 140, 146, 149, 185 n.
    10
Giudici del Proprio, 17, 149–150
Giudici di Petizion, 108
Goleno, Andrea—husband of Laura
    Belfante, 106
gondolas, 16
gondoliers, 18
gonorrhea, 98
gossip, 6, 8, 18, 126, 158
    and the courts, 158
    and female honor, 182 n. 20
    neighborhood, 60
    networks, 52
    a prerogative of women, 66
    and power, 182 n. 20
    and servants, 73
    in seventeenth-century Maryland,
    182 n. 20
    and stories for court, 6–7
    and success of women, 124
Grandajo, Francesco—husband of pe-
    titioner Lucia Grandajo, 138
grandmothers, 58
Greeks, 19
Griselda, 31
Gritti, Clara, abuse of, 128
guardians, 147
    abuse of children, 13
    Alessandro and Paolina Businelli, 57
    and arranged marriage, 40, 102
    arranging betrothal, 65
    choosing spouses, 66
    disputes with children, 10
    Favio Montagna and Isabetta
    Damiani, 50
    irresponsible behavior, 45
    neglect of children, 147
    Piero Capello and Vicenza
    Dandolo, 108
    threatening disinheritence, 49

threats of violence, 45
to be honored by children, 5
and priests, 28
and Venetian secular magistracies, 138
Guazzo, Gioseffe—husband of Laura
    Armana, 157

Hanley, Sarah—historian, 12
herbs (medicinal), 76
history, narrative, 11
honor, 16, 19, 41, 95, 113, 144, 189 n. 3
    family, 3, 51
    female, 8, 21, 120–121
    and gossip, 182 n. 20
    of husbands, 159
    male, 33, 44, 75, 78, 103, 117, 121,
    128–129, 133, 158–159
    of married women, 30, 34, 124,
    135–136, 152
    masculine operational code used by
    women, 10, 35–36, 130
    of patricians, 117
    of separated women, 131
    of unmarried women, 8
    of unwed, expectant mothers, 127
    of wayward women, 106
    of women in the neighborhood,
    182 n. 20
Hortolani, Angela—mother of Joan-
    netta Hortolani, 52–53
housing, in Venice, 18
hunger, 122, 125, 130
husbands, 5
    and dissolution of marriage, 158
    and dowries, 158
    emotional expectations, 159
    expectations of wives, 158
    flaws, 126
    misbehavior, 5, 122
    proper maintenance of wives, 136
    responsibilities, 34
    and violence, 36, 47
hymen, 80

impotence, 10, 62, 71, 75–77, 86–87,
    89, 96, 102–103
    remedies, 76–77
    and women, 97

proof of validity, 40
rates, 19
registration, 39
regulation of, 5
restricted, 20
rites, 4, 39, 108
sacrament, 4, 37
and social class, 64
wars, 6, 155, 159
Martinazzi, Santo—creditor seeking
dotal resources, 136
Martinengo (province of Brescia), 129
Mastelaria, Angela—plaintiff for dotal
resources, 137
Mazzeti, Barbera—bride of Marco
Michel, 185 n. 11
Mazzoni, Ambrosio—husband of Isabella Floriani, 64
medicinals, 76
Memo, Alessandro—uncle of Foscarina Memo, 146
Memo, Foscarina, 142–154
and Cornelia Livriera—her mother,
143-146, 148–149, 152–153
Memo, Giacomo—uncle of Foscarina
Memo, 146
Memo, Giovanni Francesco—father
of Foscarina Memo, 143
Memo, Marin—half brother of Foscarina Memo, 146
Memo, Pietro—uncle of Foscarina
Memo, 146
men, sense of entitlement, 103
Meneghetti, Giovanni—witness for
Pasquetta Peregrini, 122
merchants (German), 18
Michel, Marco—groom of Barbera
Mazzeti, 185 n. 11
midwives
and Alessandro Busellino, 82
assistance to court supplicants, 70, 103
and Camilla Benzoni, 83
control of, 95
in court, 84, 95
ecclesiastical supervision of, 95
examination of Lucieta Paduani, 91,
94
and Gasparo Centani, 83-85

importance to litigants, 95
and Lucieta Paduani, 91–93
as regulators of sexual morality, 71, 95
and sexual education, 5, 75, 94
and state examinations, 95
Paula of Zuanebragola, 92
power in the community, 95, 159
rivalry with physicians, 10
state supervision of, 95
tale, 91
testimony of Bona, 83
testimony of Catherina, 83, 91
testimony of Magdalena Scuda, 92
testimony of Marietta Filacaipo, 91
views on impotence and magic, 77
Minio, Theodoro—friend of Vittoria
Cesana, 43-44, 65
mint, of Venice, 156
Misserini, Giovanni Battista—husband
of Foscarina Memo, 148
Misserini, Niccolò—father of Giovanni Battista Misserini,
144–145, 150
modesty, of women, 72–74
monachization, 62, 66, 158, 173 n. 72,
174 n. 87
Montagna, Favio—uncle of Isabetta
Damiani, 50
Montin, Niccolò—husband of Clara
Vidali, 129–131, 135
Moro, Zuane—noble who purchased
sex from Zuana Facini, 112
Moschini, Aquilina—witness for Lucretia Balatini, 86, 89
mothers
and arranged marriage, 66
assistance to married daughters,
123, 128–129
figures of authority, 5, 50, 56
gossiping, 126
obedience to, 99
and petitions of annulment, 55
and reverential fear, 50, 56
sternness, 50, 99–100
strength, 52, 55
threatening children, 51
and violence, 47
Murano, 120–121, 123

Samitarij, Iseppo—husband of
    Vicenza Dandolo, 108
Sansoni, Iseppo—husband of Isabetta
    Damiani, 50
Sanudo, Marin—diarist, 15–16
Savioni, Giacomo—husband of Laura
    Armana, 155, 159
Scot, Reginald, author of *The Discov-
    erie of Witchcraft*, 77
Scott, Joan, 11, 12
scripts, 9, 26, 40–41, 102,159
secular courts, 8, 10
secularization, 5, 12
seed (semen), 72–73
self-description, 7
self-fashioning, 56
self-presentation, 6, 9
Senate of Venice, 17–18, 26, 39, 76
sentiments, of family life, 124
separation
    and the age gap at marriage, 63
    and arbitrators, 186 n. 17
    archival sources, 168 n. 34
    and canon law, 4
    church regulations, 21, 120
    and community attitudes, 6, 131
    in Constance, 31
    and the Council of Ten, 160
    dishonor to husbands, 129–130
    in Geneva, 31
    justifications for, 120
    narratives, 7, 133
    and the Patriarchal Court, 22
    petitions, 9, 10
    poisoning as justification for, 125
    proceedings, 120
    and property, 186 n. 17
    and property settlements, 22
    rates, 19, 29–31
    scripts, 26
    and sexual difference, 30
    successful cases, 127, 131
separation petitioners
    Camilla Belloto, 34
    Cecelia Bressan, 124
    Clara Gritti, 128
    Clara Vidali, 130– 131, 135–136,
        153–154

Cornelia Zane, 128
Faustina Gradenigo, 127
Franceschina Asolani, 129
Giovanni Battista Misserini, 142,
    145–152
Isabetta Bembo, 126
Lucia Grandajo, 137–138
Paola da Venezia, 125
Pasquetta Peregrini, 120
servants
    accounts of domestic life, 159
    and battered wives, 5
    and brides, 5
    as court witnesses, 73
    and gossip, 73
    impregnated, 127
    knowledge about sexuality and
        reproduction, 108
    and marital intimacy, 73
    portrayed in theatrical comedy, 60
    testimony, 126–128
sex
    and agency, 70
    between men, 96
    and canonical norms, 70
    coitus interruptus, 88
    crimes, 166 n. 19
    education, 5
    family planning, 5
    foreplay, 74
    gynecological and obstetric care, 5
    hymen, 80
    lovemaking, 74
    missionary position, 88
    orgasm, 80, 88
    orgasm and procreation, 88
    and pain, 74
    patrician males, 106
    pleasure and sin, 74
    and power, 70
    and procreation, 35, 70
    satisfaction of women, 74–75
    sources of information, 74
    unsatisfying, 70
sexuality, regulation of, 70
Sharp, Jane—midwife, 77, 82
Signori di Notte (night watchmen)
    and Giovanni Battista Misserini, 153

sources of, 45
tales of, 41, 120
and Vittoria Cesana, 43
virginity, 74, 78, 94
virility, 63, 71
voice and heart, 42, 45, 53, 56, 59, 132
vows
monastic, 8
of marriage, 158

Watt, Jeffrey—historian, 31
weavers, 33, 45, 125
wedding night, 5, 46
White, Hayden—historian, 11
widows
Clara Vidali, 135
and dowries, 136
and estate laws, 136
witnesses, 40, 53
credibility, 102
gondoliers, 18
to marriage rites, 39
as voices of the community, 122
vendors, 18
wives
abused, 36
battered, 121, 125
censoring husbands, 155
desire for self-improvement, 9
emotional expectations, 159

expectations of husbands, 158
misbehavior, 5
motives to file suit, 8–9
ties with natal family, 45
women
attitudes toward love, 53
aversion to arranged marriage, 66
creative agency of, 103
expectations for sex, 103
expectations of men, 35–36
latitude to make choices, 121
legal strategies, 10
modesty, 73
powers of decision, 131, 159
preferences in a mate, 66
priorities of, 59
property transactions, 135
sense of entitlement, 10, 35, 103
sex and reproduction, 103
and sexual satisfaction, 74
suicidal threats, 36

Zanchi, Antonio—litigator before the
Giudici del Procurator, 136
Zane, Marco—man who purchased
sex from Zuana Facini, 112
Zitelle Periclitanti, 147
Zoppino, Antonio—former husband
of Laura Armana, 156
Zurich, 22, 31